CNN官方授权

CNN互动英语系列

STEP BY STEP 听懂

CNN 先锋科技

CNN Science and Technology

LiveABC 编著

科学出版社
北京

图书在版编目（CIP）数据

Step by Step 听懂 CNN 先锋科技／LiveABC 编著. —北京：科学出版社，2013.1
（CNN互动英语系列）
ISBN 978-7-03-035659-8

I.①S⋯　Ⅱ.①L⋯　Ⅲ.①科学技术—英语—听说教学—自学参考资料
Ⅳ.①H319.9

中国版本图书馆CIP数据核字（2012）第229108号

责任编辑：张　培／责任校对：张林红
责任印制：赵德静／封面设计：无极书装

联系电话：010-6401 9074/电子邮箱：zhangpei@mail.sciencep.com

科 学 出 版 社 出版
北京东黄城根北街16号
邮政编码：100717
http://www.sciencep.com
北京佳信达欣艺术印刷有限公司 印刷
科学出版社发行　各地新华书店经销

*

2013年1月第　一　版　开本：B5 (720 × 1000)
2013年1月第一次印刷　印张：15
字数：410 000
定价：66.00元
（含 DVD 互动光盘 1 张）
（如有印装质量问题，我社负责调换）

听懂英语新闻，与国际接轨的最佳选择！

英语学了这么多年，想看看英语新闻却觉得听起来很吃力？看着新闻画面似乎不难猜出新闻主要事件是什么，但对于新闻细节内容却几乎听不懂？其中主要原因在于大多数人英语"听"的能力比阅读能力差，再加上不了解相关背景或专有名词、跟不上新闻播报速度等，于是对收听英语新闻望而却步。

收听国际英语新闻是与国际接轨、掌握时事最好的方式，而 CNN 是最具国际知名度的新闻媒体之一。本书内容均取材自 CNN 电视新闻网，对于想要提高英语水平及职场竞争力，同时了解科技前沿与发展脉络，拓展视野，吸收新知的读者，本书将是您的最佳选择。

本书精选 29 篇报道，依主题分为以下五大部分：

◈ 炫酷时尚

◈ 寰宇星空

◈ 生命发现

◈ 绿色革命

◈ 生命嬗变

全书的新闻报道采用中英文对照形式，除了列出单词与重要短语的解析，更适时补充相关词汇及延伸用法，还针对主题内容补充各种相关信息。随书附有互动光盘，运用多媒体科技，将文字（text）、影像（image）、声音（sound）结合在一起，如此一来将能够加深读者的学习印象，进而提高学习效率。针对苦于跟不上英语一般说话速度的读者，互动光盘中除了有正常速度的原音重视 ox-F.MP3 之外，还附有慢速的朗读 ox-S.MP3。慢速语音由专业外籍教师录制，提供清晰的发音，方便让您循序渐进，由慢至快理解新闻内容。

中文标题　　正常及慢速 MP3

新闻标题

新闻副标题

短语、惯用语及
重要词汇补充

课文单词

新闻内文中英对照

口误修正
and the responsivenes
is [are]

相关信息
补充

　　希望读者能通过本书专业的新闻报道，学习到英语中最常用的单词、实用词汇、短语用法及口语表达，并循序渐进地锻炼听力、培养语感。相信这会是您精通英文的最佳途径！

🔍 系统需求建议

[硬件]

* 处理器 Pentium 4 以上（或同等 AMD、Celeron 处理器）

* 512 MB 内存

* 全彩显卡 800×600 dpi（16K 色以上）

* 硬盘需求空间 200 MB

* 16 倍速以上 DVD 光驱

* 声卡、扬声器及麦克风（内置或外接）

[软件]

* Microsoft Windows XP、Vista、Windows 7 简体中文版系统

* Microsoft Windows Media Player 9

* Adobe Flash Player 10

🔍 请注意！

出于对版权的保护，本光盘只能在电脑上带盘运行，将光盘内容复制到电脑硬盘上再进行安装则无法运行，请读者予以谅解。

如果您的电脑装有 360 软件，请在安装光盘之前先关闭所有与 360 相关的软件，包括 360 杀毒软件、360 安全卫士、360 浏览器等。

在 Vista 系统中，如果安装互动光盘时遇到以下问题：

1. 出现【安装字体错误】的信息。

2. 出现【无法安装语音识别】的信息。

请依照下列步骤操作：

1. 卸载本产品。

2. 进入控制面板。

3. 点击"用户账户"选项。

4. 点击"开启或关闭用户账户控制"。

5. 将"使用（用户账户控制）UAC 来协助保护您的电脑"选项取消勾选。

6. 再次运行安装光盘。

在 Windows 7 系统中，安装互动光盘若遇上述问题请按以下步骤操作：

1. 进入控制面板，开启程序栏，进入程序和功能，卸载本产品。

2. 进入控制面板，点击"用户账户和家庭安全"选项。

3. 再点击"用户账户"。

4. 点击"更改用户账户控制设置"。

5. 将滑动条拖至最底端（"从不通知"的位置）。

6. 按确定后，需重新启动电脑。

7. 再次运行安装光盘。

🔍 光盘安装程序

步骤一：进入中文操作系统。

步骤二：将光盘放进光驱。

步骤三：本产品带有 Auto Run 运行功能，如果您的电脑支持 Auto Run 光盘程序自动播放功能，则将自动出现【Step by Step 听懂 CNN 先锋科技】的安装画面。

1. 如果您的电脑已安装过本系列任一产品，您可以直接点击"快速安装"图标，进行快速安装；否则，请点击"安装"图标，进行完整安装。

2. 如果您的电脑无法支持 Auto Run 光盘程序自动播放功能，请打开 Windows "我的电脑"，点击光驱，并运行光盘根目录下的 autorun.exe 程序。

3. 如果运行 autorun.exe 仍然无法安装本光碟，请进入本光盘的 setup 文件夹，并运行 setup.exe 程序，即可进行安装。

4. 如果您要删除【Step by Step 听懂 CNN 先锋科技】，请点击"开始"，选择"设置"，选择"控制面板"，选择"添加／删除程序"，并在菜单中点击"Step by Step 听懂 CNN 先锋科技"，并运行"更改／删除"即可。

5. 当语音识别系统或录音功能无法使用时，请检查声卡驱动程序是否正常，并确认硬盘空间是否足够且 Windows 录音程序可以使用。

操作说明

点击"运行"，即进入本光盘的学习内容。按顺序说明如下：

主画面

说明：

1. 主画面右下角共有五个图标，分别为：炫酷时尚、寰宇星空、生命发现、绿色革命、生活嬗变。中间有听力大考验图标。画面左下角有索引、说明、科学出版社网站及退出四个图标。

2. 点击五大类主题中任一类别，将在屏幕中列出该类课程内容，点击后可进入该则新闻的影片学习画面。

课程学习画面

影片学习

说明：

在主画面中点击任一单元，即进入本学习画面。

工具栏说明：

1. 画面右侧由上至下依次为：自动播放、播放／暂停、停止、播下一句、播上一句、反复播放本句、全屏幕播放、设置。

2. 点击"设置"图标，即可设置"反复朗读"的播放次数及间隔的秒数；若您想恢复为一直播放的模式，只要将次数调回 0 即可。

3. 画面左侧由上至下依次为：目录、上一篇、下一篇、单词解释、文字学习、主画面、退出。

4. 画面下方的英文及中文字幕，通过选取字幕前的图标，可选择出现或隐藏字幕，以便做听力练习。

5. 字幕下方有一个影片播放点控制栏，可决定影片播放的起点。

文字学习

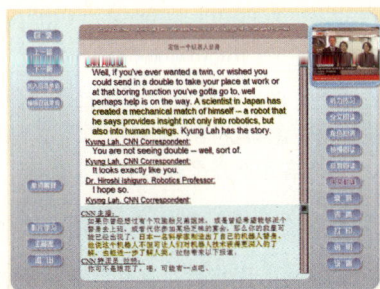

说明：

1. 在影片学习中，点击"文字学习"图标，即进入本画面。

2. 在画面的右上方有一个影片视窗，在播放原声的同时，您可以在此视窗看到该段声音的影片。

工具栏说明：

听力练习

点击"听力练习"图标，屏幕中的学习内容将会消失，读者只能通过右上角的影片画面进行听力练习。

全文朗读

点击"全文朗读"图标，电脑将自动朗读本段新闻的内容。

角色扮演

点击"角色扮演"图标，则会在图标左侧列出该段新闻的角色人名。此时，您可选择想扮演的角色，程序将关闭该角色的声音，由您和电脑进行对话练习。如果您的发音不正确，则会出现一个窗口，您可以选择"再读一次"、"略过"或"读给我听"来完成或略过该对话；也可以调整语音识别的灵敏度。若您的发音正确，则对话会一直进行下去。

快慢朗读

当您觉得对话速度太快时，可以点击"快慢朗读"图标，再点击"全文朗读"图标或任一句子，朗读速度将变慢，让您听得更清楚。慢速朗读时，为了让您更容易学习，我们将一句话断成几小段，逐段录音。若您觉得速度太慢，想恢复为一般速度时，只要再次点击"快慢朗读"图标，即可恢复成一般速度。

反复朗读

点击"反复朗读"图标后，再选取任一句子，电脑将反复播放该句。您可以点击"设置"自行设置"反复朗读"的播放次数，若您想恢复为一直播放的模式，只要将次数调回 0 即可。

中文翻译

点击"中文翻译"图标后，画面下方将出现中文翻译框，您可在中文翻译框内看到本段新闻内容时，听到对应的英文句子；同样，点击文中的任一句子，也会朗读该句英文，并显示其中文翻译。

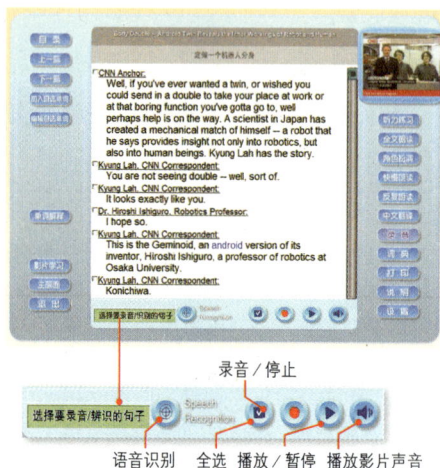

录音／停止

选择要录音/辨识的句子

语音识别　全选　播放／暂停　播放影片声音

录音

1. 点击"录音"图标后，开启录音功能控制栏。

2. 按键功能由左至右为：全选、录音／停止、播放／暂停以及播放影片声音。按左方的"全选"图标，会出现全部句子录音；若您只想选择某段内文，只要在该段前方的方框（□）点击一下即可。若您点击右边的"播放影片声音"图标，则在您进行录音或播放录音前，都将会播放该段影片原声。

3. 录音步骤如下：

   (1) 先点击您要进行录音的句子，并选择是否要在录音前播放原声。

   (2) 点击"录音"键。

   (3) 请在电脑"播放原声"后，对着麦克风读出您所选取的句子。

   (4) 当您完成该句录音后，请按键盘上的"空格键"（space bar），结束录音。

   (5) 点击"播放"键，即可听到您所录的声音。

4. 点击左边的"Speech Recognition"图标，将启动"语音识别"功能，请依照以下步骤进行语音识别：

   (1) 先选择要进行语音识别的句子，并选择是否要在语音识别前播放原声。

   (2) 点击"Speech Recognition"图标。

   (3) 当画面出现"请录音"时，您必须对麦克风读出您所选取的句子，如果您的发音正确，则将继续进行下一句；如果发音不正确，则会出现一窗口，您可选择"再读一次"、"略过"或"读给我听"来完成或略过该对话；也可在此调整语音识别的灵敏度。

5. 若您要在中途结束录音或语音识别，请在任意处点击一下即可。

词典

当您点击"词典"图标后，在画面下方将出现词典框，此时点击文中的任意一个单词，词典框内会出现该单词的音标及中文翻译，并读出该词发音。

打印

当您点击"打印"图标后，在画面下方将出现打印控制键。您可选择"全部打印"或"部分打印"；打印内容可选择是否包括中文翻译。

说明

当您点击"说明"图标后，将开启辅助说明页。您可借此了解本光盘内容的各项操作说明及用法。

学习重点

当您在点击文中蓝色文字的学习重点，画面下方会出现说明框，并配有发音；若在开启"中文翻译"功能时点击，则朗读您点击的句子。

段落朗读

当您点击文中的人名时，程序将自动朗读此人该段会话。若您是处于"慢速朗读"模式，则播放该段话时，声音及反白文字将以小段方式出现。

加入及编辑自选单词

点击"加入自订单词"图标后，可以点击您要记录的单词。在此，您可以进行单词学习，也可以删除或打印任意一个单词。

单词解释

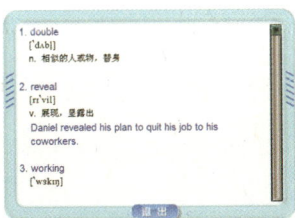

列出本课的重点单词（词性、音标、中文解释），点击该单词会发音。

听力大考验画面说明

1. 点击"听力大考验"后，可看到"听力填空"及"听力理解"两类测验题型。

2. 在"听力填空"中，请点击影片右下方的"Play"图标，你会看到一段 CNN 报道，段落中有几处空格，请在空格处填入你听到的词。

3. 在"听力理解"中，请点击影片右下方的"Play"图标播放影片并作答，完成该题后，点击"下一题"图标进行下一题，完成该测验题型后，可继续进行其他测验，或点击"退出"退出测验界面。

题型界面如下

(1) 听力填空：

(2) 听力理解：

索引

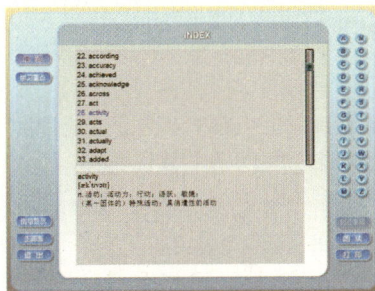

说明：

1. 在主画面点击"索引"图标，进入索引画面，内含单词检索及学习重点索引。

2. 单词检索：

   (1) 在此将所有的单词依字母分类，点击单词会出现该单词的音标、中文翻译及发音。

   (2) 连续点击单词两次或选取某一单词后点击"显示例句"图标，即会显现该单词的课文例句。

   (3) 连续点击例句两次或选取任一例句后点击"连接课文"图标，即跳至该例句的"文字学习"画面。

   (4) 点击"自选单词"图标，即可在此看到您在学习过程中加入的自选单词。

   (5) 点击"朗读"图标，则会将所选字母开头的单词从头到尾读一次；点击"打印"图标，则将以该字母开头的所有单词打印出来。

   (6) 点击任一单词后，再点击"打印"图标，则可打印该单词的内容。

3. 学习重点：

   (1) 在此列出本光盘内容的学习重点。用鼠标点击任一学习重点，会自动朗读。

   (2) 连续点击两次或选取任一学习重点后点击"连接课文"图标，即跳至该学习重点的"文字学习"画面。

   (3) 点击"返回"图标，则回到单词检索画面。

   (4) 点击"朗读"图标，则会将所有的学习重点从头到尾读一次；点击"打印"图标，则将所有的学习重点打印出来。

说明

1. 在主画面点击"说明"图标，在此提供"操作说明"及"语音识别设置说明"。

2. 您可借此了解本光盘内容的各项操作说明、用法及语音识别设置说明。

网站

点击"网站"图标，将连接至科学出版社官方网站。

原文朗读 MP3

互动光盘中含有新闻原声及慢速朗读 MP3 内容，您可以放在 MP3 播放器中收听，也可以将光盘放在电脑中，从"我的电脑"中点击您的光驱，再从中选择光盘文件里的 MP3 的文件夹，使用播放软件将文件打开收听 MP3 的内容。

目　　录

前言　　　　　　　　　　　　　　　　　　　　　　　　　　　　　*i*

光盘使用方法　　　　　　　　　　　　　　　　　　　　　　　　*iii*

炫酷时尚　　　　　　　　　　　　　　　　　　　　　　　　　*1*

❶ 游戏机科技争霸战，Sony又出新招
   Sony's Next Move
   PlayStation 3 Takes a Stab at Motion Sensor Gaming　　　*2*

❷ 定做一个机器人替身
   Body Double
   Android Twin Reveals the Inner Workings of Robot and Human　*10*

❸ 微软Xbox科技大跃进，用身体玩游戏
   Total Control
   Xbox Jumps on the Motion Gaming Bandwagon with Kinect　*18*

❹ 体验如梦似幻的高科技未来旅馆
   Hotel of Tomorrow
   Tech-Driven Creature Comforts Future Travelers Can Look Forward To　*24*

❺ 用意念控制行动——神奇的脑电波遥控科技
   Mind Games
   Gadgets Put You in Control with Brain Power　　　　　*30*

寰宇星空　　　　　　　　　　　　　　　　　　　　　　　　*39*

❻ 月球上有水，人类移居不是梦？
   Our Not-So-Dry Neighbor
   The Discovery of Lunar Water May Hold Key to Human Colonies on the Moon　*40*

7 火星生命之谜即将揭晓
Our Martian Neighbors
Scientists Search for Signs of Life on the Red Planet   48

8 开启太空时代的人造卫星迎来 50 岁生日
Celebrating Sputnik
The Tiny Satellite that Sparked the Space Race Turns 50   56

9 CNN 记者的太空体验
Blast from the Past
Vintage Technology Launches Russia's Star City to the Forefront of the Space Race   64

10 下一个大地震将发生在……
Living on Shaky Ground
Is Your City at Risk for the Next Big Quake?   72

11 美国太空计划未来出路
NASA's Next Step
The Space Administration Ponders a Future Beyond the Shuttle   82

12 以生物飞行本能为师的未来航空科技
The Nature of Flight
Science Draws Inspiration from the Animal Kingdom's Aerial Masters   90

13 英国 UFO 档案大揭秘
Britain's X-Files
Defense Ministry Releases Secret Reports on UFO Sighting   98

生命发现   105

14 演化史大发现——最早古人类化石出土
Missing Link?
Scientists Unveil the Earliest Fossil of Primate Ancestor   106

15 定做 DNA，人造生命科技大跃进
Making Life in a Lab
Geneticist Creates First Synthetic Organism   **114**

16 天文物理大师史蒂芬·霍金谈宇宙与人类的未来
The Final Frontier
Physicist Stephen Hawking Journeys into the Future of Space Exploration   **122**

17 濒危物种新希望——DNA 冷冻方舟
The Bar Code1 of Life
Creating a Genetic Ark to Preserve the Earth's Endangered Species   **128**

18 日本真的是为了研究捕鲸？生物学家告诉你真相
A Whale of a Discovery
Researchers Offer a Humane Alternative to Japan's Lethal Science   **136**

绿色革命   **143**

19 实用又环保的超薄电子报纸
Hot off the (Paperless) Presses
Eco-Friendly E-Reader Delivers the News While Saving Trees   **144**

20 替代能源新里程——生物燃料客机首航
Green Flight
Virgin Atlantic Launches First Biofuel-Powered Airliner   **150**

21 回顾环保科技 10 年轨迹
The Eco-Decade
Tracking Environmental Advancements of the Past 10 Years   **158**

生命嬗变 167

22 爱它就为它装上义肢——动物义肢新科技
Pet Prosthetics
Technology Gives Furry Friends a Leg Up 168

23 从 Walkman 到 iPod，随身听走过 30 年
Walking Away from Walkman
Sony Pulls the Plug on the Original Personal Music Player 172

24 "以牙还眼" 创新手术让盲人重见光明
A Tooth for an Eye
Florida Woman Gives Her Eyetooth to Regain Sight 180

25 新型手机揭示通信科技新风貌
Dialed in
Connecting to the Future of Mobile Communication in Barcelona 188

26 信息时代的噩梦——无线网络
Hijacked Data
Airport Wi-Fi May Expose Your Laptop to Lurking Hackers 194

27 顺应高龄化时代的护理机器人登场
Robo-Nurse
Mechanical Helper Lends a Hand to the Elderly 202

28 3D 科技带你游历古罗马
Virtual Rome
3D Technology Takes Visitors on a Walk Through the Ancient City 208

29 瘫痪病人的新希望——鳗鱼
Eels that Heal
Lampreys Offer New Hope to Spinal Injury Patients 214

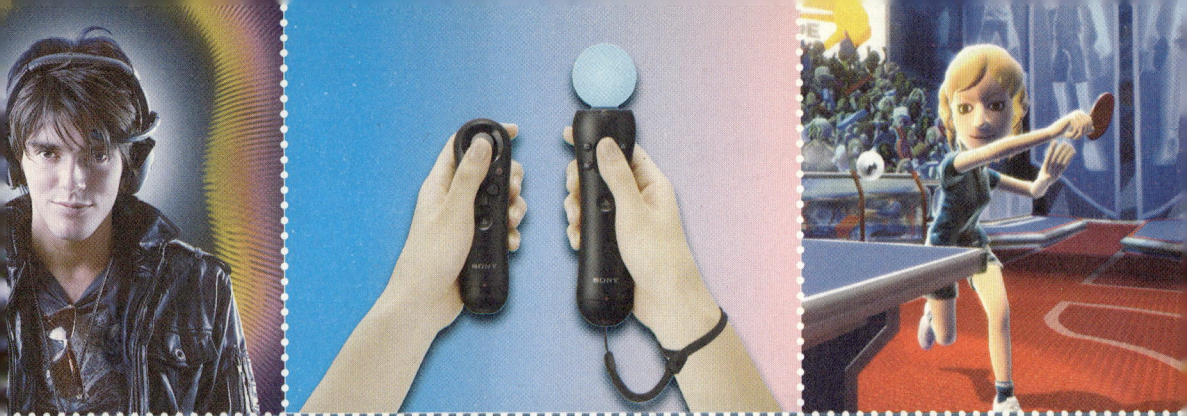

炫酷时尚

① 游戏机科技争霸战，Sony又出新招

② 定做一个机器人替身

③ 微软Xbox科技大跃进，用身体玩游戏

④ 体验如梦似幻的高科技未来旅馆

⑤ 用意念控制行动——神奇的脑电波遥控科技

PlayStation®Move

游戏机科技争霸战，Sony 又出新招

Sony's Next Move

PlayStation 3 Takes a Stab at Motion Sensor[1] Gaming

图片提供　SONY COMPUTER ENTERTAINMENT/PR NEWSWIRE

ANDREW STEVENS, CNN ANCHOR

Sony has just unveiled[2] its latest weapon in the closely fought console[3] war with Nintendo and Microsoft. It's called the Move controller, and Sony claims it's an improvement on the technology in Nintendo's Wii, which allows you to play games using the controller's own sensors to track your own movements. Now, Sony has some catching up to do.

As of the end of June, Sony had sold just over 38 million PlayStation 3s worldwide. That's still behind, but closing the gap on Microsoft's Xbox 360, which has global sales of almost 42 million, and the Xbox has appealed to the hard-core[4] gaming community. But both trail[5] far behind the Wii, with a whopping[6] 71 million units sold since its debut in 2006, largely due to the success of those wireless controllers, which have made the Wii popular with families, although perhaps less popular with serious gamers. Well, our Colleen McEdwards went to find out how the new Move actually works.

炫酷时尚 寰宇星空 生命发现 绿色革命 生活嬗变

Language Notes

标题扫描：

take a stab at 尝试一下

stab 原指"刺，戳，捅"，在此指"尝试，企图"，take a stab 表示"尝试一下"，后面用 at 加上尝试做的事物。

例 Jake took a stab at the *New York Times* crossword puzzle while he finished his coffee.
杰克在喝咖啡的时候玩了一下《纽约时报》的填字游戏。

close the gap 缩小差距

gap 是指"差距，隔阂"，close the gap 表示"缩小差距，减少隔阂"，后面用 on 加上拉近距离的对象。

例 The mobile phone maker closed the gap on its closest competitor by lowering prices.
那家手机制造商通过降价拉近与最相近的竞争对手的差距。

CNN 主播 安德鲁·史蒂文斯

在与任天堂及微软激烈的游戏机大战竞争中，索尼刚刚推出最新武器一较高下，新武器称作 Move 控制器。索尼宣称这是任天堂 Wii 的技术再升级，让你可以通过控制器里的感应器追踪动作来玩游戏。现在，索尼要加紧脚步了。

截至6月底，索尼在全球已经售出 3 800 万台 PlayStation 3 游戏机。虽然这个数字仍然落后于微软 Xbox 360 全球近 4 200 万台的销售量，但差距已经缩小。Xbox 则是成功吸引了游戏发烧友。但这两种游戏机的销量却仍远远落后于 Wii。自从 Wii 2006 年问世以来一共售出惊人的 7 100 万台；这主要归功于 Wii 的无线控制器，让 Wii 受到家庭游戏爱好者的欢迎，但却可能不太受游戏迷的青睐。本台记者科琳·麦克爱德华兹带你看看新的 Move 究竟如何工作。

Vocabulary

1. **sensor** ['sɛnsɚ] *n.*（探测光、热、压力等的）感应器
2. **unveil** [ʌn'vel] *v.*（首次）展示，推出
The car company unveiled its new hybrid model at the auto show.
3. **console** ['kɑn,sol] *n.*（电子设备的）主机，控制台
4. **hard-core** [,hɑrd'kɔr] *adj.* 中坚的，核心的
Danny considers himself to be a hard-core sports fan.
5. **trail** [trel] *v.* 落后，失利
The incumbent trails his opponent by 20 percentage points with just two weeks left before the election.
6. **whopping** ['wɑpɪŋ] *adj.* 巨大的，很大的
Kobe Bryant scored a whopping 38 points in last night's game.

COLLEEN MCEDWARDS, CNN CORRESPONDENT
Joining me now is Richard Marks with Sony to explain what this and all of this actually does. Come on in here. Tell us about PlayStation Move.

RICHARD MARKS, SONY R&D MANAGER
This is our new controller for PlayStation 3. It combines our PlayStation Eye camera and internal[7] sensors in our controller to give a new way to play PlayStation 3.

COLLEEN MCEDWARDS, CNN CORRESPONDENT
Now how . . . who are you targeting with this new product?

RICHARD MARKS, SONY R&D MANAGER
Actually, we're targeting everybody. We have very casual experiences for people who have never played games, but because it's so precise[8] and responsive[9], we also have games that would appeal to people who are really good at games—core[10] players.

COLLEEN MCEDWARDS, CNN CORRESPONDENT
Ok, I have a seven-year-old. We have a Wii. We play it as a family. We love it, but show me what this can do. I'm curious to see. Let's have a look.

RICHARD MARKS, SONY R&D MANAGER
OK, maybe the first thing you see right away is that we use our camera, so we can actually take video of the player and use the controller [to] insert[11] virtual[12] objects right into the video. One of our games called *Start the Party* actually does this very well where you can switch between lots of different objects, do different things. Things are flying at you. You have to hit them with a stick or you …

COLLEEN MCEDWARDS, CNN CORRESPONDENT
I'm still getting used to myself standing here with this giant sword.

CNN 特派员　科琳·麦克爱德华兹

　　即将到来的是索尼公司的理查德·马克斯，他要解释这个问题并说明这些东西究竟有何功用。过来吧，为我们讲解一下 PlayStation Move。

索尼公司研发部经理　理查德·马克斯

　　这是我们为 PlayStation 3 新推出的控制器。它结合了我们的 PlayStation Eye 摄像机，以及控制器中内置的感应器，使 PlayStation 3 可以一种新的玩法。

CNN 特派员　科琳·麦克爱德华兹

　　那怎么做……贵公司这款新商品锁定的对象是谁?

索尼公司研发部经理　理查德·马克斯

　　其实我们锁定的是每一个人。针对从未玩过游戏机的人，我们提供了非常轻松的游戏体验，但是因为它很精确而且反应灵敏，我们也有吸引那些相当擅长打游戏机的，也就是核心游戏爱好者的游戏。

CNN 特派员　科琳·麦克爱德华兹

　　我有个 7 岁的孩子，我们家有一台 Wii。我们全家都爱玩，也很喜欢。让我看看这台游戏机有些什么能耐。我很想看看。咱们来瞧瞧吧。

索尼公司研发部经理　理查德·马克斯

　　也许你马上会看到的是我们使用的是我们的摄像机，所以我们可以把游戏爱好者的影像拍摄下来，再用控制器将虚拟角色放进影片中。我们有一个叫《派对总动员》的游戏在这方面做得很棒，你可以更换很多不同的角色，做不同的事。东西会朝你飞过来，你必须用棍子去击打它们，否则你就会……

CNN 特派员　科琳·麦克爱德华兹

　　我还在试着习惯手拿这把巨剑站在这里。

Vocabulary

7. internal [ɪnˈtɜːnəl] *adj.* 内部的，内置的
   The factory assembles internal components for personal computers.
8. precise [prɪˈsaɪs] *adj.* 准确的，精确的
   The scale takes very precise weight measurements.
9. responsive [rɪˈspɑnsɪv] *adj.* 反应敏捷的
   Sports cars often have more responsive steering controls.
10. core [kɔr] *n.* 核心，最重要的部分
11. insert [ɪnˈsɜt] *v.* 插入，嵌入
    Donna inserted herself into a photo using an image editing program.
12. virtual [ˈvɜtʃuəl] *adj.* 模拟的，虚拟的
    The video game takes place in a virtual world.

RICHARD MARKS, SONY R&D MANAGER
Yeah, this is called augmented[13] reality. You see yourself and you also see virtual objects rendered in[1] with us. So I can switch between ... if you push the big middle button, the Move button there, you can switch between many different objects.

COLLEEN MCEDWARDS, CNN CORRESPONDENT
You see, my seven-year-old would have this figured out already. Ah!

RICHARD MARKS, SONY R&D MANAGER
It could be sports games; it could be a fighting game. You can do all sorts of different things. Of course, we wouldn't have to see video of ourselves. We could switch it to more of a normal virtual experience where you just see the object that you're holding, but the video really shows you how well it's tracking. It's rendering it right over the top of the controller perfectly.

COLLEEN MCEDWARDS, CNN CORRESPONDENT
So you think the hard-core gamer is gonna see a difference between this and what you would get in a Wii with your controller playing tennis or, you know, lightsaber duels, or whatever you're doing?

RICHARD MARKS, SONY R&D MANAGER
Definitely, the accuracy[14] and the responsiveness is [are] very different.

COLLEEN MCEDWARDS, CNN CORRESPONDENT
So why is Sony coming out with this now. It's such a difficult economy. How concerned are you about that?

RICHARD MARKS, SONY R&D MANAGER
We decided to make PlayStation Move when we could make the kind of experience we wanted to for both our casual and core players. But also I think now is a great time for our PlayStation 3. It's a great value for families. It does so many different things for a really good price point.

索尼公司研发部经理　理查德·马克斯

对，这叫做扩展现实。你会看到你自己，也会看到虚拟角色跟我们一起呈现出来。所以我可以切换……如果你按中间那个大按钮，那个 Move 按钮，你就可以在很多不同的角色之间切换。

CNN 特派员　科琳·麦克爱德华兹

你瞧，我那 7 岁的孩子早就搞明白怎么操作了。嘿！

索尼公司研发部经理　理查德·马克斯

它可以是运动游戏，可以是格斗游戏。你可以做各式各样不同的事。当然，我们不一定要看自己的影像。我们可以将它转换成一般的虚拟体验，你只会看到你手上握的东西，但是从影像上你可以看得出来它追踪得好不好。它正把东西准确地放到控制器的正上方。

CNN 特派员　科琳·麦克爱德华兹

所以你觉得游戏发烧友会看得出用这台游戏机的控制器来打网球，或玩光剑对决，或者做其他任何事，都和你从 Wii 中体验到的有所不同？

索尼公司研发部经理　理查德·马克斯

那是一定的。两者之间的精确性和反应速度天差地别。

CNN 特派员　科琳·麦克爱德华兹

为何索尼要选这个时候推出这台游戏机？经济那么不景气，你们会担心这点吗？

索尼公司研发部经理　理查德·马克斯

在我们可以带给一般游戏爱好者和游戏发烧友我们想要给他们的体验时，我们就决定要生产 PlayStation Move 了。我也认为现在是我们推出 PlayStation 3 的大好时机。它对一般家庭而言价值极高。它的功能如此之多，以它的价位来看太划算了。**CNN**

Phrases

1. render in 呈现
   Many of the creatures in the movie were rendered in high-definition computer graphics.

Vocabulary

13. augment ['ɔgmənt] v. 增加，提高，扩大
    Phil augmented his car with custom parts.
14. accuracy ['ækjərəsɪ] n. 准确性，精确

炫酷时尚　寰宇星空　生命发现　绿色革命　生活嬗变

Step by Step 听懂 CNN 先锋科技

LED sphere 彩色发光圆球

T button 扳机按钮

action buttons 动作键
按键功能可能因游戏不同而
不同，大部分用法介绍如下：

Move button 选取按钮

select 选择

□ menu/document
   目录／文件
✕ cancel 取消
△ option menu 功能目录
○ confirm 确认

home button 主画面按钮

start 开始

status indicator 状态显示灯

motion controller 动态控制器

AC adaptor
变压器

AC power cord
电线

D-pad (directional pad) 方向按钮

navigation controller
导航控制器

charging station
充电座

webcam
视频摄像机

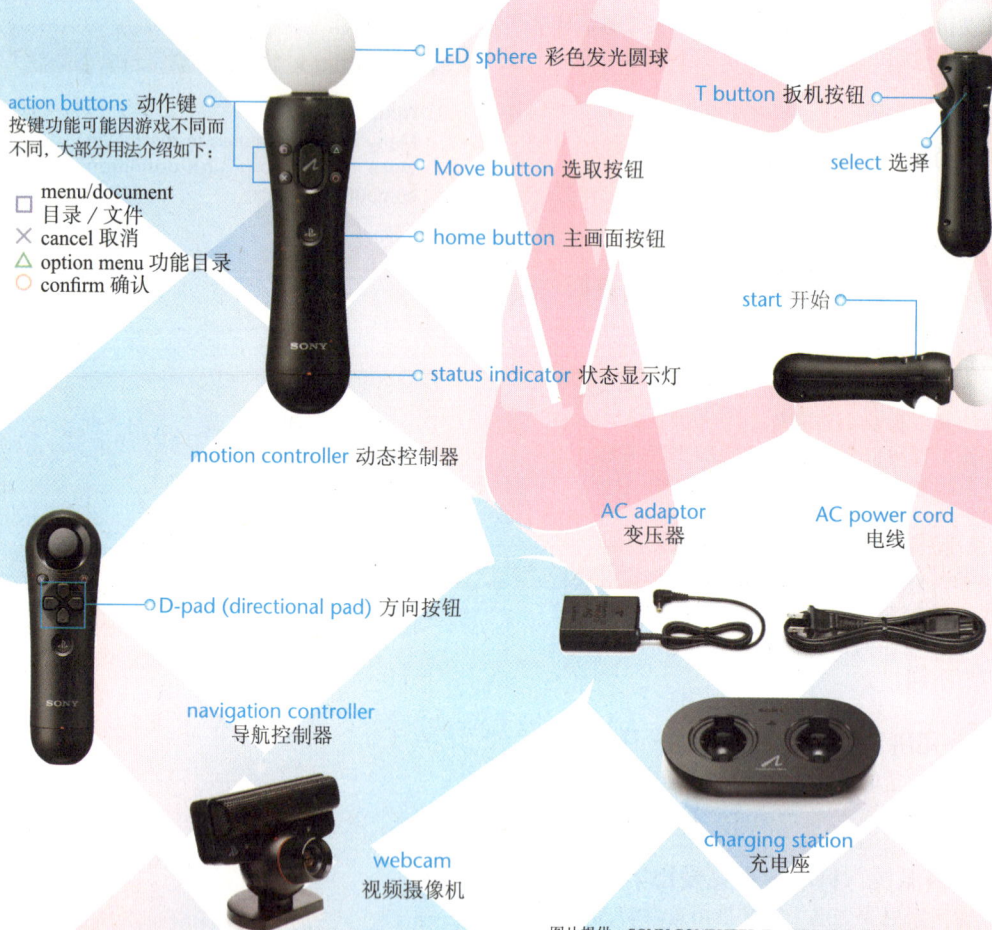

图片提供　SONY COMPUTER ENTERTAINMENT/PR NEWSWIRE

Lightsaber Duels 光剑对决

lightsaber ['laɪt'sebə] "光剑" 是《星际大战》
中知名的武器，也是许多星战迷憧憬的武
器，体感游戏《星球大战：克隆人之战——
光剑对决》（Star Wars: The Clone Wars—
Lightsaber Duels）可以用无线遥控器作为游戏
中光剑的操作媒介，让游戏爱好者可以做出
各种攻击和防御动作。

Notes

炫酷时尚

寰宇星空

生命发现

绿色革命

生活嬗变

定做一个机器人替身

Body Double[1]

Android Twin Reveals[2] the Inner Workings[3] of Robot and Human

图片提供　Geminoid was developed by ATR Intelligent Robotics and Communication Laboratories

CNN ANCHOR

Well, if you've ever wanted a twin, or wished you could send in a double to take your place at work or at that boring function[4] you've gotta go to, well perhaps help is on the way. A scientist in Japan has created a mechanical[5] match of himself—a robot that he says provides insight[6] not only into robotics[7], but also into human beings. Kyung Lah has the story.

KYUNG LAH, CNN CORRESPONDENT

You are not seeing double—well, sort of.
It looks exactly like you.

DR. HIROSHI ISHIGURO, ROBOTICS PROFESSOR, OSAKA UNIVERSITY

I hope so.

KYUNG LAH, CNN CORRESPONDENT

This is the Geminoid, an android version of its inventor, Hiroshi Ishiguro, a professor of robotics at Osaka University. Konichiwa.

CNN 主播

如果你曾经想过有个双胞胎兄弟姐妹，或是曾经希望能够派个替身去上班，或者代你参加某场乏味的宴会，那么你的救星可能已经出现了。日本一名科学家制造出了自己的机器人替身。他说这个机器人不但可让人们对机器人技术获得更深入的了解，也能进一步了解人类。拉赫带来以下报道。

CNN 特派员 拉赫

你可不是眼花了。嗯，可能有一点吧。
看起来和你一模一样。

大阪大学机器人学教授 石黑浩博士

希望如此。

CNN 特派员 拉赫

这是仿真双胞胎，也就是发明人石黑浩的机器人翻版。石黑浩是大阪大学的机器人学教授。

你好。

Language Notes

android 仿真机器人

android [ˌænˈdrɔɪd] 这个词源自希腊文 androeides，andr 是 "man"，eides 则是 "alike"，合起来就是 "仿真人" 的意思。英文 gynoid 又特指 "女仿真机器人"。

石黑浩博士是发明第一个仿真机器人的科学家，他希望能让替身在不同的课堂上教学（lecture），而他则在家里遥控。

图片提供　Geminoid was developed by ATR Intelligent Robotics and Communication Laboratories.

Vocabulary

1. double [ˌdʌbl] *n.* 相似的人或物，替身
2. reveal [rɪˈvil] *v.* 展现，显露出
   Daniel revealed his plan to quit his job to his coworkers.
3. working [ˌwɜkɪŋ] *n.* 运转，活动
4. fuction [ˌfʌŋkʃən] *n.* 职务，职责
5. mechanical [mɪˈkænɪkl] *adj.* 机械的
   The scientist invented a mechanical device that performs surgical procedures.
6. inside [ˌɪnˈsaɪd] *n.* 内幕，内情
7. robotics [roˈbɑtɪks] *n.*（用作单数）机器人技术

THE GEMINOID, ANDROID
Konichiwa.

KYUNG LAH, CNN CORRESPONDENT
Blinks[8] like you.

DR. HIROSHI ISHIGURO, ROBOTICS PROFESSOR, OSAKA UNIVERSITY
And the hair is also mine. This is him as a twins.

KYUNG LAH, CNN CORRESPONDENT
But not quite. An operator using multiple[9] cameras and infrared[10] detectors[11] for lip movement runs a Geminoid from another room. Dr. Ishiguro steps behind the curtain and we continue our talk from here.

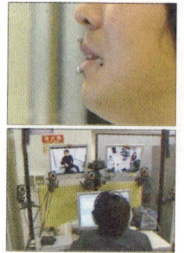

DR. HIROSHI ISHIGURO, ROBOTICS PROFESSOR, OSAKA UNIVERSITY
I can have another personality or another presence[12]. I can control this robot from anywhere.

KYUNG LAH, CNN CORRESPONDENT
The ability to be in two places at once, say roboting into the office while you work from home. After a few minutes, I even forget that the Geminoid is separate from Dr. Ishiguru.
Does that feel like I was touching you?

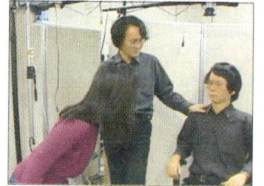

DR. HIROSHI ISHIGURO, ROBOTICS PROFESSOR, OSAKA UNIVERSITY
You know, I cannot feel something.

KYUNG LAH, CNN CORRESPONDENT
Professor, are you studying humans or androids?

DR. HIROSHI ISHIGURO, ROBOTICS PROFESSOR, OSAKA UNIVERSITY
Both. By developing [an] android, I am studying a humans.

KYUNG LAH, CNN CORRESPONDENT
Dr. Ishiguro has been developing robots like this for years, but they didn't look human. He believes this machine that looks so much like a man can be used to study human behavior.

机器人　仿真双胞胎

你好。

CNN 特派员　拉赫

他眨起眼来也和你一样。

大阪大学机器人学教授　石黑浩博士

头发也跟我一样。他是我的双胞胎。

CNN 特派员　拉赫

但也不完全是。有个操作员在另一个房间使用多台摄像机以及操控嘴唇动作的红外线探测器。石黑博士走到幕后，在此继续接受采访。

大阪大学机器人学教授　石黑浩博士

我可以拥有另一个性格，或者出现在另一个地方。我可以从任何角落控制这个机器人。

CNN 特派员　拉赫

他可以同时出现在两个地方，例如把机器人派到办公室，自己则在家工作。过了几分钟之后，我甚至忘了仿真双胞胎和石黑博士是两个不同的个体。

你觉得我像是在触摸你吗?

大阪大学机器人学教授　石黑浩博士

其实我什么都感觉不到。

CNN 特派员　拉赫

教授，你研究的对象是人类还是机器人?

大阪大学机器人学教授　石黑浩博士

两者都有。我通过研发机器人研究人类。

CNN 特派员　拉赫

石黑博士研发这样的机器人，已经有好几年的时间，可是先前那些机器人看起来都不像人。他认为这个外表非常近似人类的机器可以用来研究人类行为。

Language Notes

behind the curtain　幕后，私底下

behind the curtain 按照字面解释为"在布幔的后面"，比喻"在幕后，私底下"的意思。

例 The visit to the film studio offered a glimpse behind the curtain to see how movie magic was made.

到电影工作室参观可以让人了解电影的神奇是如何创造的。

Vocabulary

8. blink [blɪŋk] v. 眨眼睛
   Chuck blinked when the doctor put drops in his eyes.
9. multiple [ˈmʌltəpl] adj. 多样的，复合的
   Dave's mom gave him multiple reasons why he couldn't take flying lessons.
10. infrared [ˌɪnfrəˈrɛd] adj. 红外线的
    The infrared binoculars can see in the dark.
11. detector [dɪˈtɛktə] n. 探测器
12. presence [ˈprɛzəns] n. 在场，出席

DR. HIROSHI ISHIGURO, ROBOTICS PROFESSOR, OSAKA UNIVERSITY

If we replace[13] the all human functions with the technologies ... OK, then we can understand what is a human's.

KYUNG LAH, CNN CORRESPONDENT

Trying to understand the human soul by building from the outside in.

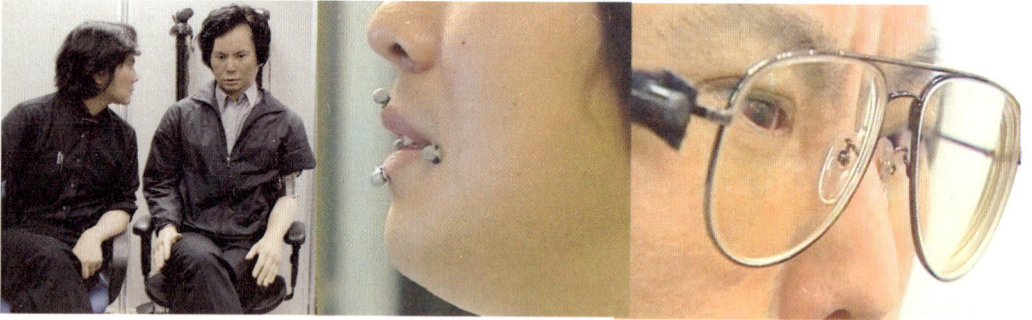

大阪大学机器人学教授　石黑浩博士
　　我们如果以科技取代人类的所有功能……
那么我们就可以了解人类究竟是什么。

CNN 特派员　拉赫
　　由外而内探究人类的灵魂。CNN

图片提供　Geminoid was developed by ATR Intelligent Robotics and Communication Laboratories

炫酷时尚　寰宇星空　生命发现　绿色革命　生活嬗变

Vocabulary

13. replace [rɪˈpleɪs] *v.* 替换，替代
Donna replaced the tires on her car before her trip.

日本仿真机器人发展时期

> **2004 年**

石黑浩博士研发了第一个仿真机器人，取名"Repliee Q1"。

> **2005 年**

日本国际博览会（Expo 2005）石黑浩博士研发并展出仿真机器人"DER 01"。

> **2006 年**

日本 Kokoro 有限公司推出身高约 165 厘米的仿真机器人"DER 02"。

> **2006 年**

石黑浩博士创造出替身机器人"Geminoid HI-1"。

图片提供

commons.wikimedia.org

Give It a Try 请选出正确答案

1. Brett saw someone at the mall that could be his _____.
   a. detector　　　　b. double
   c. presence　　　　d. robotics

2. The bright light caused Joe to _____ his eyes.
   a. blink　　　　b. replace
   c. reveal　　　　d. double

3. The special camera can see _____ light.
   a. multiple　　　　b. mechanical
   c. double　　　　d. infrared

Answers: 1.b 2.a 3.d

Notes

Total Control

微软 Xbox 科技大跃进，用身体玩游戏

Xbox Jumps on the Motion Gaming Bandwagon with Kinect

KRISTIE LU STOUT, CNN ANCHOR

Now it is the mother of all gaming expos, and once again the Tokyo Game Show hasn't failed[1] to deliver[2]. Now all the talk this year is about Microsoft's latest offering the Xbox Kinect, and Kyung Lah gave it a test run[3].

MICROSOFT EMPLOYEE

OK, you ready?

KYUNG LAH, CNN CORRESPONDENT

OK.

Why am I running like a fool? Because this is the future of gaming, or so believes Microsoft. It's called Xbox 360 Kinect. No controller—the machine has sensors, turning you into the controller.

MICROSOFT EMPLOYEE

OK, you just hold it there. You don't have to push. You just hold your hand over it. Perfect.

KYUNG LAH, CNN CORRESPONDENT

[Explain] how it's seeing what we're doing.

Language Notes

标题扫描：

jump on the bandwagon
加入行列，跟上流行

bandwagon 原本是指游行队伍中的载着乐手的"乐队花车"，引申比喻为"新潮流，流行趋势"，jump on the bandwagon 则表示"加入行列，赶时髦"。

例 Judy jumped on the bandwagon and started her own blog.
朱蒂赶时髦开始创建她的博客。

CNN 主播　克里斯蒂·卢·斯托特

东京游戏展是游戏展之母，而今年的展览同样没有令人失望。今年最热门的话题就是微软推出的最新产品 Xbox Kinect。拉赫柔身测试了一番。

微软员工

好，准备好了吗？

CNN 特派员　拉赫

好了。

我为什么像个傻瓜一样一直跑？因为这就是游戏的未来，至少微软这么认为。这套系统叫做 Xbox 360 Kinect。不需要控制器——机器上有感测仪，所以你本身就是控制器。

微软员工

好，你保持不动。不用按，只要把手放在上面。太好了。

CNN 特派员　拉赫

请你说明一下这套系统是怎么看见我们的动作的。

Vocabulary

1. fail [fel] v. 未能做到，使失望，负于
   James failed to notify his secretary that he would be out of the office.
2. deliver [dɪ'lɪvə] v. 达成所愿，不负期望，履行
   Every time Jake gives Susan a difficult task, she delivers.
3. test run [tɛst][rʌn] 试运营，试用

MICROSOFT EMPLOYEE
    Well, it can see each of the little, like, differences in depth to just track your body. So, anything you do with your body, it's instantly ... your character will do it on screen.

KYUNG LAH, CNN CORRESPONDENT
    This is me?

MICROSOFT EMPLOYEE
    Yep. You jump. Another jump. Jump.

KYUNG LAH, CNN CORRESPONDENT
    No skills required. Even a novice[4] gamer like yours truly gets sucked in[1] quickly.

MICROSOFT EMPLOYEE
    And you can see the pictures of us playing, and you'll be able to share those out with friends on email or on Facebook or whatever you like.

KYUNG LAH, CNN CORRESPONDENT
    Are you breaking down yet another wall between people and technology?

DON MATTRICK, MICROSOFT SENIOR V.P.
    Absolutely. The goal is for technology to be more receptive[5] to the things that we do naturally.

KYUNG LAH, CNN CORRESPONDENT
    The Nintendo Wii introduced wire-free controllers that track motion—a commercial hit introducing gaming to non-gamers. Kinect goes one step further.

KEVIN EYKEN, JOURNALIST
    It might be a good step towards something new, but it's a baby step. It's just the beginning of something different, and I'm not sure this is it, just motion gaming.

KYUNG LAH, CNN CORRESPONDENT
    Keeping consumers interested, say critics[6] at the Tokyo Game Show, will be the challenge, saying the technology is cool. As far as[2] the games ...

微软员工

这套系统可以看见各种细微的，诸如影像深度的差异，以此追踪你的身体动作。所以，你的身体只要有任何动作，它就会立刻…… 你的人物在屏幕上就会跟着做。

CNN 特派员 拉赫

这是我吗？

微软员工

没错。你跳一下，再跳，跳。

CNN 特派员 拉赫

完全不需要技巧。即便是像我这样的游戏新手，也立刻沉醉其中了。

微软员工

你可以看到我们正在玩的画面，也可以通过电子邮件或脸谱网等各种你喜欢的渠道和朋友分享这些照片。

CNN 特派员 拉赫

你们是不是又打破了人与科技之间的另一道障碍？

微软资深副总裁 唐·马特里克

的确如此。我们的目标就是让科技更能接受我们生来能做的动作。

CNN 特派员 拉赫

任天堂的 Wii 带来了能够追踪动作的无线控制器，结果大为热卖，让许多原本不是游戏迷的人都踏入了游戏的世界。Kinect 又向前迈进了一步。

记者 凯文·艾肯

这也许是迈向某种新技术的一步，但只是小小的一步。这只是某种不同技术的开端而已，我也不确定这真的就是游戏的未来。这只不过是动作感应式游戏而已。

CNN 特派员 拉赫

东京游戏展的评论家指出，要让消费者兴趣不减将是一大挑战，但他们也说这项技术很酷。至于配套的游戏……

Phrases

1. **get sucked in/into** 被吸引，无端卷入
Danny got sucked into the book's plot after just a few pages.
2. **as far as** 至于
As far as long-term cost is concerned, a car with low gas mileage is a better value.

Vocabulary

4. **novice** ['nɑvəs] *n.* 初学者，新手
5. **receptive** [rɪ'sɛptɪv] *adj.* 易于接受的，有接受力的
Alex is always receptive to constructive criticism.
6. **critic** ['krɪtɪk] *n.* 批评者，评论家

炫酷时尚　寰宇星空　生命发现　绿色革命　生活嬗变

RAPHAEL GUYOT, SANQUA MAGAZINE

Well, there's nothing really original in the games itself [themselves], so for the technology to work and the market to change, I think Microsoft has to show some really innovative[7] piece of software that goes with the new hardware.

MICROSOFT EMPLOYEE

I just think it's a lot more immersive[8], a lot more fun.

KYUNG LAH, CNN CORRESPONDENT

Consumers will weigh in this November when Xbox Kinect rolls out[3] worldwide. Microsoft says it will be one of the biggest gaming launches[9] ever, betting the bank that this new technology will be a runaway[10] hit.

MICROSOFT EMPLOYEE

Oh, super close!

《Sanqua 杂志》 拉菲尔·盖特

这些游戏本身没有什么原创性，所以这项科技如果真的要发挥作用，真的要改变市场，我想微软就必须为这种新硬件开发一些真正的创新性软件。

微软员工

我真的觉得这样玩更具现场感，更加有趣。

CNN 特派员 拉赫

Xbox Kinect 将于今年11月在全球正式推出，届时消费者就可以表达他们的意见了。微软表示，这将会是有史以来声势最浩大的游戏上市活动，他们把所有精力都投入在这项新的科技产品上，笃定这件产品一定会非常成功。

微软员工

哦，只差一点点！

CNN

Language Notes

weigh in   评价，发表意见

weigh 原意为"称重，重达"，引申为"衡量，对……有重要性或影响力"的意思，weigh in 常表示"发表意见，提出看法"，另外也指体育竞赛前选手"称重"。

例 On the talk show, several former politicians weighed in on the candidates in the current election.
数名曾经从政的人士在谈话节目中发表对目前选举候选人的看法。

例 The boxers weighed in before their fight.
拳击选手们比赛前先称重。

bet the bank   投入全部资金

bank 是"银行"或"本金"，bet the bank 表示"投入全部资金"，就好像把赌金全部下注一样，也可用 bet the farm 或 bet the ranch 表示。

例 Many wise investors wouldn't bet the bank on the long term strength of the local housing market.
许多明智的投资者不会把钱全部用来长期投资当地房地产。

Phrases

3. roll out 推出（产品）
The mobile phone manufacturer rolled out several new models this year.

Vocabulary

7. innovative ['ɪnə'veɪtɪv] *adj.* 创新的，革新的
The product has many innovative features.

8. immersive [ɪ'mɜːsɪv] *adj.* 有现场感的，身临其境的
Some studios believe 3-D movies are a more immersive experience.

9. launch [lɔːntʃ] *n.* 启动

10. runaway ['rʌnə'weɪ] *adj.* 大幅领先的，非常成功的
The video game was a runaway success.

炫酷时尚 寰宇星空 生命发现 绿色革命 生活嬗变

体验如梦似幻的
高科技未来旅馆

Hotel of
Tomorrow

Tech-Driven Creature Comforts[1] Future Travelers Can Look Forward To

RICHARD QUEST, BUSINESS TRAVELLER

Venice is built on a series of islands, so space is at a premium, as you can clearly see here in room 131. The room is so small that after opening the bag, well, there's no room for my suitcase. I've had to leave it on the floor. Some would call this snug[2]. I call it tiny.

To be sure, all the technology's here—the television, the telephone and the pretty lights. So, there is some technology, although I can't get Wi-Fi. What will the room of the future look like? Hopefully it will be a bit bigger. CNN's Jim Boulden has been to Germany to see how technology and hotels will look tomorrow.

JIM BOULDEN, CNN CORRESPONDENT

This is my hotel room today—comfortable bed, nice mini bar, wide-screen television. But fast-forward[3] a few years, and a hotel room could look like this.

DIGITAL PERSONAL CONCIERGE

Welcome, Jim, to the hotel room of the future.

图片提供　© gee-ly, Zürich und Fraunhofer IAO, Design: LAVA

4　体验如梦似幻的高科技未来旅馆

Language Notes

标题扫描：

-driven　受……驱动的

动词 drive 有"推动，驱赶，驱使"的意思，过去分词 -driven 当词尾，前面加上名词表示"受……驱动的，由……主导的"。

例 The electronics manufacturer prides itself on being innovation-driven.

那家电子制造商以创新研发为目标而自豪。

at a premium　稀少，难得

premium [ˈpriːmɪəm] 是"加价，溢价"，at a premium 原本是指"以超过面值的价格，以高价"，引申为"难得，稀少"，因而价值相对较高。

例 During the holidays, vacant rooms are at a premium in the city.

放假期间很难在该市找到空房间。

Vocabulary

1. **comfort** [ˈkʌmfət] *n.* 舒适的设施、条件（常用复数形式）
2. **snug** [snʌg] *adj.* 舒适的，温暖的
Martin could only afford a snug bungalow for his honeymoon accommodation.
3. **fast-forward** [ˌfæstˈfɔːwəd] *v.* 快速前进
The couple seems happy now, but fast-forward a year or so and I think you will find a much different situation.

《商务旅行家》 理查德·奎斯特

威尼斯建立在一系列群岛上，所以空间就显得弥足珍贵，从 131 号房你就能清楚看出。这个房间小到我把包打开后，就没地方放手提箱了，我得把它放在地上。有人会说它小巧温馨，我会说它小得可怜。

当然啦，这里有很多科技产品，例如电视、电话、精美灯座，的确是有一些科技产品，但我没有无线网络可用。未来的客房会是什么样子？希望能够大一点，本台的吉姆·博尔登已经到了德国，要带大家看看明日的科技和旅馆是什么模样。

CNN 特派员 吉姆·博尔登

这是我今天的客房，舒适的床铺、精美的小冰箱、宽屏幕电视，往以后快进几年，客房可能会像这个样子。

计算机私人管家

吉姆，欢迎光临未来饭店。

炫酷时尚　寰宇星空　生命发现　商海拾趣　生活嬗变

JIM BOULDEN, CNN CORRESPONDENT

Well, with all these white walls and curves, this room certainly has a futuristic[4] feel, but what's so special about it? What can it do that's so different?

DIGITAL PERSONAL CONCIERGE[5]

Well, Jim, if you lay back, the bed of the future can rock you to sleep.

VANESSA BORKMANN, FRAUNHOFER IAO

We started the Future Hotel Project about two years ago. The purpose is to find out the perfect hotel, today and in the future. We use it to integrate[6] different technologies, new products and try it [them] out[7].

JIM BOULDEN, CNN CORRESPONDENT

The accent[8] here is on living well rather than just looking good. The result has to be as soothing[9] to the mind as it is pleasing[10] to the eye.

VANESSA BORKMANN, FRAUNHOFER IAO

Everything is curved, and nothing is really, really straight. It is psychological. You feel like a little fetus[11]. And it's the shape that you also find in the nature.

JIM BOULDEN, CNN CORRESPONDENT

So, where are all the light switches in this room?

DIGITAL PERSONAL CONCIERGE

In the hotel room of the future, there will be no light switches. Instead, we will use sensor[12].

JIM BOULDEN, CNN CORRESPONDENT

In the future, these sensor could be used to monitor[13] heart rate and temperature. Accidental falls could trigger[14] alarm bells. Getting checked in could become synonymous with getting checked up[15]. Blue, green and purple light may just be a gimmick[16], but the intensity[17] of the LED white light could be usefully programmed to mimic[18] the waxing and waning of the sun.

So, are you a television?

DIGITAL PERSONAL CONCIERGE

No, Jim. I am you personal concierge, able to answer any question you may have from what time breakfast is to what floor the business center is on.

CNN 特派员　吉姆·博尔登

有了全白的墙面和曲线，这间客房很具未来感，但它有何特别之处？可以做些什么不一样的事情呢？

计算机私人管家

吉姆，如果你躺下，这张未来之床会摇你入睡。

弗劳恩霍夫工业工程研究所　瓦内莎·伯克曼

我们大概两年前开始了这项未来旅馆的计划，目的是要找出现在和未来最完美的旅馆，我们整合不同的科技和新产品，并付诸试验。

CNN 特派员　吉姆·博尔登

这里强调的是住得舒服而不只是样子好看，结果必须让心灵感到抚慰，视觉上也要舒服愉悦。

弗劳恩霍夫工业工程研究所　瓦内莎·伯克曼

所有东西的线条都是弯曲的，没有一样东西的线条是完全直的，这牵涉心理层面，你会觉得自己像个小胚胎，而这就是大自然的形状。

CNN 特派员　吉姆·博尔登

这个房间所有灯光的开关在哪呢？

计算机私人管家

在未来客房中没有灯光开关，我们使用的是感应器。

CNN 特派员　吉姆·博尔登

未来，这些感应器可以用来侦测心跳和温度，不小心跌倒可能就会触动警报器，所以登记入住很可能等于是在接受健康检查。蓝灯、绿灯和紫灯可能只是些小花招，但是 LED 白灯的强度对于模仿日光强弱的设计就很有用了。

那么你是电视吗？

计算机私人管家

不，吉姆，我是你的私人管家，可以回答你任何问题，包括早餐何时提供以及商务中心在哪个楼层。

Language Notes

synonymous with　等同于……

形容词 synonymous [sɪ'nɑnəməs] 是指"同义的，等同的"，通常与介词 with 连用，后面加上相比的事物，来表示"与……同义，等同于……"。

例 The hotel is synonymous with good service.
那家旅馆是优良服务的代名词。

wax and wane　明暗变化，强弱

wax 是指月亮"逐渐盈满"，wane 则是月亮"逐渐亏缺"，惯用语 wax and wane 即月亮的"阴晴圆缺"，也比喻事物的"盛衰，兴衰枯荣"，文中是说用灯光模拟日光强弱、天色明暗的变化。

例 Before calendars, people measured the months by the waxing and waning of the moon.
在历法发明之前，人们靠月亮的阴晴圆缺来估算一个月的时间。

Vocabulary

4. futuristic [ˌfjutʃə'rɪstɪk] adj. 未来感的，未来的
The new car has a very futuristic features.
5. concierge [kɑn'sjɛrʒ] n. 看门人，门房
6. integrate [ˌɪntə'gret] v. 整合，融合一体
7. try out [ʧraɪ][aʊt] 试验，试用
8. accent [ˈæksɛnt] n. 着重点，强调
9. soothing [ˈsuðɪŋ] adj. 抚慰性的，舒缓的
10. pleasing [ˈplizɪŋ] adj. 令人愉快的，令人满意的
11. fetus [ˈfitəs] n. 胎儿
12. sensor [ˌsɛnsə] n. 感应器（光、温度、重量等）
13. monitor [ˌmɑnətə] v. 监视，监控
14. trigger [ˈtrɪɡə] v. 引发，触发
15. check up [ʧɛk][ʌp] 检查，（尤指）身体检查
16. gimmick [ˈɡɪmɪk] n. 花招
17. intensity [ɪn'tɛnsəti] n. 强度（光、色彩、情感等）
18. mimic [ˌmɪmɪk] v. 模仿

VANESSA BORKMANN, FRAUNHOFER IAO

It's more than only a concierge; you can also use it to have your e-mails read, for example, to make a phone call or to ask for the music you like. Even a real concierge cannot help you in [with] these questions.

I want to mention that we still want to have people in a hotel. It's not to have the robotic hotel of the future.

JIM BOULDEN, CNN CORRESPONDENT

And apparently behind these walls, you could have infrared[19] lighting, which could rejuvenate[20] the skin. You could actually look younger while you're staying in the hotel.

So, fast-forward to the hotel room of the future. I don't think I would be checking out any time too soon.

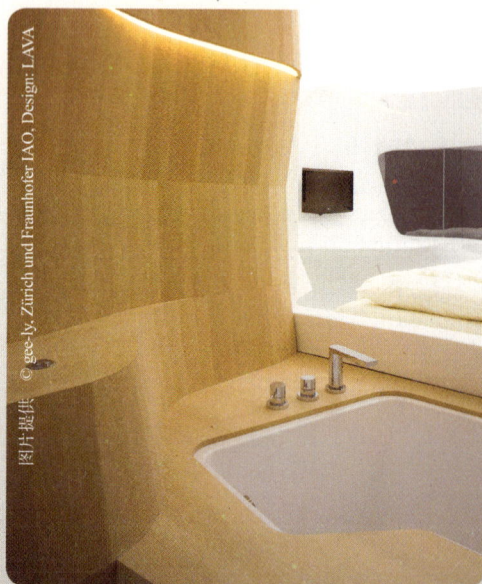

图片提供 ©gee-ly, Zürich und Fraunhofer IAO, Design: LAVA

弗劳恩霍夫工业工程研究所　瓦内莎·伯克曼

它可不只是管家而已，例如你可以用它来读取电子邮件、拨打电话、要求播放你喜欢的音乐，即使真人管家也无法帮你解决这些问题。

我想特别提出的是，我们还是希望未来旅馆里有活生生的人，并不是要发展成机器人旅馆。

CNN 特派员　吉姆·博尔登

而且你可以清楚看到，在这些墙后头你可以享受能让肌肤恢复活力的红外线照明，待在这家旅馆中真的可以让你看来更年轻。

快进入几年后的客房，我想我可不愿意太快退房呢！

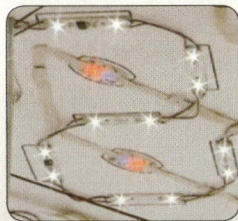

Vocabulary

19. infrared [ˌɪnfrəˈrɛd] *adj.* （使用）红外线的
Humans cannot see infrared light.
20. rejuvenate [rɪˈdʒuvəˈnet] *v.* 使年轻，复原
Many people rejuvenate themselves at hot springs.

用意念控制行动——

神奇的脑电波遥控科技

Mind Games

Gadgets[1] Put You in Control with Brain Power

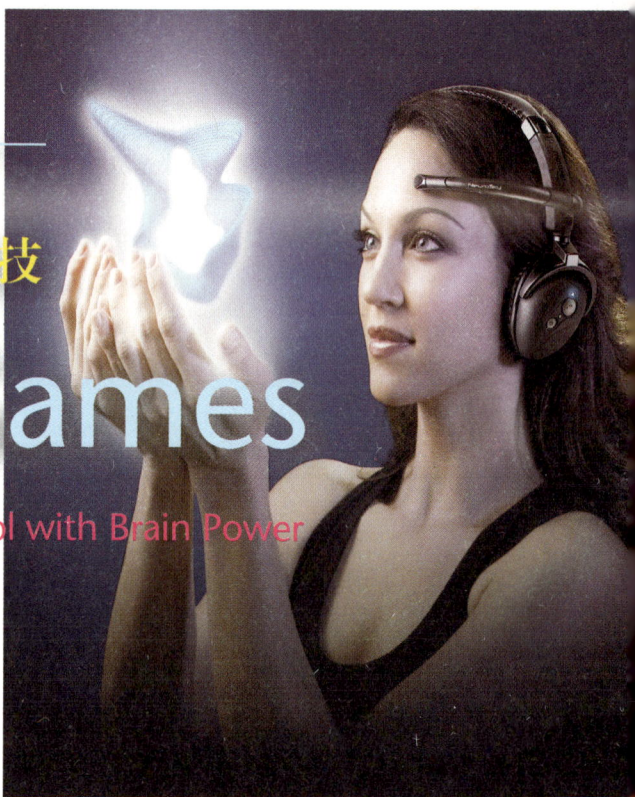

图片提供　NeuroSky

KRISTIE LU STOUT, CNN ANCHOR

Some new mind-controlled inventions could dramatically[2] change how we work and play. Brooke Baldwin visited a futuristic lab in California to check it all out[1].

TANSY BROOK, NEUROSKY

So, right here.

BROOKE BALDWIN, CNN CORRESPONDENT

I am moving this ball with only my mind.

TANSY BROOK, NEUROSKY

Just try to relax just a little bit.

BROOKE BALDWIN, CNN CORRESPONDENT

No keyboard, no game controls, just pure brain power. This is brain wave technology taken to a whole new level by a Silicon Valley based company called NeuroSky.

CNN 主播　克里斯蒂·卢·斯托特

　　新式的意念操控设备可能会大大改变我们工作与娱乐的方式。布鲁克·鲍德温采访了加利福尼亚一所充满未来色彩的实验室，要好好看看这项设备。

NeuroSky 公司　唐思·布鲁克

　　就在这里。

CNN 特派员　布鲁克·鲍德温

　　我只靠着意念移动这个球。

NeuroSky 公司　唐思·布鲁克

　　再放松一点。

CNN 特派员　布鲁克·鲍德温

　　没有键盘，没有游戏控制器，单纯靠脑力。设立于硅谷的 NeuroSky 公司把脑电波科技带到了全新的境界。

Phrases

1. check out 【口】试试，看看
   John went to the zoo to check out the panda exhibit.

Vocabulary

1. gadget ['gædʒət] *n.* 小器具，科技小产品
2. dramatically [drə'mætɪklɪ] *adv.* 剧烈地

TANSY BROOK, NEUROSKY

It's kind of the first application[3] of telekinesis[4].

BROOKE BALDWIN, CNN CORRESPONDENT

Engineers here have big plans to revolutionize[5] the way people work, play and live, using just their thoughts, and it starts with this— Uncle Milton's Star Wars Science Force Trainer, a new game that goes for about a hundred dollars.

TANSY BROOK, NEUROSKY

Well, the goal is to get the ball to rise and control it.

BROOKE BALDWIN, CNN CORRESPONDENT

This headset[6] has a sensor that reads my brain's electrical signals. It then sends them to a wireless receiver[7] inside the game's base, which lights up when I'm concentrating[8].

Too much concentration. Relax my brain. That's tough[9]. And your brain waves can control bigger objects, too. This is what NeuroSky calls the brain race, and I have this headset on, which is measuring my brain waves, and the second I start concentrating, this cart[10] should move forward. Let's see.

OK, that is kind of cool.

Now imagine a reality TV show like CBS's *Survivor* and throw in[2] this type of technology. NeuroSky is in talks with TV producers to develop[11] new reality shows that will do just that.

TANSY BROOK, NEUROSKY

Wouldn't it be fun to have a reality show? Wouldn't it be fun if people can change their environments using their minds? Could you light things on fire? Could you raise a drawbridge[12] by concentrating? Could you have to relax enough to have something levitate[13] to move you to the next level?

BROOKE BALDWIN, CNN CORRESPONDENT

But right now, the technology is being used to help train world class athletes like the U.S. archery[14] team.

Brady Ellison is one of the youngest U.S. archers to compete in the Olympics. He says a strong mental game is everything. That is exactly why he and his teammates were among the first to test brain wave technology to keep them in the zone.

NeuroSky 公司　唐思·布鲁克

这算是首款使用心灵遥感能力的设备。

CNN 特派员　布鲁克·鲍德温

这里的工程师有着远大的计划，打算彻底革新人们工作、娱乐与生活的方式，让人只靠着意念行事。而这就是这项计划的起点——米尔顿叔叔玩具公司的星际大战原力训练仪，这套新玩具要价约 100 美元。

NeuroSky 公司　唐思·布鲁克

目标就是要让球上升，然后加以控制。

CNN 特派员　布鲁克·鲍德温

这个头戴式装置有个感应器，可以读取我大脑的电子信号，然后把这些信号传送到玩具基座的无线式接收器。我只要集中注意力，玩具基座的灯光就会点亮。

太专注了。要放松我的大脑。好难啊。你的脑电波还可以控制更大的物体。这就是 NeuroSky 公司所谓的头脑赛车。我戴着这个头戴式装置，让它测量我的脑波。我一旦开始专注，这辆车应该就会前进。试试看吧。

好，这样确实很酷。

想想看，如果一部像 CBS 电视台《幸存者》这样的真人实境秀加入这种科技会变得怎样吧。NeuroSky 公司正与电视制作人洽谈制播这样的真人实境节目。

NeuroSky 公司　唐思·布鲁克

如果有一部这样的实境节目不是很好玩吗？如果人可以用意念改变周遭环境，不是很好玩吗？你能不能让东西着火？能不能利用专注力升起活动吊桥？你能不能放松，好让东西飘浮起来，把你带到下一关？

CNN 特派员　布鲁克·鲍德温

不过，现在这项科技被用来训练像美国射箭队这样的世界级运动员。

布雷迪·艾利森是美国最年轻的奥运射箭选手。他说，全神贯注是最重要的，所以他和他的队友才会率先测试脑电波科技，好让自己保持专注的状态。

Phrases

2. throw in 增添，添入
   Sue threw in some irises when making the flower arrangement.

Vocabulary

3. application [ˌæpləˈkeʃən] n. 应用（理论、发明等）
4. telekinesis [ˌtɛlɪkəˈnisəs] n. 心灵遥感
5. revolutionize [ˌrɛvəˈluʃəˌnaɪz] v. 彻底改变
   The iPhone revolutionized mobile handsets.
6. headset [ˈhɛdˌsɛt] n. 头戴式装置（如耳机）
7. receiver [rɪˈsivər] n. 接收器
8. concentrate [ˈkɑnsṇˌtret] v. 集中（注意力）
   Jeff concentrated on the test question before selecting his answer.
9. tough [tʌf] adj. 艰难的，棘手的
   Brian found it tough to maintain two jobs at the same time.
10. cart [kɑrt] n. 手推车
11. develop [dɪˈvɛləp] v. 构思，开发
    The company developed new technology for sharing video over the Internet.
12. drawbridge [ˈdrɔˌbrɪdʒ] n. 活动吊桥
13. levitate [ˈlɛvəˌtet] v. 使升空，使漂浮（尤指靠魔力或法力）
    The magician's assistant levitated above the stage.
14. archery [ˈɑrtʃərɪ] n. 射箭运动，射箭

炫酷时尚｜寰宇星空｜生命发现｜绿色革命｜生活嬗变

How many of you have seen a concrete[15] change in the way you've been shooting since this headset?

UNIDENTIFIED MALE ARCHER
I have.

U.S. ARCHERY TEAM
All of us.

BROOKE BALDWIN, CNN CORRESPONDENT
NeuroSky is sharing its technology with other companies, and there are unlimited possibilities for its use. For example, it might one day, be used to keep drowsy[16] drivers off[3] the road.

TANSY BROOK, NEUROSKY
Say the car could detect that and do something like turn on your radio or set off[4] a little alarm warning you that you need to pull over[5] and get some coffee.

你们开始使用这种头戴式装置之后，有多少人看到自己在射箭方面有了具体的变化？

未提供姓名的射箭男选手

我有。

美国射箭队

我们全部都有。

CNN 特派员　布鲁克·鲍德温

NeuroSky 公司和其他公司分享了这项科技，其应用方式可谓无穷无尽。举例而言，有一天也许可以利用这种科技防止精神不佳的驾驶员上路。

NeuroSky 公司　唐思·布鲁克

譬如车子可以侦测驾驶员的精神状况，然后做出类似打开收音机或是发出一点警报声这类的反应，以警告你得把车停到路边喝点咖啡。

Phrases

3. **keep sb. off** 使某人远离……
   Don put a fence around his yard to **keep** kids **off** his lawn.
4. **set off sth.** 使（警报）响起
   Ben's cooking always **sets off** the smoke alarm in the kitchen.
5. **pull over** （车辆）停靠路边
   Phil **pulled over** to ask for directions.

Vocabulary

15. **concrete** [ˌkɑŋkrit] *adj.* 具体的
    The instructor gave several **concrete** examples to make his point.
16. **drowsy** [ˌdrauzı] *adj.* 昏昏欲睡的，困倦的
    The cough medicine made the bus driver **drowsy**.

mind control 意念控制

人类脑电波主要分为 α、β、θ 及 δ 四种。α 波和 β 波是清醒时的脑波，θ 波和 δ 波则是睡眠时才会出现的脑电波。相对于精神专注时就会产生

的 β 波而言，α 波是在大脑空白（go blank）、呈半休息状态的时候会出现的一种脑电波。

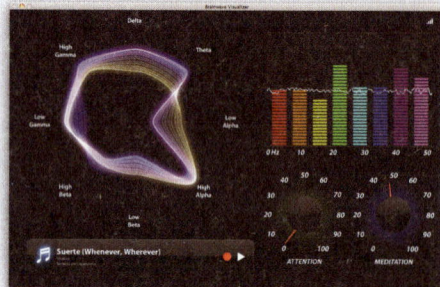

NeuroSky 公司的科技是用 α 波来启动（trigger）或操纵（manipulate）意念控制仪器。操纵者必须让脑部放松，让大脑只留下指挥仪器的指令（command）。α 波也会在人们昏昏欲睡时出现，因此可以用来侦测（detect）驾驶员清醒与否，然后实时发出警告或直接控制车辆，以避免交通意外发生。

Notes

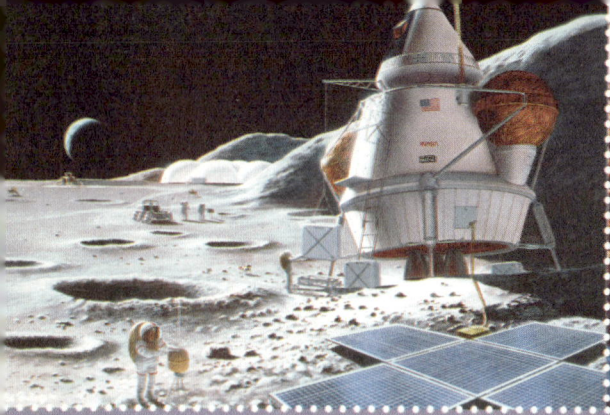

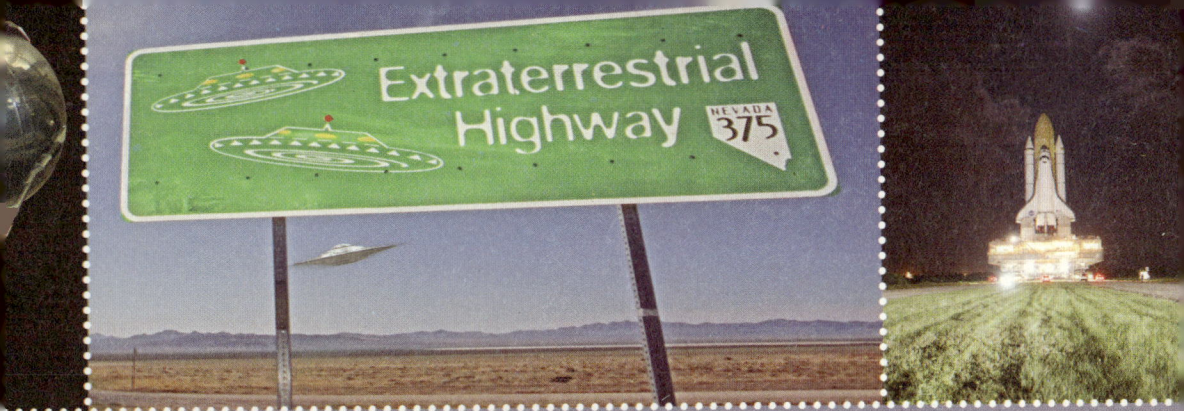

寰宇星空

⑥ 月球上有水，人类移居不是梦？

⑦ 火星生命之谜即将揭晓

⑧ 开启太空时代的人造卫星迎来 50 岁生日

⑨ CNN 记者的太空体验

⑩ 下一个大地震将发生在……

⑪ 美国太空计划未来出路

⑫ 以生物飞行本能为师的未来航空科技

⑬ 英国 UFO 档案大揭秘

月球上有水，

人类移居不是梦？

Our Not-So-Dry
Neighbor

The Discovery of Lunar Water
May Hold Key to Human
Colonies[1] on the Moon

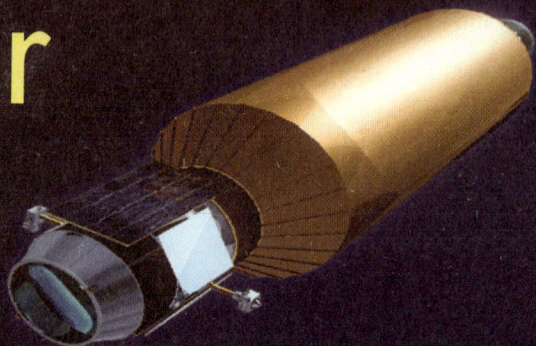

图片提供 NASA

ANNA COREN, CNN ANCHOR

Well, since the earliest days of modern astronomy[2], scientists believed the moon was a bone-dry[3] ball of rock and dust. But now some surprising new findings— there's water all over the moon. It'll take a bit of distilling[4], but the implications[5] are enormous, as Nina Nannar explains.

CHARLES DUKE, APOLLO ASTRONAUT

Oh, spectacular. Just spectacular.

NINA NANNAR, ITN REPORTER

It's even more spectacular than these early astronauts can have imagined because our dry and dusty moon has at last yielded[6] a huge secret—it's covered in water. It's not dripping in it, by any means, but it is there, hidden stores[7] of water molecules[8] in the moon's top layers. It's not yet the drinking kind. It's not even in liquid form, but it is instead bound up with minerals in lunar dust.

ISRO CONTROLLER

Three, two, one, zero, plus one, plus two …

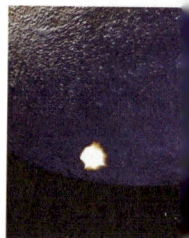

6 月球上有水，人类移居不是梦？

炫酷时尚

寰宇星空

生命发现

绿色革命

生活嬗变

Language Notes

标题扫描：

hold key to 是……的关键

以"拿着……的钥匙"比喻"是……的关键"，另外也可以用 be the key to 表示"是……的关键、秘诀或解决之道"。而标题在此是指月球上有水的这个发现，对未来人类居住月球的计划来说至关重要。

例 Many believe that stem cell research holds the key to curing many diseases.
许多人相信干细胞研究是治疗许多疾病的关键。

not . . . by any means 绝非

by any means 是指"无论如何"，加上 not 表示否定，与 by no means"绝不，绝非"同义。另外，表示肯定的 by all means 则是"当然，务必，没问题"的意思。

例 In spite of his injury, the player said his season is not over by any means.
这名球员虽然受伤，但他说他的运动生涯绝没结束。

例 You are by all means welcome to bring a guest to the party.
我们绝对欢迎您带宾客出席派对。

Vocabulary

1. colony [ˌkɑlənɪ] n. 殖民地
2. astronomy [əˈstrɑnəmɪ] n. 天文学
3. bone-dry [ˌbonˈdraɪ] adj. 干涸的
   Camels thrive in a bone-dry desert climate.
4. distill [dɪˈstɪl] v. 萃取，提炼
   The company distills its whisky from local grains.
5. implication [ˌɪmpləˈkeʃən] n. 含意，可能的影响（常为复数形式）
6. yield [jild] v. 提供，出产
   The area's ore yields high-quality metal.
7. store [stɔr] n. 储存物
8. molecule [ˈmɑləˌkjul] n. 分子

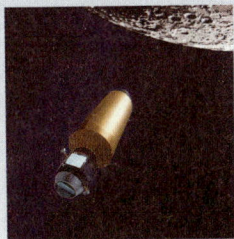

CNN 主播　安娜·科伦

　　在早期的现代天文学中，科学家们认为月球是个由石砾和粉尘构成的干燥球体。但现在却出现了一些令人惊讶的发现：月球上布满了水。月球上的水多少还需要净化，但其含意却相当深远。以下是妮娜·南娜的报道。

阿波罗航天员　查尔斯·杜克

　　太壮观了，实在太壮观了。

ITN 记者　妮娜·南娜

　　这比那些早期航天员所能想象的还要壮观，因为我们这颗干燥且满布尘土的月球最终透露了一个天大的秘密——它遍布着水。水并非在月球上滴流着，但它确实存在，以水分子的形式蕴藏在月球表层中。它还算不上饮用水，甚至还不是液体形态，而是蕴藏于月球尘土中的矿物。

印度太空研究组织控制员

　　三、二、一、零、正一、正二……

NINA NANNAR, ITN REPORTER

The discovery was made by India's lunar craft Chandrayaan-1, launched a year ago on the country's first moon mission, and scientists are thrilled[9].

CARLE PIETERS, NASA PROFESSOR

You have to think outside of the box on this. This is not what any of us expected a decade ago, but widespread water has been detected on the surface of the moon.

NINA NANNAR, ITN REPORTER

One of the Chandrayaan probe's main objectives was to search for signs of water, but when it came, it was still a surprise. The unmanned[10] craft was equipped with NASA's Moon Mineralogy[11] Mapper, which looks for water by picking up[12] the electromagnetic[13] radiation emitted[14] by minerals.

It's thought earlier missions missed the lunar dust because they didn't look at the moon's poles. The Erlanger Crater near the north pole is one of the areas being analyzed for signs of water.

NASA may here be imagining a permanent[15] base on the moon, but, say scientists, the discovery of water brings that a lot closer, as with the right technology, water could be extracted[16] from moon dust and stored ready for lunar visitors.

CARL PILCHER, DIRECTOR, NASA ASTROBIOLOGY INST.

[It is] water that might be used some day by lunar explorers—human lunar explorers —who return to the moon to do science on the moon and perhaps as a stepping-stone[17] out into the rest of the solar system.

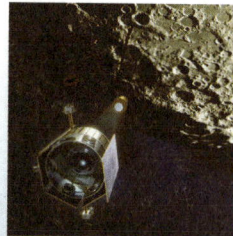

ITN 记者　妮娜·南娜

这是印度登月飞船"月球飞船一号"的一项发现。这艘飞船在一年前发射，是印度的首次月球任务，科学家对此深感兴奋。

美国太空总署专家　卡尔·彼得斯

你必须跳出框架来思考这件事。10 年前没有任何人预见到这件事，但目前月球表面已经被探测出有大面积的水存在。

ITN 记者　妮娜·南娜

"月球飞船一号"探勘任务的主要目标之一是搜寻水的迹象，但当找到它时，仍旧令人感到惊讶。该艘无人驾驶的飞行器配备了美国太空总署的矿源绘图仪，通过接收矿物所发散的电磁波辐射来找寻水的踪迹。

有人认为早期的探月任务之所以遗漏了月球的尘土，是因为他们并未探勘月球的极区。靠近月球北极的厄兰格陨石坑，就是其中一个用来分析是否标志有水的区域。

太空总署现在可能想在月球上设立一个永久基地，但科学家说，发现水让这个可能性大为提升，因为只要用正确的科技，就能从月球的尘土中提取出水，并贮存起来供月球访客使用。

美国太空总署太空生物研究所
卡尔·皮尔丘

那些水可能某天会供月球探索者使用，这里是指人类月球探索者，他们回到月球上做月球科学研究，或许还可以以月球为跳板前往太阳系其余的地方。

Language Notes

think outside of the box
跳出既有思考模式

字面上意思是"跳出箱子思考"，"箱子"比喻"限制、封闭的范围，固定的框架"，所以该词组就表示"摆脱窠臼，跳出既有思维模式"，以自由、有创意的方式来思考。

例 Carl encouraged his creative team to think outside the box when planning ad campaigns. 卡尔鼓励他的创意团队在构思广告活动时跳出既有的思考模式。

Vocabulary

9. **thrilled** [θrɪld] *adj.* 非常兴奋的、激动的
   Jane was thrilled that her son was accepted to a top university.

10. **unmanned** [ˌʌnˈmænd] *adj.* 无人操作的，未载人的
   NASA sent an unmanned probe to Mars.

11. **mineralogy** [ˌmɪnəˈrɑlədʒɪ] *n.* (某地区、岩层、岩石结构的)矿物特质

12. **pick up** [pɪk][ʌp] 辨识，收集，接收（信号）
   Nathan sometimes picks up broadcasts from Europe on his shortwave radio.

13. **electromagnetic** [ɪˈlɛktromæɡˈnɛtɪk] *adj.* 电磁的
   The satellite signal was knocked out by electromagnetic interference.

14. **emit** [ɪˈmɪt] *v.* 发散
   The alarm emitted a loud buzzing noise.

15. **permanent** [ˌpɜˈmənənt] *adj.* 长久的，长期的
   Janet switched to a full-time position and became a permanent member of the staff.

16. **extract** [ɛkˈstrækt] *v.* 提取，萃取
   The machine extracts oil from coal.

17. **stepping-stone** [ˌstɛpɪŋˈston] *n.* 踏脚石，敲门砖

NINA NANNAR, ITN REPORTER

The next generation of rocket is being prepared. The international race to set foot on the moon again is heating up[18], and now we know there's water, the notion of living there is perhaps no longer so fantastical.

图片提供：NASA

ITN 记者　妮娜·南娜

　　下一代的火箭正在筹备中。国际上的登月竞赛再度白热化。现在我们知道月球上有水了，在月球上居住的想法或许将不再那么不切实际了。⃝

图片提供：NASA

set foot on　踏上，到达某地

set foot 是"将脚踏上，到达"的意思，后面用 on 加地点表示"到达某处"，用 in 加地点则表示"进入某处"，如进入建筑物、国家等。另外结构相近的 set eyes on sth. 则是指"看到某物"。

例 Many historians believe Vikings were the first Europeans to set foot on American soil.
许多历史学家相信维京海盗是最早踏上美国土地的欧洲人。

例 Wilma set foot in the restaurant for the first time last week and has been back every day since.
威玛自从上周第一次来到这家餐厅之后就每天报到。

例 Daphne fell in love the moment she first set eyes on her future husband.
达芙妮第一次看到她现在的丈夫时就瞬间坠入了爱河。

Vocabulary

18. **heat up** ['hit,ʌp] 加温，激烈起来
The baseball championship heated up with pairing of two longtime rivals.

月球飞船一号 Chandrayaan-1

由印度太空研究组织（Indian Space Research Organisation, ISRO）打造的绕月卫星（orbiter），使印度成为全球第四个登月的国家。月球飞船一号于 2008 年 10 月升空，2009 年 9 月发现大范围的月球土壤中存在水分子。

这个新发现让科学家们大为兴奋，因为如果月球有水就表示可能有生物存在，人类在月球上生活的可能性也会提高，这激励着各国太空机构持续探测月球。

例如美国太空总署就在 2009 年 10 月进行了 LCROSS 撞月行动，利用火箭将探测器投掷到月球表面激起浮尘，加以收集后进行分析，确认月球有水的事实及含水量多少。

图片提供：NASA

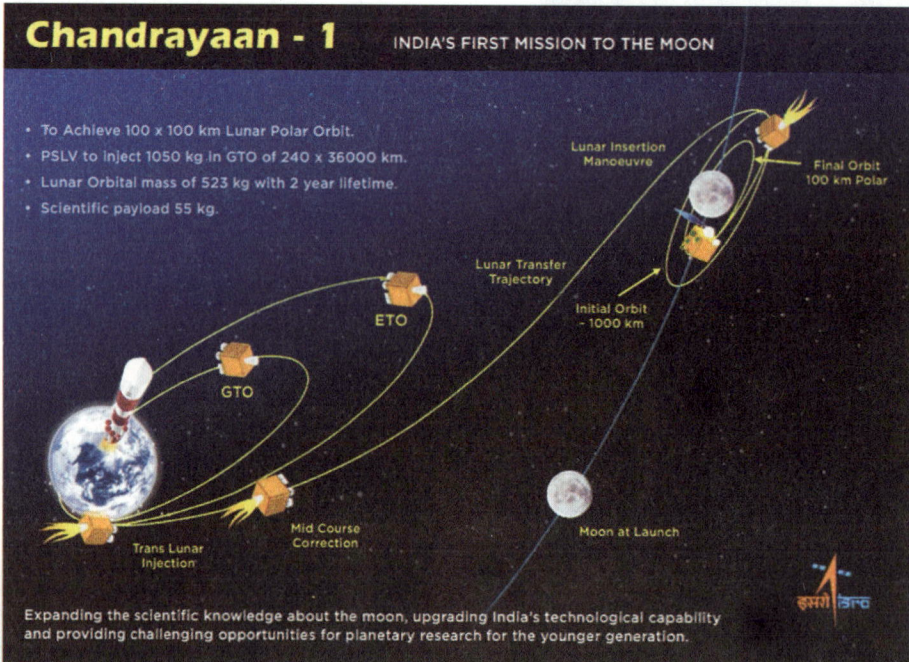

Chandrayaan - 1   INDIA'S FIRST MISSION TO THE MOON

- To Achieve 100 x 100 km Lunar Polar Orbit.
- PSLV to inject 1050 kg in GTO of 240 x 36000 km.
- Lunar Orbital mass of 523 kg with 2 year lifetime.
- Scientific payload 55 kg.

Lunar Insertion Manoeuvre

Final Orbit 100 km Polar

Lunar Transfer Trajectory

ETO

GTO

Initial Orbit - 1000 km

Mid Course Correction

Trans Lunar Injection

Moon at Launch

Expanding the scientific knowledge about the moon, upgrading India's technological capability and providing challenging opportunities for planetary research for the younger generation.

Moon Mineralogy Mapper 矿源绘图仪

　　这是"月球飞船一号"其中的一台"装载设备"（payload），也就是装载（on board）于人造卫星或飞行器上、用来进行实验或通信的仪器。矿源绘图仪主要用来绘制月球的矿源立体光谱图，以显示月球表面与其矿物组成的关系。

　　月球在形成后就几乎停止活动，不像其他星球大多持续进行地壳变动、气候变化等。因此，通过分析月球的矿物组成，不但能一窥月球的奥秘，也可能找到太阳系形成初期的线索。

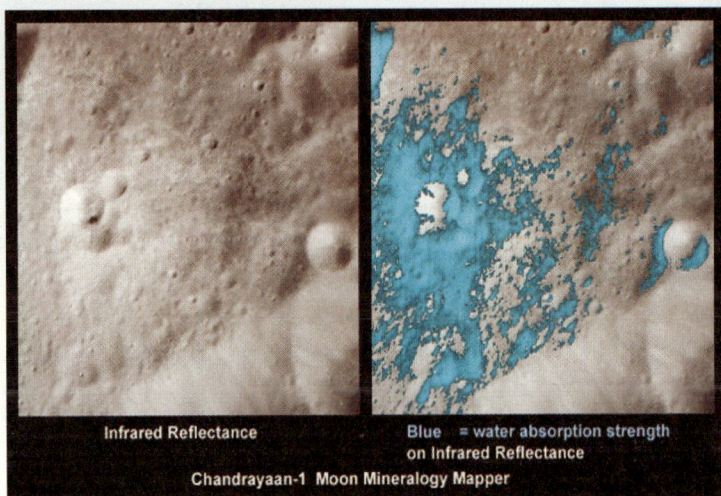

图片提供：NASA

Infrared Reflectance

Blue = water absorption strength on Infrared Reflectance

Chandrayaan-1 Moon Mineralogy Mapper

炫酷时尚

寰宇星空

生命发现

绿色革命

生活嬗变

火　星

生命之谜即将揭晓

Our Martian[1] Neighbors

Scientists Search for Signs of Life on the Red Planet

图片提供：NASA

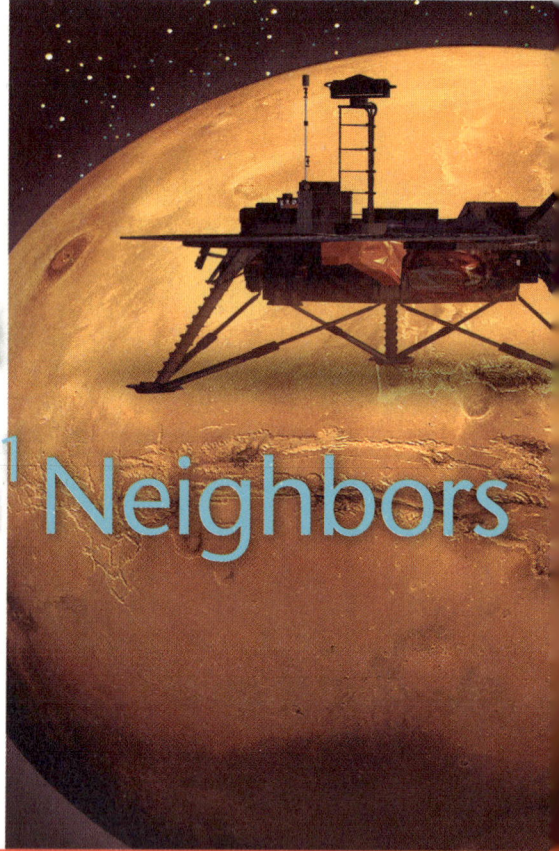

CNN ANCHOR

Well, many have looked up at the night sky and wondered if our nearest neighbor can actually support life, and if so, what sort of life. Miles O'Brien met one of the scientists trying to answer those cosmic[2] questions.

MILES O'BRIEN, CNN TECHNOLOGY CORRESPONDENT

Mars is a place of contradictions[3], alien[4] yet familiar; so close it seems reachable[5], yet far enough to protect its secrets. For as long as we have looked at the night sky, we have wondered about that reddish[6] star, what mysteries might it hold and whether one day we might pay a visit.

Steve Squyres is the top scientist for NASA's Mars Rover[7] expeditions[8], which rolled out the intrepid[9] robots Spirit and Opportunity on the Martian surface in January 2004.

Language Notes

roll out　送出，推出

roll out 原意是"推出新产品"，在本文中的火星探测机器人有车轮装置协助行驶，因此取 roll 字面上"滚动"的意思来表示将这两架机器人送上了火星。

例 The pit crew rolled out the racecar onto the track.

维修站的人员将赛车送入车道中。

Vocabulary

1. **Martian** ['mɑrʃən] *adj.* 火星的
   The Martian atmosphere is much thinner than that of Earth.
2. **cosmic** ['kɑzmɪk] *adj.* 宇宙的
   The spaceship's cosmic journey lasted three years.
3. **contradiction** [ˌkɑntrə'dɪkʃən] *n.* 矛盾
4. **alien** ['elɪən] *n.* 外星人
5. **reachable** ['ritʃəbl] *adj.* 可到达的
   The island is reachable only by plane or ship.
6. **reddish** ['rɛdɪʃ] *adj.* 偏红色的
   Phyllis dyed her hair reddish-brown.
7. **rover** ['rovə] *n.* 流浪者，漫游者
8. **expedition** [ˌɛkspɪ'dɪʃən] *n.* 探险队，考察队
9. **intrepid** [ɪn'trɛpɪd] *n.* 勇敢的，大胆的
   The intrepid explorer led several expeditions through the heart of Borneo.

CNN 主播

许多人都曾经仰望夜空，想着最邻近我们的星球是否适合生存。如果答案是肯定的话，又适合什么样的生物？迈尔斯·欧布莱恩访问了一位试图回答这些关于宇宙问题的科学家。

CNN 科技特派员　迈尔斯·欧布莱恩

火星是个充满矛盾的地方。一方面显得陌生，另一方面又相当熟悉；一方面近得似乎能够到达，另一方面又远得足以保持神秘感。自从人类开始仰望夜空以来，我们就一直对这颗红色星球充满好奇，心想着这颗星球有什么样的奥秘，以及我们是否有一天能够探访这颗星球。

史蒂夫·斯奎尔斯是美国航天总署火星探测车任务的顶尖科学家，他们在 2004 年 1 月把"勇气号"与"机遇号"这两个勇敢无畏的机器人送上了火星表面。

STEVE SQUYRES, MARS ROVER SCIENTIST

Here we go, keep going, keep going. Keep going. These two spots to north and the south are the ones that we've been looking at.

MILES O'BRIEN, CNN TECHNOLOGY CORRESPONDENT

The red planet for him is a means to an end; a great place to answer some questions that have burned inside him all his life.

STEVE SQUYRES, MARS ROVER SCIENTIST

How common is life throughout[10] the universe? And how does life first arise[11]?

MILES O'BRIEN, CNN TECHNOLOGY CORRESPONDENT

Do you remember the first time you asked that question of yourself?

STEVE SQUYRES, MARS ROVER SCIENTIST

I can't remember a time when I didn't.

MILES O'BRIEN, CNN TECHNOLOGY CORRESPONDENT

From day one?

STEVE SQUYRES, MARS ROVER SCIENTIST

Yeah, I mean, and I think that just speaks to how normal and natural it is for anybody. You could ask that question of anybody I think, you'd get almost the same answer. Six-year-old kid, go out and look at the sky at night, look at the stars. You know, what's out there? Didn't you wonder[12]?

MILES O'BRIEN, CNN TECHNOLOGY CORRESPONDENT

Sure.

STEVE SQUYRES, MARS ROVER SCIENTIST

We all have.

MILES O'BRIEN, CNN TECHNOLOGY CORRESPONDENT

Mars may be just the place to find the Holy Grail.

火星探测车科学家　史蒂夫·斯奎尔斯

　　好，继续前进，继续前进。继续前进。我们一直在观察的就是北边和南边这两个点。

CNN 科技特派员　迈尔斯·欧布莱恩

　　对他而言，火星是他永远的研究重点，在这里可以为他内心思索了一辈子的一些问题找到答案。

火星探测车科学家　史蒂夫·斯奎尔斯

　　宇宙间存在生命的现象有多么普遍？生命又是如何开始的？

CNN 科技特派员　迈尔斯·欧布莱恩

　　你还记得自己什么时候第一次对自己提出这个问题吗？

火星探测车科学家　史蒂夫·斯奎尔斯

　　我都记不得自己什么时候停止问这个问题了。

CNN 科技特派员　迈尔斯·欧布莱恩

　　从出生那一天就开始了吗？

火星探测车科学家　史蒂夫·斯奎尔斯

　　是啊。我是说，我认为由此可见每个人都自然而然会问这样的问题。问谁都会得到几乎相同的答案。6 岁的小孩抬头看着夜空，看着星星，也一样会问，天上有什么东西？你难道不曾好奇过吗？

CNN 科技特派员　迈尔斯·欧布莱恩

　　当然好奇过。

火星探测车科学家　史蒂夫·斯奎尔斯

　　大家都想过。

CNN 科技特派员　迈尔斯·欧布莱恩

　　火星很可能正是能够找到答案的地方。

Language Notes

a means to an end　达到目的的方法

means 表示"方法，手段"，a means to an end 是"达到目的的方法或手段"，文中是说他通过研究火星，来探究宇宙中的其他生命并寻找生命的起源。

例 Hal didn't like his job, but it was a means to end.
哈尔不喜欢他的工作，但那是他的生计。

speak to sth.　为……举例说明

speak to sth. 意思是 be an example of sth.，也就是指"举例说明，提供了某事的一个例子"。

例 The documentary film speaks to the fragile state of our environment.
这部纪录片清楚说明了我们的环境的脆弱状态。

Holy Grail　圣杯，最终目标

Holy Grail 原本是指耶稣在受难时，用来盛接耶稣鲜血的圣餐杯，另有一种说法是耶稣在最后的晚餐使用的杯子。传说如果能找到圣杯并喝下盛装其中的水，就能青春永驻，长生不老。后来 Holy Grail 引申为"所追寻的最终目标"。

Vocabulary

10. **throughout** [θruˈaʊt] *prep.* 遍及，遍布
11. **arise** [əˈraɪz] *v.* 产生，出现
Archeologists and historians believe the first human civilizations arose in area around the Tigris and Euphrates rivers.
12. **wonder** [ˈwʌndə] *v.* 想知道

STEVE SQUYRES, MARS ROVER SCIENTIST

If you can go to just another planet in this solar[13] system and find that even just in this one solar system, life has independently arisen twice, then it requires no great leap of faith or anything else to believe that it may, in fact, be common when you consider the multitude[14] of worlds that there are out there.

图片提供：NASA

火星探测车科学家　史蒂夫·斯奎尔斯

　　你如果能够前往太阳系里的另外一颗行星，就会发现单单在这个太阳系里，生命就独立出现过两次，那么就不难相信外星生物很可能普遍存在了。想想看，在外层空间还有多少个不同的世界啊。CNN

leap of faith　无条件的信任

leap of faith 通常是指在宗教信仰上"无条件的信任"的意思。leap 是"跳跃，跨越"，在这里也就是说跳出逻辑思考，对某事保持全然的信任。

Vocabulary

13. **solar** ['solə] *adj.* 太阳的，日光的
    Solar flares often interfere with radio and television signals.
14. **multitude** [,mʌltə'tjud] *n.* 许多

炫酷时尚

寰宇星空

生命发现

绿色革命

生活嬗变

Mars Exploration Rover Mission
火星探测车任务

火星探险车任务（简称 MER）是美国太空总署 2003 年开始进行的外层空间探索计划。2003 年 6 月 10 日发送了"勇气号"，同年 7 月 7 日发送"机遇号"，当时的主要任务是探测火星表面及地质状况（geology）。带领此项任务计划的人员为美国太空总署喷射推进实验（NASA's Jet Propulsion Laboratory）的项目经理（project manager）彼得·薛辛格（Peter Theisinger），以及康奈尔大学天文系的首席科学家（principal investigator）史蒂夫·斯奎尔斯博士（Dr. Steve Squyres）。

图片提供：NASA

Give It a Try 请选出正确答案

1. The temple is _____ only by a perilous mountain path.
   a. readable   b. rentable
   c. reachable   d. reasonable

2. The _____ expedition reached the river's source.
   a. intrepid   b. interested
   c. interned   d. interim

Answers: 1.c 2.a

Notes

....
....
....
....
....
....
....
....
....
....
....
....
....
....
....
....
....
....
....
....
....

炫酷时尚

寰宇星空

生命发现

绿色革命

生活嬗变

开启太空时代的人造卫星迎来 50 岁生日

Celebrating Sputnik

The Tiny Satellite[1] that Sparked
the Space Race Turns 50

图片提供：NASA

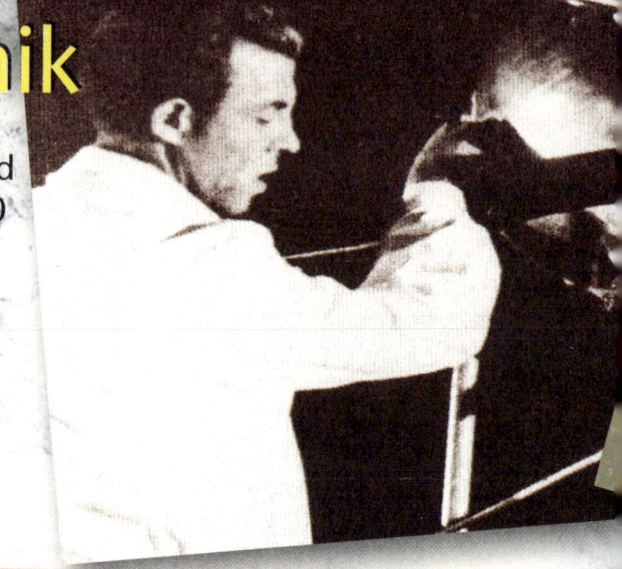

CNN ANCHOR
In an era of space shuttles[2] and orbiting[3] space stations with human crews[4], it's a little hard to imagine that just 50 years ago it was all science fiction[5].

CNN ANCHOR
Yes, and then a new word in the world's vocabulary came about—Sputnik. Jill Dougherty looks back five decades to the event that launched the space age. Just 50 years.

JILL DOUGHERTY, CNN CORRESPONDENT
It streaked[6] across the night sky October 4, 1957: a tiny, shiny sphere circling the globe every hour and a half, emitting[7] radio signals; the first man-made object in space, launched by the Soviet Union. People around the world searched the heavens, some in awe, some in fear.

UNIDENTIFIED WOMAN
It gets the American people alarmed that a foreign country, especially an enemy country, can do this. We fear this.

JILL DOUGHERTY, CNN CORRESPONDENT
Fifty years later, retired science professor Cameron Pulliam still remembers that sound.

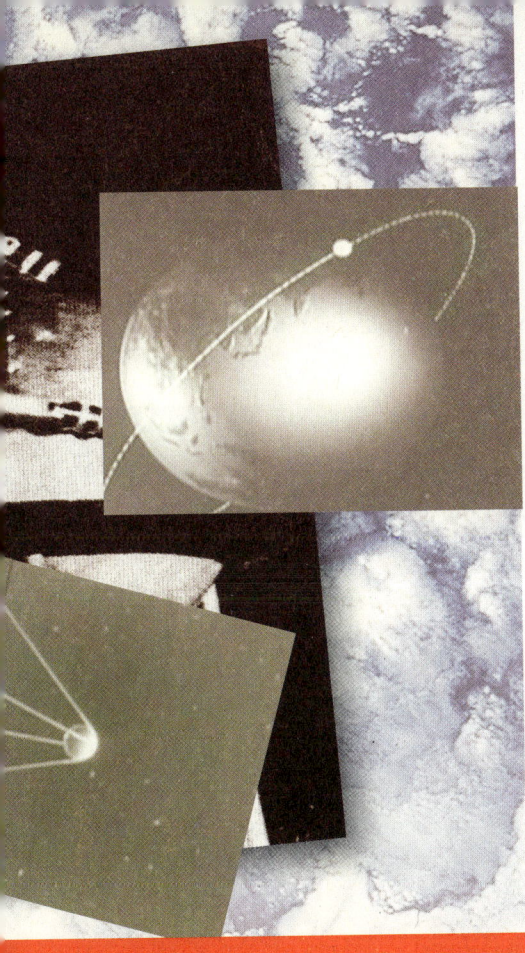

8 开启太空时代的人造卫星迎来 50 岁生日

Language Notes

come about 发生，出现

用来表示某事件或问题"发生"，通常是指经过一段时间的酝酿或发展，意思和 happen 或 take place 类似。

例 Ben's promotion came about through hard work and persistence.
本的升迁来自于努力和勤奋。

in awe 敬畏地

awe 当名词是指"敬畏"，in awe 表示抱着又敬又怕的心态，后面可用介词 of 加上敬畏的人或事物。

例 Steve is in awe of his older brother.
史蒂夫对他的兄长又敬又怕。

CNN 主播

在这个航天飞机与驻人太空站的时代，实在很难想象这些东西在 50 年前都还只是科幻想象。

CNN 主播

没错，但后来世界上出现了一个新词汇——斯普特尼克 1 号。吉尔·杜尔迪回顾 50 年前那个开启了太空时代的事件。才 50 年。

CNN 特派员 吉尔·杜尔迪

它在 1957 年 10 月 4 日划过夜空：一个渺小闪亮的球体，每 1.5 小时绕行地球一周，同时发出无线电信号。这是太空中第一个人造物体，由苏联发射。世界各地的人都搜寻着天际，有些人怀着敬畏，有些人带着恐惧。

不知名女性

外国竟然做得到这样的事情，尤其还是敌国，这种情形让美国人民深感不安。我们很害怕。

CNN 特派员 吉尔·杜尔迪

50 年后，退休科学教授卡梅伦·普廉姆仍然记得那个声音。

Vocabulary

1. **satellite** ['sætə,laɪt] *n.* 卫星
2. **space shuttle** [spes]['ʃʌtl] 航天飞机
3. **orbit** ['ɔrbɪt] *v.* 绕轨道运行
   The space station orbits the earth.
4. **crew** [kru] *n.* 全体成员，全体工作人员
5. **science fiction** ['saɪəns]['fɪkʃən] 科幻小说
6. **streak** [strik] *v.* 闪现，飞奔
   The meteor streaked across the sky.
7. **emit** [i'mɪt] *v.* 发出，散发
   The alarm emitted a piercing noise.

CAMERON, PULLIAM, RETIRED
SCIENCE PROFESSOR

We heard it. We heard the "beep, beep, beep." And I remember listening on the radio to the sounds of the beeping satellite and how shocking it was that someone could have done better than we did in scientific endeavors[8].

JILL DOUGHERTY, CNN CORRESPONDENT

But Sputnik inspired as well.

FEMALE RADIO ANNOUNCER

This is Radio Moscow and here is the news.

MALE RADIO ANNOUNCER

Our satellite Sputnik lifted off at 22 hours 28 minutes Moscow time and entered orbit around the Earth.

MALE RADIO ANNOUNCER

The first artificial[9] Earth satellite in the world.

JILL DOUGHERTY, CNN CORRESPONDENT

A new documentary[10] *Sputnik Mania* shows John Glenn on a TV game show just three hours after Sputnik was launched. Four years later, he would become the first American to orbit the Earth.

JOHN GLENN, TEST PILOT AND ASTRONAUT

This is probably the first step toward space travel or moon travel, something we'll probably run into maybe in Eddie's lifetime here, at least.

GEORGE DEWITT, NAME THAT TUNE HOST

Eddie, would you like to take a trip to the moon?

EDDIE HODGES, NAME THAT TUNE CONTESTANT

No sir, I like it fine right here.

JILL DOUGHERTY, CNN CORRESPONDENT

It's hard to imagine today how technologically primitive[11] Sputnik actually was, just a battery and a radio transmitter[12], not even close to today's cell phone. The real Sputnik burned up after three months in space. The National Air and Space Museum in Washington D.C. has a copy given to it by the Soviet Academy of Sciences. The size of it is so amazingly small compared to what you think.

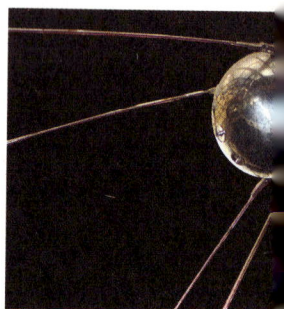

MARTIN COLLINS, NATIONAL AIR AND SPACE MUSEUM

There is a reason. It takes a tremendous[13] amount of energy to lift an object from the surface of the Earth, so to get something even small up into space requires a rocket of substantial[14] size.

退休科学教授　卡梅伦·普廉姆

我们听到那个声音，听到"哔，哔，哔"。我记得当时在收音机上听着卫星的哔哔声，对于别人竟然能够在科学成就上超越我们深感震惊。

CNN 特派员　吉尔·杜尔迪

但斯普特尼克 1 号也激励了许多人。

电台女播音员

这是莫斯科广播电台，以下是最新新闻。

电台男播音员

我们的卫星斯普特尼克 1 号在莫斯科时间 22 时 28 分升空，并且进入了地球轨道。

电台男播音员

这是全世界第一颗人造地球卫星。

CNN 特派员　吉尔·杜尔迪

在《斯普特尼克 1 号狂潮》这部新推出的纪录片里，可以看到约翰·格伦在斯普特尼克 1 号发射 3 小时后参加电视猜谜节目的画面。4 年后，他就成了第一位绕行地球的美国人。

测试飞行员兼航天员　约翰·格伦

这大概是迈向太空旅游或月球旅行的第一步，这个梦想至少在艾迪有生之年应该就会实现。

《歌名大挑战》节目主持人　乔治·德威特

艾迪，你想不想到月球去？

《歌名大挑战》节目参赛者　艾迪·哈吉斯

不想。我觉得在地球上很好。

CNN 特派员　吉尔·杜尔迪

今天很难想象斯普特尼克 1 号使用的科技实际上是多么原始，只有一块电池和一台无线电发送机，连今天的手机都比不上。真正的斯普特尼克 1 号在太空中绕行 3 个月后就烧毁了。华盛顿的国家航空太空博物馆收藏了前苏联科学院赠送的复制品。这颗卫星的体积比你想象的还小很多。

美国国家航空太空博物馆　马丁·科林斯

这是有原因的，因为要把物体推离地球表面需要非常大量的能量。所以，即便是把一个小东西送上太空，也需要体积相当大的火箭。

Vocabulary

8. endeavor [ɪnˈdɛvə] *n.* 努力
9. artificial [ˌɑrtəˈfɪʃəl] *adj.* 人造的
10. documentary [ˌdɑkjuˈmɛntəri] *n.* 纪录片
11. primitive [ˈprɪmɪtɪv] *adj.* 原始的，最初的
    The anthropologists visited a primitive village in the Amazon jungle.
12. transmitter [trænsˈmɪtə] *n.* 发送机
13. tremendous [trɪˈmɛndəs] *adj.* 极度的，惊人的
    Once the test was over, Tina felt a tremendous amount of relief.
14. substantial [sʌbˈstænʃəl] *adj.* 极大的，大量的
    Gina received a substantial discount on her airline tickets.

JILL DOUGHERTY, CNN CORRESPONDENT

Ultimately[15], Sputnik was the byproduct[16] of Soviet efforts to develop the intercontinental[17] ballistic missile[18].

MARTIN COLLINS, NATIONAL AIR AND SPACE MUSEUM

The 1950s was defined by fear, nuclear fear in particular[19], whether weapons delivered[20] by airplanes or by this new technology of the long-range missile.

JILL DOUGHERTY, CNN CORRESPONDENT

Sputnik led the Eisenhower administration[21] to create the U.S. space agency NASA less than a year later. Fifty years after Sputnik, it means little or nothing to the younger generation.

UNIDENTIFIED GIRL

I'm not too sure, but Mom's just mentioned[22] it a few times and I'm like, "What's that?"

JILL DOUGHERTY, CNN CORRESPONDENT

But Sputnik changed the world forever. The Cold War deepened. The U.S. and the Soviet Union began the dash[23] to test hydrogen bombs[24] .Yet as people stared at the night sky half a century ago, they marveled at what the mind of man can do and listened.

1962

1969

1975

CNN 特派员　吉尔·杜尔迪

不过，斯普特尼克 1 号其实是（前）苏联发展洲际弹道飞弹的副产品。

美国国家航空太空博物馆　马丁·科林斯

20 世纪 50 年代是个充满恐惧的年代，尤其是对核武的恐惧，不论武器的载体是飞机还是长程飞弹这种新的科技产物。

CNN 特派员　吉尔·杜尔迪

斯普特尼克 1 号促使艾森豪威尔政府在不到 1 年后随即成立美国太空机构"美国国家航空航天局"。在斯普特尼克 1 号发射 50 年后，这颗卫星在年轻一代的心目中已经没有什么意义了。

不知名女孩

我不太确定，我妈提到过几次，我只说："那是什么东西？"

CNN 特派员　吉尔·杜尔迪

但是斯普特尼克 1 号永远改变了世界。冷战因此更为激烈。美国和（前）苏联开始竞相测试氢弹。不过，世人在半个世纪前仰望夜空的时候，他们确实赞叹于人类智慧能够创造的成就，并且静静聆听卫星的声音。 **CNN**

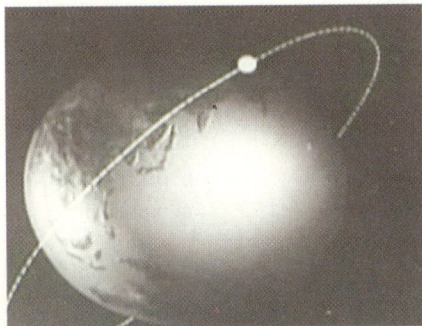

Language Notes

marvel at　惊讶，吃惊

marvel 当动词是"感到惊讶或钦佩"的意思，后面用介词 at 加上惊讶的事物。marvel 也可当名词，意思是"令人惊讶的事物或人"。

例 Julia marveled at her sister's expensive engagement ring.
朱莉娅对她姐姐的昂贵订婚戒指感到吃惊。

例 The cleaning fluid worked marvels on Janice's kitchen floor.
那种清洁剂让珍妮丝的地板焕然一新。

Vocabulary

15. **ultimately** [ˈʌltəmətlɪ] *adv.* 终究地，最后地
16. **byproduct** [ˈbaɪˌprɑdəkt] *n.* 副产品
17. **intercontinental** [ˌɪntəˌkɑntəˈnɛntl] *adj.* 洲际的
    Many intercontinental flights were delayed by holiday crowds and bad weather.
18. **ballistic missile** [bəˈlɪstɪk][ˈmɪsl] 弹道飞弹
19. **in particular** [ɪn][pəˈtɪkjələ] 尤其，特别地
    Lucy had several suggestions for improving Nathan's life, and his love life in particular.
20. **deliver** [dɪˈlɪvə] *v.* 投递，递送
    Wendy delivered gifts to her friends on Christmas Eve.
21. **administration** [ədˌmɪnəˈstreʃən] *n.* 政权
22. **mention** [ˈmɛnʃən] *v.* 提及
    Tammy mentioned that she may be quitting her job.
23. **dash** [dæʃ] *n.* 急冲，冲刺
24. **hydrogen bomb** [ˈhaɪdrədʒən][bɑm] 氢弹

Space Race
美苏太空竞赛

苏 联		美 国
· 发射人造卫星 · 送 Laika 上太空	1957	
	1958	· 发射人造卫星 · 成立 NASA
· 传回月球背面影像 · 探测器坠落月球	1959	
	1960	· 气象卫星传回 2 万多张地表气象画面
· 探测器飞跃金星 · 人类首次上太空	1961	
	1962	· 探测器传送金星数据 · 探测器登陆月球传送月球表面影像
· 首位女性航天员	1963	
	1964	· 探测器传送火星影像
· 航天员太空漫步 （space walk）	1965	· 宇宙飞船轨道会合
· 探测器登陆月球传送影像	1966	· 宇宙飞船对接（docking）
	1968	
	1969	· 人类首次登陆月球 · 进行火星探测
· 设立首个太空站 （space station）	1971	· 发射火星卫星
	1973	· 设立太空实验站（Skylab） · 木星、土星和水星探测
· 美苏载人宇宙飞船合作进行对接	1975	

Sputnik 1

斯普特尼克 1 号
小档案

重量： 83.6 千克

体积： 直径约 58 厘米，大小如篮球，有两组天线。

构造： 外壳为铝镁钛合金（alloy），前端发射器以 20.005 或 40.002 MHz 发送信号，中间有银锌（silver-zinc）电池提供动力，末端有通风扇（ventilation fan）。

发射： 1957 年 10 月 4 日，发射于苏联哈萨克拜科努尔太空中心（Baikonur Cosmodrome）

目的： 为国际地球物理学年（International Geophysical Year, IGY）的研究计划之一，主要是为了研究大气层的密度及其离子（ion）组成，并取得太阳辐射、地球磁场（magnetic field）和宇宙射线（cosmic ray）等数据。

运行： 以椭圆（elliptical）轨道绕行地球，绕行一周约 96 分钟。发送信息 22 天，绕行约 3 个月，最后在进入大气层（reentry）时焚毁。

Give It a Try 请选出正确答案

1. The villagers were _____ of the erupting volcano.
   a. in awe
   b. in pain
   c. in vain
   d. in repose

2. The old computer used a _____ operating system.
   a. primary
   b. privileged
   c. primitive
   d. probable

Answers: 1.a 2.c

Notes

CNN 记者的太空体验

Blast from the Past

Vintage[1] Technology Launches Russia's Star City to the Forefront[2] of the Space Race

图片提供：Reuters 达志

CNN ANCHOR

All this week, CNN has its eye on Russia as we explore the country's dynamic[3] political, social and economic landscape. Its legacy[4] in technology is legendary given the fact that Russia was the first in space and continues to push toward the final frontier. Matthew Chance found that out firsthand at Russia's Star City and had an unexpected experience during his visit.

MATTHEW CHANCE, CNN CORRESPONDENT

Space is a very important place, certainly for Russia. Its satellite was the first to orbit[5] Earth, its cosmonauts[6], pioneers of space travel. And with NASA's space shuttle due to fly its last mission in 2010, Russian rockets are set to become the only means[7] of reaching space until the next generation of NASA-manned[8] spacecraft comes online in 2015.

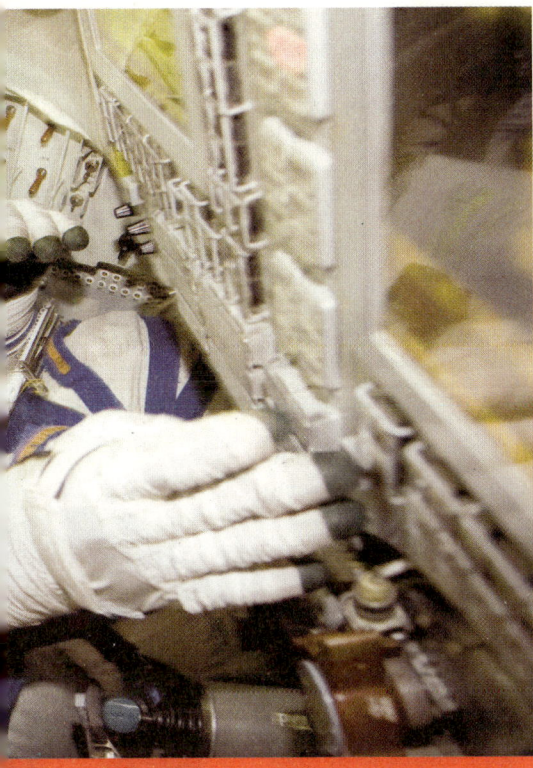

CNN 主播

这一周，CNN都把焦点集中在俄罗斯，探究这个国家充满活力的政治、社会与经济环境。这个国家的科技成就充满传奇，因为俄罗斯是最早上太空的国家，也持续不断向最终的边界推进。马修·钱斯到俄罗斯的星城目睹了这一切，并且在访问期间获得了一次出乎意料的体验。

CNN 特派员　马修·钱斯

太空是个非常重要的地方，至少对俄罗斯来说绝对如此。俄罗斯发射了第一颗绕行地球的卫星，俄罗斯的航天员也是太空旅行的开路先锋。随着美国太空总署的航天飞机在 2010年的最后一次飞行任务后退役，俄罗斯的火箭也将成为人类前往太空的唯一载体，直到太空总署于 2015 年推出下个世代的载人宇宙飞船为止。

Vocabulary

1. vintage ['vɪntɪdʒ] *adj.* 老式的，古色古香的
   Alexander drove a vintage car in the parade.
2. forefront ['fɔr,frʌnt] *n.* 最前部，（活动等的）中心
3. dynamic [daɪ'næmɪk] *adj.* 生气蓬勃的
   The company offers a dynamic work environment.
4. legacy ['lɛgəsɪ] *n.* 遗赠，贡献
5. orbit ['ɔrbɪt] *v.* 环绕……的轨道运行
   The asteroid orbits the earth every 18 years.
6. cosmonaut ['kɑzmə,nɑt] *n.* （尤指前苏联）航天员
7. means [minz] *n.* 手段，方法，工具
8. man [wʌnz] *v.* 操纵，执行，操作
   Janice manned the ladder during the fire drill.

Well, this is a mock-up[9] of a Russian Soyuz capsule[10]. It's the same weight, the same height; it's got all the same instruments as one of the actual craft[11] that goes into space. In fact, this is the habitat[12] module[13] where the astronauts live on long missions. It's not exactly new technology. In fact, it's been around since the middle of the 1960s, but the incredible[14] thing is it's still the most reliable[15] means of getting to places like the International Space Station. In fact, there's a NASA astronaut inside this one training to do just that.

Katie Coleman is a two-time veteran[16] shuttle astronaut, but next time she'll be going up in a Russian Soyuz.

Russia's so central to reaching space after 2010, NASA is now putting all of its astronauts, like Katie, through Soyuz training—training that someone convinced me to volunteer for.

It's like giving the money to the executioner[17]. I crossed his palm with some silver.

The Russian Space Agency has had to turn to the private sector[18] for some of its money, which means that if you pay, you know, $30 million or so, they'll send you up on a Soyuz capsule to the International Space Station. Well, you know, CNN didn't stretch that far, but I am about to take a sample of what it's like to train as a cosmonaut, and this is the instrument of torture in which I will be doing that.

It's a centrifuge[19] that simulates[20] the crushing pressures placed on astronauts when they blast off. Goodbye. Look at this, it's outrageous[21] that I'm doing this. OK, I've changed my mind. I've changed my mind.

OK, we're off. In the words of Yuri Gagarin, "I loexa ! [Let's go!]."

Ooh, wow! Ooh, ow, ow, ow ow, ow, ow ow, ow, ow, ow. It's really bad. I've got four Gs now. I'm really quite having to push back on my face. I don't think my arms. . .oh, I can't do it. It's really amazing. What is incredible is that astronauts endure[22] eight Gs on their first training session. It's four gs, which mean its four times the weight of gravity[23]— very heavy weight on me.

这是俄罗斯联合号宇宙飞船的仿造品，重量一样，高度一样，所有仪器也都和实物一模一样。实际上，这是航天员在长程任务上赖以维生的居住舱。这项科技其实并不新颖，早在20世纪60年代中期就已经出现。但让人讶异的是，这艘太空船至今仍是前往太空最可靠的载体，譬如你如果要到国际太空站，就得搭乘这艘太空船。实际上，这里就有个美国太空总署的航天员正在接受登上国际太空站的训练。

凯蒂·科尔曼是两度搭乘航天飞机进行任务的资深航天员。不过，她的下一次任务将会搭乘俄罗斯的联合号宇宙飞船。

2010年之后，只有通过俄罗斯才能前往太空，所以美国太空总署已派遣所有航天员——例如凯蒂——接受联合号宇宙飞船的训练。有人说服我自愿参与了这项训练。

感觉像是付钱给自己的刽子手一样，我用银子贿赂他。

俄罗斯太空署必须私募经费，所以你只要付3 000万美元左右，他们就会让你搭乘联合号太空舱上国际太空站。CNN虽然没有那么出手大方，但我还是可以尝试一下航天员所接受的训练。这就是我要体验的刑具。

这是一台离心机，用于模拟宇宙飞船发射之时产生的巨大压力。再见。你看，我这么做实在是疯了。我改变主意了，我改变主意了。

好，就像尤里·加加林说的，（俄语）"出发！"

哇！哦哦哦哦哦！真惨。现在的重力已高达4G了（注）。我得努力把脸往后仰。我觉得我的手臂……唉，没办法。实在太神奇了。无法置信的是，航天员第一次受训就得承受8G的重力。我现在承受的是4G，也就是平常重力的4倍——对我来说实在是很重。

> 注：G 是 g-force，为一个万有引力常数（gravitational constant），原是航空专有名词，现在泛指高速移动时承受力量的单位。

Language Notes

cross one's palm 贿赂某人

此词组后面常接 with silver/tip/money 等，表示"贿赂某人"的意思。动词 cross 意指将金钱放在某人手掌中。

例 Jonathan crossed the doorman's palm with a tip to get inside the club.
乔纳森给了俱乐部门卫些钱，好让他可以进去。

Vocabulary

9. **mock-up** ['mɑk,ʌp] *n.* （实验或教学用的）实物大小的模型
10. **capsule** ['kæpsl] *n.* 太空舱，（飞机的）可弹射座舱
11. **craft** [kræft] *n.* 飞机，宇宙飞船
12. **habitat** ['hæbə,tæt] *n.* 栖息地
13. **module** ['mɑdʒul] *n.* （航空器的）舱，组件
14. **incredible** [ɪn'krɛdəbl] *adj.* 惊人的，难以置信的
The acrobat performed several incredible stunts for the crowd.
15. **reliable** [rɪ'laɪəbl] *adj.* 可信赖的，可靠的
It was difficult to find a reliable mobile phone signal while traveling outside the city.
16. **veteran** ['vɛtərən] *adj.* 经验丰富的
The team welcomed back several veteran players for the exhibition game.
17. **executioner** [,ɛksɪ'kjuʃənə] *n.* 死刑执行者
18. **sector** ['sɛktə] *n.* 部分，部门
19. **centrifuge** ['sɛntrə,fjudʒ] *n.* 离心机
20. **simulate** ['sɪmjə,let] *v.* 模仿，模拟
The computer program simulates the experience of flying a jumbo jet.
21. **outrageous** [aʊt'redʒəs] *adj.* 令人吃惊的
The tabloid article made several outrageous claims about the actor's love life.
22. **endure** [ɪn'djur] *v.* 忍耐，忍受
Some breeds of sled dog can endure extremely low temperatures.
23. **gravity** ['grævətɪ] *n.* 重力，地心引力

TRAINING INSTRRUCTOR
　　Show us your hands.

MATTHEW CHANCE, CNN CORRESPONDENT
　　Ah, I'm trying to pick up my hand. Here it is. Hi. Oh, wow. That's tough. It's the kind of feeling you get when you're taking off in a Soyuz rocket, blasting off to the International Space Station.

　　I was taken out after a few minutes, exhausted and cramped[24]. But with its facilities and long experience, Russia is thrusting itself into the future of space travel.

TRAINING INSTRUCTOR
　　Welcome to Earth.

MATTHEW CHANCE, CNN CORRESPONDENT
　　Thank you very much. It was a long flight, but I'm glad to be safely back on the ground again.

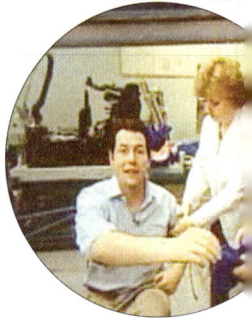

指导员

伸出手来。

CNN 特派员　马修·钱斯

我努力把手抬起来。好了。嗨。哇。真是困难。你如果搭乘联合号宇宙飞船，升空飞往国际太空站，就会有这种感觉。

我在几分钟后被人扶了出来，全身又累又酸痛。不过，利用这些设施和长久以来的经验，俄罗斯正不断往太空旅行的未来迈进。

指导员

欢迎回到地球。

CNN 特派员　马修·钱斯

谢谢你。这次飞行真久，但我很高兴自己总算安然回到了地面。CNN

Language Notes

> **thrust ... into**　猛推，猛塞

动词 thrust 是指一股力量用力往前推，词组 thrust sth./sb. into 是"将……猛地推入"，有强迫的意思。

例 The scandal thrust the reclusive former politician back into the spotlight.
这桩丑闻让那位低调的前政治家成为所有人的焦点。

Vocabulary

24. cramped [ˈkræmpt] *adj.* 抽筋的
Jack moved from his cramped cubical into a spacious office.

炫酷时尚　寰宇星空　生命发现　绿色革命　生活嬗变

Star City　星城

星城是苏联一个军事研究与训练场所（facility），位于首都莫斯科东北方约 32 公里。自 20 世纪 60 年代起，苏联的航天员就开始在星城的加加林太空训练中心（Yuri Gagarin Cosmonaut Training Center）受训。该中心是以世界第一位进入外层空间的宇航员尤里·加加林（1934~1968）命名。

在苏联时代，该城镇被列为极机密的地方，严密地与世界及该国其他地方隔离。许多苏联的航天员会将全家搬迁到星城，那里有自己的邮局、学校、商店、托儿所（child day care）和娱乐设施。

到了 20 世纪 90 年代中期，星城的学生首次参加与美俄文化交流计划，赴纽约几所学校就读。星城目前与美国得克萨斯州拿索湾市（Nassau Bay）为姐妹城市。

Notes

炫酷时尚

寰宇星空

生命发现

绿色革命

生活嬗变

10–F.MP3
10–S.MP3

下一个

大地震 将发生在……

Living o
Sha
Groun

Is Your City at Risk for the Next Big Quake?

ANDERSON COOPER, AC 360

We've seen two major earthquakes this year. Seismologists[1] predict more likely—well, we're likely to see more if not shortly, then certainly within the near future. The question is where? Experts say five cities face the greatest risk.

Jakarta, Indonesia, a country still recovering from the deadly quake and tsunami[2] in 2004. Seattle, big ones don't hit Seattle very often, but if one does, neither it nor any of the nearby Pacific Northwest cities is as well prepared as, say, San Francisco. Iran's capital, Tehran, is number three on the list. The entire country frankly vulnerable[3]; more than 30,000 died when a quake hit the city of Bam in 2003.

Tokyo is number two on the list. They get plenty of quakes. They're prepared, but so many people living in so little space means casualties[4] could be high.

《360° 全面视野》 安德森·库珀

　　我们今年已目睹了两次大地震。地震学家预测可能会有更多——我们接下来可能会看到更多地震，即使不是在最近，也必然是在不久的将来。问题是，会发生在哪里？专家说目前有 5 座城市面临的风险最高。

　　印度尼西亚的雅加达经历了 2004 年的致命地震与海啸，目前还在恢复中。西雅图——西雅图不常发生大规模地震，但一旦发生，西雅图与邻近的太平洋沿岸西北部城市的地震应变能力，都不及旧金山。伊朗首都德黑兰在这份名单上排名第三。老实说，伊朗全国都相当不堪一击。2003 年，巴姆市遭受地震袭击，死亡人数超过 3 万人。

　　东京在名单中排名第二。那里地震很频繁，所以他们已有所准备。但那么多人居住在那么小的空间，伤亡人数一定会很多。

Vocabulary

1. **seismologist** [ˌsaɪzˈmɒlədʒɪst] *n.* 地震学家
2. **tsunami** [tsuˈnɑmɪ] *n.* 海啸（源自日语）
3. **vulnerable** [ˈvʌlnərəbl] *adj.* 有弱点的，脆弱的
   The computer network is vulnerable to attack.
4. **casualty** [ˈkæʒəltɪ] *n.* 死伤，伤亡

炫酷时尚　寰宇星空　生命发现　绿色革命　生活嬗变

And the number one on the danger list is Los Angeles, California. The last so-called big one hit the city in 1857. Seismologists say it gets one every 150 years, so it is due.

With us now is Arthur Lerner-Lam, Associate Director for Seismology at Columbia University. Let's start in Los Angeles. How prepared is that city?

ARTHUR LERNER-LAM, COLUMBIA UNIVERSITY

Well, Los Angeles is one of the best-prepared cities in the world, actually. The earthquake probabilities[5], the occurrence is well known. There are very, very strict building codes[6] and the emergency responders are very well-trained.

ANDERSON COOPER, AC 360

The way you determine, though, I mean, you can't say, well, the next five years—you guys do it in 30-year timeframes.[7] Why is that?

ARTHUR LERNER-LAM, COLUMBIA UNIVERSITY

Well, 30 years is sort of a time scale that people can understand in terms of[1] their property. It's the length of a typical[8] mortgage[9], for example. But really, from a physics[10] point of view, we can't do much better than trying to forecast[11] earthquakes on decade time scales.

ANDERSON COOPER, AC 360

I read that 80 percent of California's buildings, some that were built before 1971, which I think is when the last time there was a major earthquake, and a lot of the building standards were changed, how big of a concern is that?

危机名单上排名第一的是加利福尼亚的洛杉矶。该市上一次所谓的大地震发生于 1857 年。地震学家说这里每 150 年会发生一次大地震，所以时间已经到了。

今天的特别来宾是阿瑟·勒纳拉姆，哥伦比亚大学地震学系副主任。我们先从洛杉矶谈起。这座城市准备好了吗？

哥伦比亚大学　阿瑟·勒纳拉姆

洛杉矶其实是全世界准备最充分的城市之一。这里发生地震的概率及受灾情形已广为人知，所以不但建筑标准要求非常严格，紧急应变人员也受过良好的训练。

《360° 全面视野》　安德森·库珀

你们对地震的预测，我是说，你们连未来 5 年的状况都无法确知——你们的预测却都以 30 年为期，为什么？

哥伦比亚大学　阿瑟·勒纳拉姆

30 年是一般人对财产的期限认定标准，譬如一般房贷的时限就是 30 年。但从物理学的角度而言，我们预测地震的时间范围也不可能低于 10 年。

《360° 全面视野》　安德森·库珀

我读过一些报道指出，加利福尼亚有 80% 的建筑物建于 1971 年之前，那正是上次发生大地震的时候，而许多建筑标准都改变了。这样的问题大不大？

Phrases

1. **in terms of** 在……方面
   Jack is feeling better **in terms of** personal health.

Vocabulary

5. **probability** [ˌprɑbəˈbɪlətɪ] *n.* 可能性
6. **code** [kod] *n.* 法规，规则
7. **timeframe** [ˈtaɪmˌfrem] *n.* 时间范围，一段时间
8. **typical** [ˈtɪpɪkl] *adj.* 典型的，代表性的
   The **typical** action movie fan is a male between the ages of 16 and 25.
9. **mortgage** [ˈmɔrgɪdʒ] *n.* 房贷，抵押
10. **physics** [ˈfɪzɪks] *n.* 物理学
11. **forecast** [ˈforˌkæst] *v.* 预测，预报
    The weatherman **forecast** rain for the weekend.

ARTHUR LERNER-LAM, COLUMBIA UNIVERSITY

Well, that's a big concern not just in California but worldwide. Engineers, of course, know a lot more about earthquakes and the way to build strong buildings. But any building that's constructed[12] prior to[2] the imposition[13] of building codes can be very weak. And that's a major concern.

ANDERSON COOPER, AC 360

Let's move up the coast to Seattle. How is Seattle prepared and what's the likelihood of something there?

ARTHUR LERNER-LAM, COLUMBIA UNIVERSITY

Well, the last major earthquake along the coast of Washington and Oregon occurred around 1700, and that was very large. It's very much like the earthquake that occurred in Chile. It produced a tsunami, and in recent years Seattle has become more prepared for an event of that nature.

ANDERSON COOPER, AC 360

And this red line is ... these are fault[14] lines?

ARTHUR LERNER-LAM, COLUMBIA UNIVERSITY

Yeah. This red line is a plate[15] boundary. In fact, there are two plate boundaries here. This is a small plate that's moving below Washington and Oregon. And it's moving along this trench.[16] This is called a subduction zone[17] and it causes the volcanoes in the Cascade Range and earthquakes along the coast.

ANDERSON COOPER, AC 360

Now, this looks relatively far away from Seattle. I mean, should people take comfort in[3] that it's not right there, or does that not matter?

ARTHUR LERNER-LAM, COLUMBIA UNIVERSITY

Well, it is relatively far away from Seattle, so there won't be that much shaking perhaps, or the shaking will be somewhat attenuated[18], but the problem here might be a coastal tsunami just like we saw in Chile.

ANDERSON COOPER, AC 360

Let's go to Jakarta, Indonesia, a place ... the whole region is called the "Ring of Fire." This is obviously where we saw the tsunami a little bit further up north.

哥伦比亚大学　阿瑟·勒纳拉姆

这是个很大的问题，不只在加利福尼亚，在世界各地都一样。当然，工程师更加了解地震，也更懂得如何建造坚固的建筑。但在建筑规范强制执行前所建的建筑物，有可能非常脆弱，这种情况很令人担忧。

《360°全面视野》　安德森·库珀

接下来谈谈北方沿岸的西雅图。西雅图做了怎样的准备，发生地震的可能性又有多高？

哥伦比亚大学　阿瑟·勒纳拉姆

沿岸的华盛顿州与俄勒冈州，最近一次的大地震发生于 1700 年左右，而且强度非常大，和智利大地震非常相似。那场地震引发了海啸，近年来西雅图对于这类自然灾害已做了较多的准备。

《360°全面视野》　安德森·库珀

这条红线……是断层线吗？

哥伦比亚大学　阿瑟·勒纳拉姆

没错，这条红线是板块边缘。其实这里有两条板块边缘。这是个小板块，在华盛顿州与俄勒冈州下面移动，沿着这条海沟移动。这个地方称为隐没带，造成喀斯喀特山脉的火山与沿岸的地震。

《360°全面视野》　安德森·库珀

这里看来离西雅图相当远。我是说，人们是否该因此区不位于西雅图而感到宽慰，还是根本没有分别？

哥伦比亚大学　阿瑟·勒纳拉姆

这里离西雅图相对较远，所以摇晃可能会比较小，程度也可能较轻微，但问题是，这里的沿岸也可能发生海啸，就像我们在智利看到的一样。

《360°全面视野》　安德森·库珀

接下来看到印度尼西亚雅加达……这整个区域又称为"火环"。这里往北一点，就是当初发生海啸的地方。

Phrases

2. **prior to** 在……之前
   Prior to his accident, Tim ran every day.
3. **take comfort in** 因……感到安慰、宽心
   Phyllis **took comfort in** the fact that she did not have a mortgage.

Vocabulary

12. **construct** [kən'strʌkt] v. 建立，建造
    The workers **constructed** a bridge across the river.
13. **imposition** [ˌɪmpə'zɪʃən] n. 施行，实施
14. **fault** [fɔlt] n. 断层
15. **plate boundary** [plet]['baʊndərɪ] 板块边缘
16. **trench** [trɛntʃ] n. 海沟
17. **subduction zone** [səb'dʌkʃən][zon] 隐没带
18. **attenuate** [ə'tɛnjʊet] v. 减弱，变小
    The sales graph **attenuated** in the latter half of the year.

炫酷时尚　寰宇星空　生命发现　绿色革命　生活嬗变

ARTHUR LERNER-LAM, COLUMBIA UNIVERSITY

Right, this is called … this is part of what seismologists call the circum-Pacific seismic belt, or more colloquially[19], "Ring of Fire."

ANDERSON COOPER, AC 360

So they've got a line running down, right now.

ARTHUR LERNER-LAM, COLUMBIA UNIVERSITY

They've got a line running down the center of Sumatra. Here is Jakarta, over here. This is the island of Java. The earthquake in 2004 occurred right around up here and this basically, this whole region has volcanoes. It has earthquakes and we know that there have been large earthquakes in the past.

ANDERSON COOPER, AC 360

How can you tell that a tsunami is the bigger threat than the earthquake might be?

ARTHUR LERNER-LAM, COLUMBIA UNIVERSITY

Well, that's really rough[20]. We know from past history that earthquakes along faults such as off Indonesia do cause tsunamis. But we have very little evidence of past damage. They don't occur very frequently. But generally speaking, a tsunami can be a very dangerous threat. The good thing about it—if there is a good thing—is that often its comes with a few hours warning.

ANDERSON COOPER, AC 360

Yeah, Tokyo and Tehran, the other cities on the list. Professor, I appreciate you being with us. Thank you so much.

哥伦比亚大学　阿瑟·勒纳拉姆

没错，这里就是地震学家所谓的环太平洋地震带，一般俗称为"火环"。

《360° 全面视野》 安德森·库珀

所以这里有一条线。

哥伦比亚大学　阿瑟·勒纳拉姆

这里有一条线通过苏门答腊中央。这里是雅加达，这是爪哇岛。2004 年的地震就发生在这附近，基本上这整个区域都是火山。这里常发生地震，我们也知道过去发生过大地震。

《360° 全面视野》 安德森·库珀

你怎么知道海啸会是比地震更大的威胁？

哥伦比亚大学　阿瑟·勒纳拉姆

这其实只是大致的预测。从过去的历史可知，发生在印度尼西亚外海这类断层上的地震，都会引发海啸，但能证明曾造成多大损害的证据并不多。这种情形发生的频率不高。但一般而言，海啸可能是非常危险的灾害。唯一的好处是——如果海啸还有所谓的好处的话——就是通常能提前几小时得到预警。

《360° 全面视野》 安德森·库珀

没错。东京和德黑兰是名单上的另外两个城市。教授，感谢你到我们节目来。非常谢谢你。 CNN

3. TEHRAN

Iran

Vocabulary

19. **colloquially** [kəˈlokwɪəlɪ] *adv.* 口语地，通俗地说

20. **rough** [rʌf] *adj.* 粗糙的，粗略的
The rough surface of the road made driving uncomfortable.

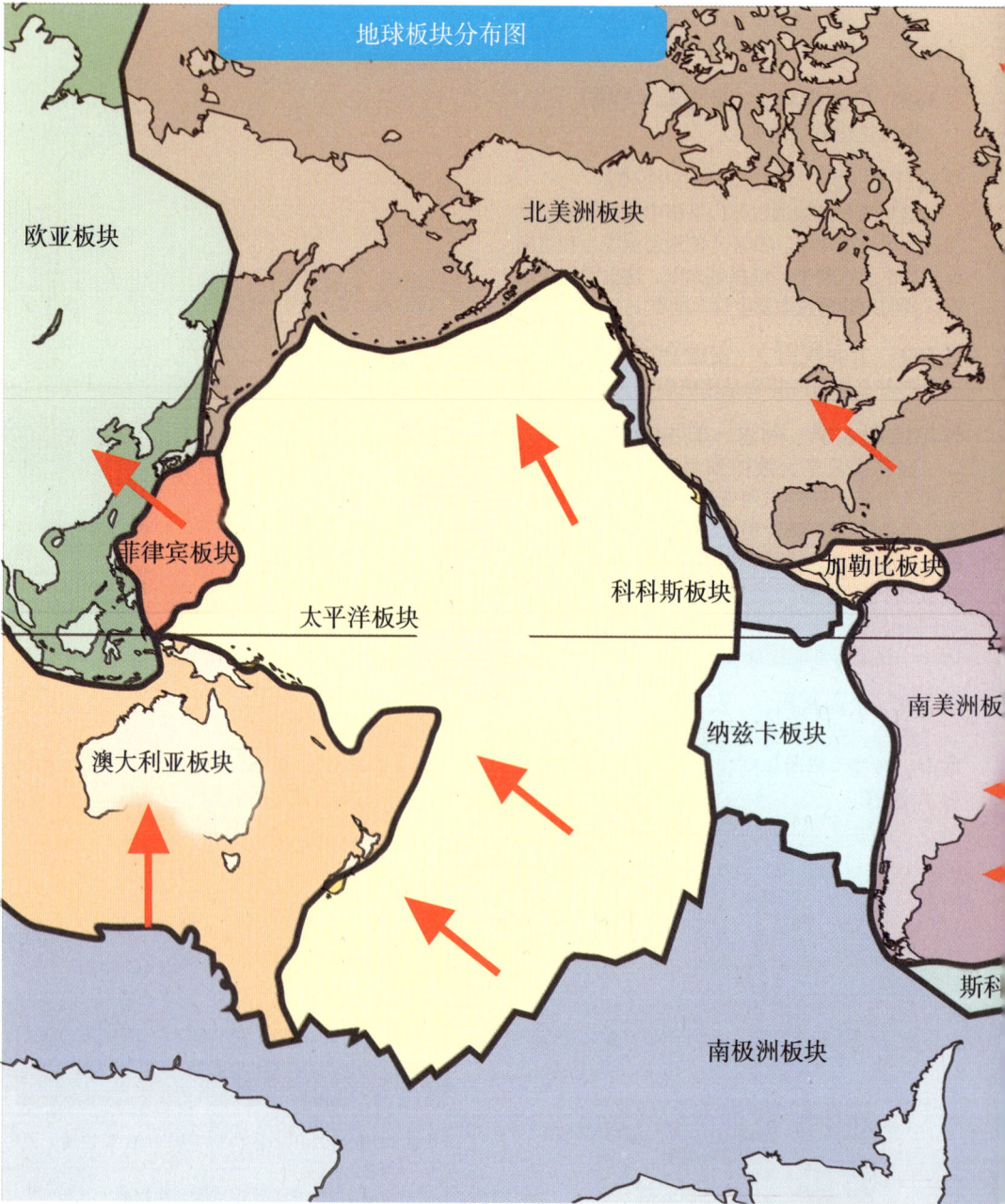

地球板块分布图

欧亚板块

北美洲板块

菲律宾板块

太平洋板块

科科斯板块

加勒比板块

澳大利亚板块

纳兹卡板块

南美洲板

南极洲板块

斯科

欧亚板块

印度板块

阿拉伯板块

非洲板块

南极洲板块

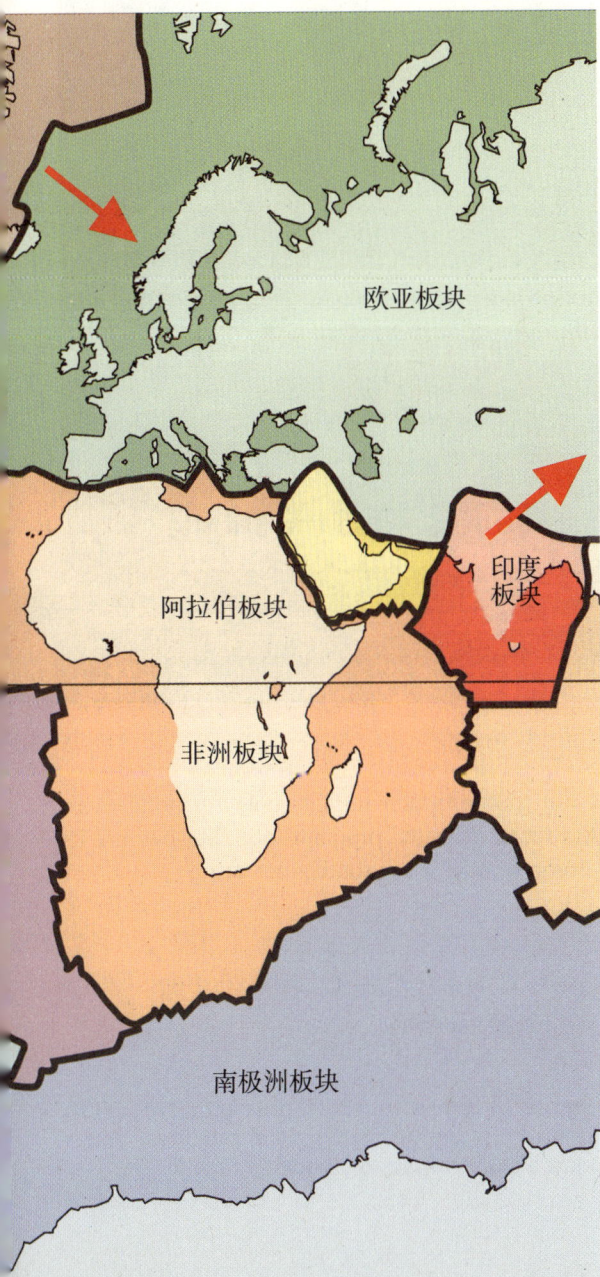

地球板块分布

地球板块一般分为七大板块，包括欧亚板块、北美洲板块、南美洲板块、非洲板块、印度—澳大利亚板块、太平洋板块及南极洲板块，另外还有数个较小的板块。板块受到张力、压力、重力及地幔对流的作用，每年以几厘米的相对速度缓慢移动，大部分的地震、火山及造山运动皆因相邻板块的互相作用而发生。

板块交界处主要有三种形态：

分离板块交界处（divergent boundaries）：地壳在这里由于张力作用向两侧扩张延伸，地幔上部经熔融作用冒出产生新的岩石圈，形成洋脊（ocean ridge）。

聚合板块交界处（convergent boundaries）：两板块相互碰撞，较重的板块会插入较轻板块的下方，称为隐没带（subduction zone），岩石圈进入地幔消失形成海沟（oceanic trench），上方板块被推挤形成山脉。

守恒板块交界处（conservative boundaries）：相邻两板块彼此横向移动摩擦，不产生新的岩石圈也没有岩石圈消失。

炫酷时尚　寰宇星空　生命发现　绿色革命　生活嬗变

美国太空计划
未来出路

NASA's Next Step

The Space Administration Ponders a Future Beyond the Shuttle.

ers a Future Beyond the Shuttle

图片提供：NASA.gov

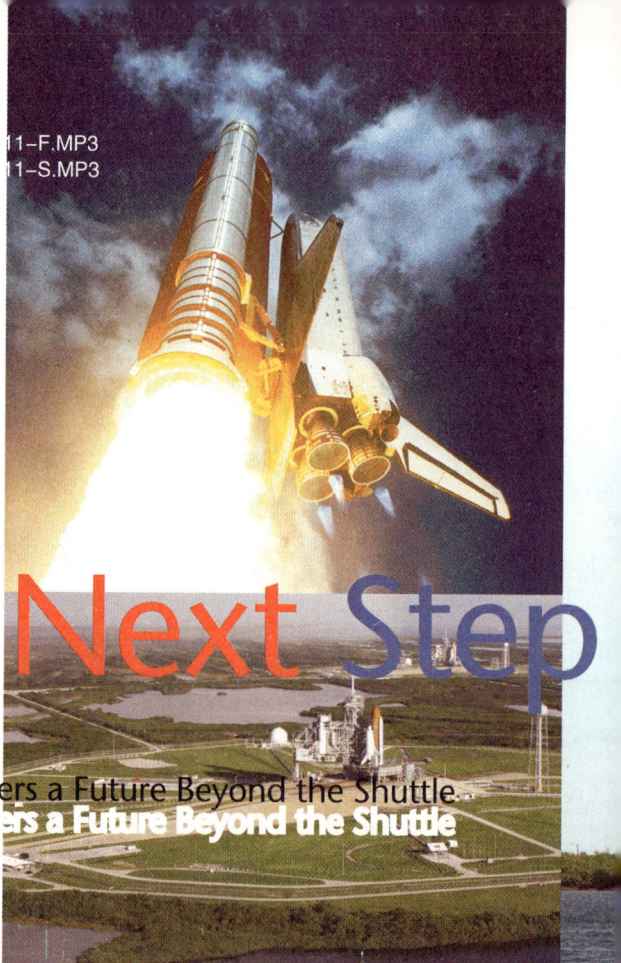

CNN ANCHOR

Well, I hope you got a good look at that shuttle launch[1] because only a handful[2] more of them are on tap for the future. NASA is set to retire the program soon, but because its replacement isn't quite ready for liftoff[3], some wonder if the shuttles are being phased out prematurely[4]. John Zarella explains.

NASA ENGINEER

Three, two, one. Booster[5] ignition[6] and liftoff of Endeavor.

JOHN ZARRELLA, CNN CORRESPONDENT

And now there are seven, the number of space shuttle flights left. Nearly 30 years of flying astronauts[7] in a reusable[8] space plane, fixing crippled[9] satellites[10] and a telescope, building a space station—soon just a chapter in history books.

DAVID LECKRONE, HUBBLE SPACE TELESCOPE SCIENTIST

And it just makes me want to cry to think that this is the end of it.

Language Notes

on tap 立即可得的

tap 是"水龙头",由于水龙头一转就会有水立刻流出来,后来 on tap 就引申指"立即可得的,随时可用的"。

例 Jeffrey is on tap to replace Pat as the chess club president.
杰弗里随时能取代帕特成为棋社负责人。

phase out 逐步淘汰

phase 做动词用时意指"分阶段进行",所以 phase out 就表示"分阶段撤销,逐步淘汰",反之,phase in 则指"逐步实施,分阶段引进"。

例 The phone maker phased out some older models to concentrate on the smart-phone market.
这家手机制造商逐步淘汰较旧的机型,好专攻智能手机。

CNN 主播

希望各位认真观赏了刚才的航天飞机发射画面,因为未来这种画面可是不多了。美国太空总署即将终止航天飞机计划,但因为接替的飞行器还没准备完毕,有些人于是对航天飞机是否太早退役有所质疑。约翰·札瑞拉对此给出解释。

美国太空总署工程师

三,二,一。推进器点火,奋进号升空。

CNN 特派员 约翰·札瑞拉

接下来还剩下七次的航天飞机飞行任务。将近三十年来,这种可重复使用的太空飞机不断搭载航天员升空,修理有故障的人造卫星与望远镜,还建造了一座太空站。但不久之后,这一切将只是史书上的一篇章节了。

哈伯太空望远镜科学家 大卫·莱克龙

想到航天飞机的时代就要结束,我实在情不自禁想哭。

Vocabulary

1. **launch** [lɔntʃ] n. 发射
2. **handful** ['hænd,ful] n. 少量
3. **liftoff** ['lɪft,ɔf] n. 发射
4. **prematurely** [,primə'tjurlɪ] adv. 过早地
5. **booster** ['bustə] n. 推进器
6. **ignition** [ɪg'nɪʃən] n.【机】点火
7. **astronaut** ['æstrə,nɔt] n. 航天员
8. **reusable** [,rɪ'juzəbl] adj. 可重复使用的
   The rechargeable batteries are reusable and save money in the long run.
9. **cripple** ['krɪpl] v. 损坏,使瘫痪
   The ship was crippled when it struck a submerged reef.
10. **satellite** ['sætə,laɪt] n. 人造卫星

炫酷时尚 | 寰宇星空 | 生命发现 | 绿色革命 | 生活嬗变

JOHN ZARRELLA, CNN CORRESPONDENT

A huge mistake says NASA scientist Dave Leckrone.

DAVID LECKRONE, HUBBLE SPACE TELESCOPES-CIENTIST

And I think that's just a shame to abandon[11] one of the most impressive, refined[12], sophisticated capabilities that this agency as a whole—human side and robotics side—has achieved.

JOHN ZARRELLA, CNN CORRESPONDENT

Besides the technological abilities lost when the last shuttle flies in September 2010, it leaves a gaping[13] hole behind. Because of NASA budget cuts, the next-generation vehicle, the Ares rocket and Orion capsule[14], key components of the Constellation program, won't be ready to fly astronauts until 2015. Until then, NASA has to carpool[15] with the Russians to get to space.

Thousands of shuttle workers not needed for the new vehicle will lose their jobs. Workers who are needed may not be around if more budget cuts further delay the next generation of spacecraft.

CHARLIE PRECOURT, ATK LAUNCH SYSTEMS

The more that gap widens, the more that these highly skilled engineers and technicians will find work elsewhere.

JOHN ZARRELLA, CNN CORRESPONDENT

And further delays are possible. An Obama administration-ordered blue-ribbon[16] panel[17] is reviewing NASA's direction after shuttle ends, i.e., the Constellation program, which Leckrone says is fuzzy[18] on direction.

DAVID LECKRONE, HUBBLE SPACE TELESCOPE SCIENTIST

And I just don't see that if that organization, within NASA, that's producing Constellation, doesn't begin talking to their customer, potential customer base, they're gonna end up with something that no one is interested in using.

JOHN ZARRELLA, CNN CORRESPONDENT

Precourt insists Constellation is clearly visionary[19].

CNN 特派员　约翰·札瑞拉

　　美国太空总署科学家大卫·莱克龙说，这项决定实在是大错特错。

哈伯太空望远镜科学家　大卫·莱克龙

　　我认为，这种相当让人惊叹、极度精密、具有极先进能力的飞行器，可说是集人力、机械技术之大成，现在居然要废弃它，这实在很可惜。

CNN 特派员　约翰·札瑞拉

　　最后一架航天飞机在 2010 年 9 月升空之后，除了相关的技术能力将就此丧失之外，也会留下一段真空期。战神火箭与猎户太空舱是下一代的太空飞行器，也是星座计划的关键要素，却因为太空总署的预算遭到删减，而必须等到 2015 年才能搭载航天员升空。在那之前，美国太空总署如果要把人员送上太空，只得搭俄罗斯的便车。

　　新型运载工具业务用不到的数千名航天飞机工作人员到时将会失业。而且如果预算再被删减的话，下一代太空飞行器的推出又会延后，留下来的工作人员可能也待不到那个时候。

ATK 发射系统公司　查理·普瑞科特

　　这段真空期拖得越久，这些具备高级技术的工程师与技师就越可能另谋高就。

CNN 特派员　约翰·札瑞拉

　　进一步延期确实有可能。奥巴马政府成立的特别评估小组正在审查美国太空总署终止航天飞机计划之后的走向，也就是所谓的星座计划。莱克龙说这项计划的方向很模糊。

哈伯太空望远镜科学家　大卫·莱克龙

　　我觉得，太空总署里那个筹备星座计划的组织如果不着手和他们的客户，也就是和潜在基础顾客群沟通，那么他们最后研发出来的将是没人有兴趣用的东西。

CNN 特派员　约翰·札瑞拉

　　普瑞科特坚决表示，星座计划分明是个具有远见的计划。

Vocabulary

11. abandon [əˈbændən] v. 放弃，中止
The driver abandoned the car on the side of the road when it ran out of fuel.
12. refined [rɪˈfaɪnd] adj. 精确的，优美的
The painter's refined style was known for its attention to detail.
13. gaping [ˈgeɪpɪŋ] adj. 开口大且深的
The explosion left a gaping hole in the side of the building.
14. capsule [ˈkæpsl] n. 太空舱
15. carpool [ˈkɑrˌpul] v. 共乘
Dan carpools to work with his colleagues.
16. blue-ribbon [ˈbluˈrɪbən] adj. 头等的，最高荣誉的，蓝绶带的
The government assembled a blue-ribbon panel to help reform the country's health care system.
17. panel [ˈpænl] n. 评估小组
18. fuzzy [ˈfʌzɪ] adj. 模糊的
The driver was a bit fuzzy on the details of what lead to the accident.
19. visionary [ˈvɪʒəˌnɛrɪ] adj. 有远见的
The hospital is being designed by a visionary architect.

CHARLIE PRECOURT, ATK LAUNCH SYSTEMS

It behooves[20] us to build an architecture that can serve a multitude[21] of missions for those next 50-plus years. And that's where this was first envisioned[22] was—to think about space station, lunar[23], asteroids[24], beyond—maybe to Mars.

JOHN ZARRELLA, CNN CORRESPONDENT

Built as less expensive than shuttles, safer for astronauts, the Constellation program is supposed to be everything shuttle is not.

Funny how perceptions change. For decades, the shuttle program was maligned[25] as too costly, too complicated a vehicle, too risky, too unreliable.

Now what do you hear? Too bad it's over.

ATK 发射系统公司　查理·普瑞科特

建造一个可在未来五十多年里供多种任务使用的建筑，是非常适当的做法。当初这项计划考虑到包括太空站、月球、小行星，甚至更远的地方，也许还会有火星。

CNN 特派员　约翰·札瑞拉

星座计划的建置成本低于航天飞机，对航天员的安全保护又更完善，可说是弥补了航天飞机的一切不足之处。

人们想法的变化实在很有趣。过去数十年来，航天飞机计划一直饱受抨击，原因包括成本太高昂，结构太复杂，风险太高，太不稳定。

结果现在听到的是什么？航天飞机计划就要终止了，真是可惜。 CNN

Vocabulary

20. **behoove** [bɪˈhuv] *v.* 对……有必要
It would **behoove** you to be on time for tomorrow's meeting since it concerns your project.
21. **multitude** [ˈmʌltəˌtud] *n.* 大量
22. **envision** [ɪnˈvɪʒən] *v.* 展望
Dr. Martin Luther King **envisioned** a future without racial prejudice.
23. **lunar** [ˈlunə] *adj.* 月亮的，月球的
The museum has a collection of **lunar** rocks and dust.
24. **asteroid** [ˈæstəˌrɔɪd] *n.* 一大群
25. **malign** [məˈlaɪn] *v.* 非议，中伤
The critic **maligned** much of the writer's catalog of work.

各国太空计划

美国 Vision for Space Exploration 计划：预定于 2020 年前回到月球建立研究基地，并为进军火星及更远处铺路。

俄罗斯 预定 2025 年前在近地轨道完成有人驻守的太空站及登陆月球，2032 年前建立月球长期考察站，2035 年后登陆火星。

印度 预定于 2012 年至 2013 年间发射火星无人探测器，并于 2015 年间载人登月。

欧洲 Aurora 计划：预计于 2020 年至 2025 年间登月，并在2030 年至 2035 年前登陆火星。

中国 天宫计划：建置太空实验室，预计于 2010 年至2015 年间实行。
神舟系列计划：在 2003 年至 2008 年间陆续完成载人飞行任务后，于 2011 年至 2012 年再发射四艘宇宙飞船，辅助太空实验室计划施行。
嫦娥计划：以探索月球为目标。2007年已成功发射探月卫星，预定于 2011 年至 2017 年完成登月并采取月球土壤样品的任务。

日本 预定于 2025 年前完成可多次使用的太空飞机，并在月球兴建以太阳能发电卫星为动力来源的研究基地。

韩国 预定于 2020 年载人升空，并开始进行探月工程。

Notes

Science Draws Inspiration[1] from the Animal Kingdom's Aerial[2] Masters

The Nature of Flight

以生物飞行本能为师的
未来航空科技

KRISTIE LU STOU, CNN ANCHOR

Now, in our *Earth's Frontiers* series we are soaring[3] high with bio-inspiration. From the wingtips[4] of an eagle to the thorax[5] of a dragonfly, we take a look at how scientists are applying the benefits of a billion years of evolution. Becky Anderson has the story.

OLIVIER CALDARA, AVIATION ENGINEER & INVENTOR

Mimicry[6], the biomimicry, but for the gliders, we have a lot to learn from those.

BECKY ANDERSON, CNN ANCHOR/CORRESPONDENT

Biomimicry—the science of replicating[7] the little details which nature has perfected[8] over billions of years of evolution. For the French, perfecting flight is about learning from the experts.

OLIVIER CALDARA, AVIATION ENGINEER & INVENTOR

Some time ago, I had some flight in paragliders[9]. Then because I'm an aviation[10] engineer, I had in mind to build my own and to design my own, but with some features from birds, because I know that evolution made very, very efficient wings. First, one feature under this wing is a winglet[11]. And normal paragliders like this at the tip of the wing (gesturing), and mine is like this (gesturing again). It makes more wing span[12]. So it flies better. For the same area, you have [a] better glider.

图片提供：Reuters

CNN 主播　克里斯蒂·卢·斯托特

现在，在我们的《地球先锋》系列中，我们将受生物飞行启发翱翔天际。从老鹰的翼尖到蜻蜓的胸腔，我们来看看科学家如何应用 10 亿年的进化成果。贝基·安德森带来以下的报道。

航空工程师兼发明家　奥利维尔·卡达拉

模仿，仿生学，就滑翔机而言，我们从中学到很多。

CNN 主播兼特派员　贝基·安德森

仿生学这门科学模仿大自然中历经数十亿年演化过程而臻于完美的小细节。对这位法国人而言，完美的飞行便是向专家学习而来的。

航空工程师兼发明家　奥利维尔·卡达拉

不久前，我曾有滑翔伞的飞行经历。由于我是航空工程师，我打算打造并设计我自己的滑翔伞，不过会多一些鸟类的特征，因为我知道进化造就了非常高效的翅膀。首先，这个伞翼的其中一项特征便是小翼。普通的滑翔伞伞翼的翼端是像这样（打手势），而我的是像这样（打手势）。这让翼延展度更大，所以它也能飞得更好。以相同伞翼面积来看，你会有更好的滑翔伞。

Vocabulary

1. **inspiration** [ˌɪnspəˈreʃən] *n.* 启发灵感的人（或事物）
2. **aerial** [ˈɛriəl] *adj.* 空中的，空气中的
   The eagles put on a magnificent aerial display.
3. **soar** [sɔr] *v.* 高飞，翱翔
   The hawk soared above the canyon looking for prey.
4. **wingtip** [ˈwɪŋˌtɪp] *n.* 翼梢
5. **thorax** [ˈθɔrˌæks] *n.* （昆虫的）胸，胸部
6. **mimicry** [ˈmɪməkrɪ] *n.* 模仿，模仿的技巧
7. **replicate** [ˈrɛpləˌket] *v.* 复制，（精确地）仿制
   Roger replicates the sounds of several wild animals to entertain his friends.
8. **perfect** [pəˈfɛkt] *v.* 使完善，使完美
   Danielle perfected her singing with a professional voice coach.
9. **paraglider** [ˈpærəˌglaɪdə] *n.* 滑翔伞
10. **aviation** [ˌeviˈeʃən] *n.* 航空，航空制造业
11. **winglet** [ˈwɪŋlət] *n.* 小翼
12. **span** [spæn] *n.* 宽度，跨度

And the second feature of birds, I do the ability to reduce area just to fly faster and to sink[13] a lot, not to be sucked in [into] the clouds. Then, the sinking of the wings is much better and the speed, also. And it flaps[14] a little bit like birds. Yeah.

BECKY ANDERSON, CNN ANCHOR/CORRESPONDENT
Big aviation companies are following the same trend.

UNIDENTIFIED SPOKESMAN, DASSAULT AVIATION
This is a Dassault Aviation's latest design, which is now manufactur[ing] the Falcon 7X, which features three engines, which has digital fly by wire and also winglet[s] at the tip of the wing[s]. The winglet[s] are just inspired from the observation of eagles. Eagles can adapt and reform[15] their wing tips due to different conditions. And then we understood that in tradition such devices reduced the drag[16] of the aircraft, and then reduces the fuel consumption[17].

BECKY ANDERSON, CNN ANCHOR/CORRESPONDENT
Up in the Alps, scientists in French aerospace[18] labs are being inspired by dragonflies.

MICHEL DE GLINIASTY, GENERAL SCIENTIFIC DIRECTOR, ONERA
We thought that it was better to try to mimic[19] insects, because when you look at the wing of an insect, the wing is nearly inert[20]. All the living parts are within the thorax, which is very [much] easier to handle with. This is a thorax, and I will show you how it works. And these are the eyes, which are, in fact, cameras.

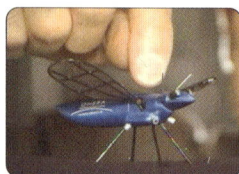

BECKY ANDERSON, CNN ANCHOR/CORRESPONDENT
Here, the latest drone[21] technology is being developed —unmanned[22] devices which can fly.

MICHEL DE GLINIASTY, GENERAL SCIENTIFIC DIRECTOR, ONERA
The drones, it's very exciting. It's very exciting, of course, because technologically, it's lots of challenges. And you can see here, the three beams[23], which allows a twist of the wing, which is totally bio-inspired.

BECKY ANDERSON, CNN ANCHOR/CORRESPONDENT
Scientists here acknowledge[24] that nature has perfected its own design solutions[25] across time.

鸟类还有第二个特点，我尽力缩小伞面就能飞得更快、下降更多，就不会被吸入云中。如此一来，伞翼的沉降变得更顺畅，速度也更快。它振翼的模样有点像鸟类。是的。

CNN 主播兼特派员　贝基·安德森

大型航空公司也追随相同的潮流。

达索航空公司　未提供姓名发言人

这是达索航空最新的设计，现在正在生产猎鹰 7X，特色是有三个引擎，能做数字线控飞行，在翼梢还有小翼。这个小翼的设计是通过观察老鹰得到的启发。老鹰可以根据不同的情况调节它们的翼梢。而以往我们了解到这样的装置可以减少飞机的阻力，并且能够降低燃料的消耗。

CNN 主播兼特派员　贝基·安德森

阿尔卑斯山上，法国航空实验室里的科学家则受到蜻蜓的启发。

法国国家航空航天研究中心科学研究主任　米歇尔·得葛林尼斯蒂

我们认为试着模仿昆虫会更好，因为你看昆虫的翅膀，这些翅膀几乎是无动力的。所有活动的零件都在胸腔内，这样处理起来就更为简单。这是胸腔，我想让你看看它如何工作。这些是眼睛，其实这是摄像机。

CNN 主播兼特派员　贝基·安德森

这里正在研发最新的飞行器科技——无人驾驶的飞行装置。

法国国家航空航天研究中心科学研究主任　米歇尔·得葛林尼斯蒂

这架无人机，令人非常兴奋。令人非常兴奋，因为在技术层面上，它面临许多挑战。你可以看到这里，这三根支架让机翼能够扭转，而这也全是受到生物的启发。

CNN 主播兼特派员　贝基·安德森

这里的科学家承认，大自然随着时间的演进已经让它的设计方案臻于完美。

Vocabulary

13. **sink** [sɪŋk] v. 下沉，沉降
The sun sank over the horizon as the day ended.
14. **flap** [flæp] v. 振（翅），摆动
The parrot flapped its wings when its owner came into the room.
15. **reform** [rɪˈfɔrm] v. 改革，改良
The line of ants reformed just minutes after Alex tried to wipe them up.
16. **drag** [dræg] n. （作用于飞机或运载工具的）空气阻力
17. **consumption** [kənˈsʌmpʃən] n. 消耗，消耗量
18. **aerospace** [ˈɛroˌspes] n. 航空航天，航空航天工业
19. **mimic** [ˈmɪmɪk] v. 模仿
The child mimicked the sound of a fire engine as he ran across the playground.
20. **inert** [ɪˈnɜt] adj. 无活动能力的，无行动力的
The cat sat inert for several minutes waiting to pounce on the mouse.
21. **drone** [dron] n. 无人驾驶飞机（或飞艇等）
22. **unmanned** [ʌnˈmænd] adj. 无人操作的，无人控制的
Scientists sent an unmanned probe to the planet.
23. **beam** [bim] n. 梁，平衡木
24. **acknowledge** [ɪkˈnɑlɪdʒ] v. 承认
Benson acknowledged that he did not work on the project alone, but had the help of several colleagues.
25. **solution** [səˈluʃən] n. 解决办法，处理手段

MICHEL DE GLINIASTY, GENERAL SCIENTIFIC DIRECTOR, ONERA
   Billions of years of evolution leads [lead] to a very complicated[26] biological system. Biomimicry, you cannot really reproduce[27] nature, but there is one thing you can do, it's try to reproduce some natural phenomenon with human technologies.

法国国家航空航天研究中心科学研究主任　米歇尔·得葛林尼斯蒂

　　数十亿年的演化过程造就了一套非常复杂的生物系统。仿生学，你无法真的复制自然，但是你仍可做到一件事，就是运用人类的科技尝试重制一些自然现象。CNN

Give It a Try 请选出正确答案

1. It took years of trial and error to ___ the car's design.
   a. perfect　　　　　　b. predict
   c. consider　　　　　d. compile

2. Jeffery sat _____ for nearly an hour while meditating.
   a. unmanned　　　　b. imperfect
   c. inert　　　　　　d. unprepared

Answers: 1. a 2. c

Vocabulary

26. **complicated** [ˈkɑmpləˌketɪd] *adj.* 复杂的
    Wendy solves complicated math calculations with ease.

27. **reproduce** [rɪˈprɑdjus] *v.* 再制造，再现
    The chemical reproduces the scent of a female panda.

滑翔伞 图解单词

top surface
上伞衣

leading edge
前缘

bottom surface
下伞衣

cell
气室

wingtip
翼梢

canopy / wing / sai
伞翼

trailing edge
后缘

lines
伞绳

brake lines
煞车绳

risers 组带

helmet 安全帽
brake handles
煞车手柄
harness 吊带

biomimicry & paraglider
仿生学与滑翔伞

　　仿生学（biomimicry）最佳的例子之一就是通过观察鸟类而促使人类飞行的研究。从达·芬奇的飞行器草图到莱特兄弟（The Wright Brothers）发明飞机，都是从鸟类获得的灵感。

　　鸟类飞行是通过上下拍动膀翅（flap），翅膀会产生前推力（thrust），让空气由下往上流动，因此这股前推力也会产生浮力（buoyancy）。

　　鸟儿升空之后，再根据环境与需求，控制翅膀的形状与大小来改变前推力与浮力。

　　滑翔伞（paraglider）的形状如鸟翼，原理也类似鸟类飞行。当空气进入气室将伞翼充满（inflate），便可带人在空中飘浮（float）。空气通过伞翼时，上伞衣距离长，下伞衣距离短，因此伞翼上方空气流速快、压力小，伞翼下方空气流速慢、压力大，因而造成一股由下往上推挤的升力（lift）。速度越快，升力就越大，因此飞行伞起飞（launch）时必须先让伞充满空气后再助跑，以速度换取升力起飞。

图片提供：dcysurfer

area 伞翼面积 A
平铺地表的面积，以平方米表示

wing span 翼展长度 B
伞翼展开自左翼端至右翼端的全长，以米计

wing loading 翼面荷重 = $\frac{kg}{A}$
滑翔伞在飞行中的重量除以翼面积的值，数值越大，速度越快

glide ratio 滑降比 = $\frac{C - D}{E}$
在无风状态下飞行，离着陆地点的高度差和飞行距离的比

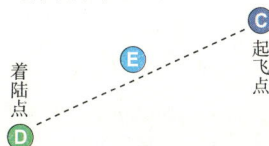

aspect ratio 展弦比 = $\frac{B^2}{A}$
翼展长度的平方除以伞翼面积的值，数值越大，滑降比越大

滑翔伞 其他相关词汇

着陆点 D　　E　　起飞点 C

炫酷时尚 寰宇星空 生命发现 绿色革命 生活嬗变

97

英国 UFO

档 案 大揭秘

Britain's X-Files

Defense[1] Ministry Releases Secret Reports on UFO Sightings[2]

CNN ANCHOR

Now, you think UFOs is [are] kind of a U.S. obsession[3], but there have been hundreds of UFO sightings in Britain over the last 10 years.

CNN ANCHOR

And if you've ever wondered whether aliens exist, well the British defense ministry is now revealing what it knows. Phil Black reports.

PHIL BLACK, CNN CORRESPONDENT

UFOs, Hollywood style. When aliens visit Earth in the movies, they're often driving that distinctive[4] flying saucer[5], from *Close Encounters of a Third Kind* to *Independence Day* and *Mars Attacks*. And this is how UFOs tend[6] to look when earthlings[7] catch them on camera—shaky[8], fuzzy[9] images of bright lights and saucer-shaped objects. Fraud[10]?

Foolishness?

UNIDENTIFIED UFO WITNESS

Dude, they're all, uh, like, moving …

炫酷时尚 | 寰宇星空 | 生命发现 | 绿色革命 | 生活嬗变

CNN 主播

你以为 UFO 好像是让美国人着迷的东西，但过去十年来，英国就曾出现数百次目击 UFO 的记录。

CNN 主播

如果您曾怀疑外星人是否存在，现在英国国防部正要对外揭露它所知道的信息。记者菲尔·布雷克带来报道。

CNN 特派员　菲尔·布雷克

这是好莱坞式的 UFO。当外星人在电影中造访地球时，他们通常都是驾驶那种特色十足的飞碟，从《第三类接触》到《ID4：星际终结者》到《星际毁灭者》都是如此。而当地球人在镜头上捕捉到 UFO 时，UFO 通常是这副模样：一团抖动、模糊的亮光和碟状的物体。这究竟是个骗局，还是件蠢事？

UFO 目击者

伙计，他们好像都在……移动。

Vocabulary

1. **defense ministry** [dɪ'fɛns]['mɪnəstrɪ] 国防部
2. **sighting** ['saɪtɪŋ] *n.* 看见，发现
3. **obsession** [əb'sɛʃən] *n.* 着迷，走火入魔
4. **distinctive** [dɪ'stɪŋktɪv] *adj.* 有特色的，特殊的
   The archeologist could see the distinctive outline of several human shapes in the cave painting.
5. **saucer** ['sɔsə] *n.* 浅碟形物
6. **tend** [tɛnd] *v.* 倾向于
   Chris tends to avoid conflict when dealing with her coworkers.
7. **earthling** ['ɜθlɪŋ] *n.* 世人，俗人
8. **shaky** ['ʃekɪ] *adj.* 摇晃的，不稳定的
   The director is know for the shaky camera technique used in his films.
9. **fuzzy** ['fʌzɪ] *adj.* 模糊不清的
   It was difficult to tell who was in the background of the fuzzy photograph.
10. **fraud** [frɔd] *n.* 诡计，骗局

PHIL BLACK, CNN CORRESPONDENT

Or proof of alien life? The British Ministry of Defense says it's now coming clean on what it knows, which it insists is not very much. It's begun releasing all its files on UFO sighting investigations[11]. The first batch[12] covers 1981 to '87.

DAVID CLARK, UFO HISTORIAN

I'm surprised at the number of them, you know, the hundreds and hundreds of reports that were being received every year, every year by the Ministry of Defense.

PHIL BLACK, CNN CORRESPONDENT

UFO buff[13] David Clark fought for the documents' release and has read them all so far. He says most of the sightings can be explained, but not all of them, like the air traffic controllers who were taken by surprise in 1984.

DAVID CLARK, UFO HISTORIAN

A ball of light, and they described seeing this thing touch down on the runway and then zoom away at some fantastic[14] speed. And they were so worried about the possible damage to their reputation[15] if they reported this officially, and it got out to the media, that they demanded[16] that their names were withheld[17].

PHIL BLACK, CNN CORRESPONDENT

The Ministry of Defense says it's releasing the documents because the public demand has been so great and to show there's no great alien cover-up. Despite some obvious similarities, these investigations aren't exactly like television's *X-Files*. The British Ministry of Defense says it's only worried about finding out whether or not its airspace has been violated,[18] and it claims to have no interest in determining whether or not alien life actually exists. Defense officials know that's unlikely to satisfy hard-core[19] conspiracy[20] theorists[21], but they hope the files will please many who are desperate[22] to know more about mysterious close encounters[23] in the skies over Britain.

DAVID CLARK, UFO HISTORIAN

Something's going on. I don't know what the answer is, and the truth, really, is in these files, whatever the truth is.

CNN 特派员　菲尔·布雷克

还是外星生物的证据？英国国防部表示，现在要公布所知道的一切，并坚称所知道的并不多。英国国防部已经开始公布所有的 UFO 目击调查档案。其中第一批档案的时间涵盖了 1981 至 1987 年。

UFO 历史学家　大卫·克拉克

我对于其中的数目感到惊讶，每年国防部都会接到数百篇的报告。

CNN 特派员　菲尔·布雷克

UFO 迷大卫·克拉克争取将该批文件公布，他目前已经读完所有报告。他说其中大部分的目击经过都可以解释，但并非全部。比方 1984 年当时那名措手不及的航空管控员。

UFO 历史学家　大卫·克拉克

一团光球，他们形容自己看到的这个东西降落在跑道上，然后飞速离开。他们非常担心万一他们正式举报这件事，可能会损害到他们的名声，结果整件事传到了媒体那里，他们要求隐匿他们的姓名。

CNN 特派员　菲尔·布雷克

国防部表示鉴于人们的呼声非常强烈，为了表示并没有大量隐瞒外星人消息的情况，国防部会对外公布文件。尽管一部分有明显的相似之处，但这些调查报告和电视上的《X 档案》不尽相同。英国国防部表示，他们只担心英国的领空是否遭到侵犯，并声称对于判定外星生物是否真的存在并不感兴趣。国防部官员知道，这么做不大可能满足难缠的阴谋论者，但他们希望这些档案能满足许多人对于了解英国上空神秘的近距离接触事件的渴望。

UFO 历史学家　大卫·克拉克

有些事正在发生，我不知道答案怎样，而真相就在这些档案里，不管真相怎样。CNN

Language Notes

come clean　坦白交代，承认

词组 come clean 是指"说实话，坦承"，通常是坦白交代某些隐藏许久，见不得光的事。

(be) taken by surprise　出乎某人意料

sb. be taken by surprise 是"某人出乎意料的事情"的意思。也可用主动式 take sb. by surprise。

touch down　降落

touch down 是指如飞机等航空器接触地面，也就是"降落，着陆"的意思。

get out (to)　走漏（消息）

get out 加上介词 to 是指"将某消息泄漏"，等于 leak to sb. to。后面的名词是接收消息的对象。

Vocabulary

11. investigation [ɪnˌvɛstəˈgeʃən] n. 研究，调查
12. batch [bætʃ] n. 一批，一组，一群
13. buff [bʌf] n.【美】【口】迷，爱好者
14. fantastic [fænˈtæstɪk] adj. 惊人的，难以置信的
15. reputation [ˌrɛpjəˈteʃən] n. 名誉
16. demand [dɪˈmænd] v. 要求
17. withhold [wɪθˈhold] v. 隐瞒，保留
18. violate [ˈvaɪəˌlet] v. 违犯，违背
19. hard-core [ˈhɑrdˌkɔr] adj. 坚定不移的，绝对的
20. conspiracy [kənˈspɪrəsi] n. 阴谋
21. theorist [ˈθɪərɪst] n. 理论家
22. desperate [ˈdɛspərət] adj. 极度渴望的
23. encounter [ɪnˈkauntə] n. 偶然（或短暂的）遇见

炫酷时尚　寰宇星空　生命发现　绿色革命　生活嬗变

THE UFO PATTERN

曾被目击的 UFO 的形状

SAUCER 碟形

ELLIPSOIDAL 椭圆形

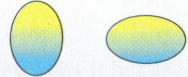

FLAT-TOPPED STRAW HAT
扁帽形

DIRIGIBLE 飞船形

DOUBLE HAT 双层扁帽形

CYLINDRICAL 雪茄形

CONICAL HAT 圆锥形

TRIANGLE OR BOOMERANG 三角形或回飞镖形

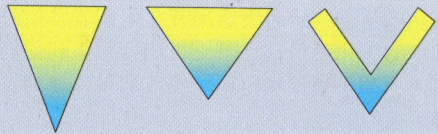

SPHERE 球形

SATURN 土星形

图片来源：Smurrayinchester

Phil Black
London

Notes

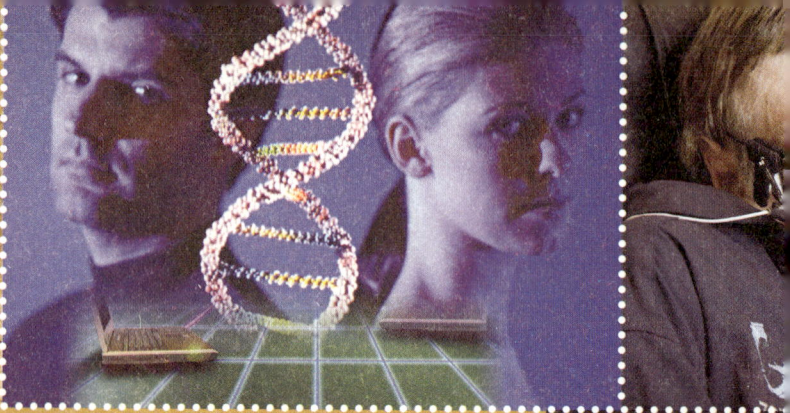

生命发现

⑭ 演化史大发现——最早古人类化石出土

⑮ 定做 DNA，人造生命科技大跃进

⑯ 天文物理大师史蒂芬·霍金谈宇宙与人类的未来

⑰ 濒危物种新希望——DNA 冷冻方舟

⑱ 日本真的是为了研究捕鲸？生物学家告诉你真相

14-F.MP3
14-S.MP3

演化史大发现——
最早古人类化石出土

Missing Link?

Scientists Unveil[1] the Earliest Fossil[2] of Primate[3] Ancestor[4]

CNN ANCHOR

Here's the story that was 47 millions years in the making. On Tuesday, scientists in New York unveiled a small primate fossil, and what makes it special, they say, is there's a possibility that it could be the missing link—[a] common[5] ancestor for monkeys, primates and humans. Richard Roth takes a look at this fascinating[6] fossil.

UNKNOWN FEMALE

Three, two, one.

RICHARD ROTH, CNN CORRESPONDENT

Could the so-called missing link be behind the curtain? Behold[7]. A 47-million-year-old primate fossil.

JOHN HURUM, UNIVERSITY OF OSLO

This is the most complete primate fossil before human burial[8].

RICHARD ROTH, CNN CORRESPONDENT

These paleontologists[9] believe the primate is a gateway[10] to discovering everything about human evolution[11]. They found humanlike nails, not claws, plus toes and teeth.

图片提供: Franzen JL, Gingerich PD, Habersetzer J, Hurum JH, von Koenigswald W & Smith BH (2009) Complete Primate Skeleton from the Middle Eocene of Messel in Germany: Morphology and Paleobiology. PLoS ONE 4(5): e5723. doi:10.1371/journal.pone.0005723

Language Notes

in the making　制造

in the making 在文中是"制造，成形"的意思，前面可加上一段时间，表示花了多久的时间制造。另外 in the making 还可表示"正在发展中、塑造中的"。

例 A new housing development is in the making on the outskirts of the town.
那个新城镇周围的住房发展项目正在筹建中。

例 The young singer is a star in the making.
那位年轻歌手是个未来巨星。

Vocabulary

1. unveil [ʌnˈvel] v. 揭露，揭开
Jim unveiled plans for a new line of products at the management meeting.
2. fossil [ˈfɑsl] n. 化石
3. primate [ˈpraɪˌmet] n. 灵长类动物
4. ancestor [ˈænˌsɛstə] n. 祖先，祖宗
5. common [ˈkɑmən] adj. 共同的，共有的
Tom and Alice have several common friends.
6. fascinating [ˈfæsəˌnetɪŋ] adj. 迷人的，极好的
Phil wrote a fascinating article on politics.
7. behold [bɪˈhold] v. 注视，看
Dave beheld an unexplored valley when he reached the mountaintop.
8. burial [ˈbɛriəl] n. 埋葬，墓葬
9. paleontologist [ˌpelianˈtɑləgɪst] n. 古生物学家
10. gateway [ˈgetˌwe] n. 入口处，通道
11. evolution [ˌɛvəˈluʃən] n. 演化，进化（论）

CNN 记者

这是一个花了4 700万年才完成的故事。周二，科学家在纽约展出了一个小灵长类化石，特别的地方是，它有可能是猴子、灵长类动物和人类共同的祖先。理查德·罗斯带我们看看这个吸引人的化石。

不知名女性

三、二、一。

CNN 特派员　理查德·罗斯

所谓的空白期就在这幕布后面吗？注意看，这是4 700万年的灵长类化石。

奥斯陆大学　约翰·赫伦

这是在人类遗骸发现之前最完整的灵长类化石。

CNN 特派员　理查德·罗斯

这些古生物学家相信，这个灵长类是发掘人类进化过程一切秘密的入口。他们发现了类似人类的指甲，不是爪子，还有脚趾和牙齿。

INGA BOSTAD, UNIVERSITY OF OSLO

I remember from my school days the discussion about the search for a missing link.

RICHARD ROTH, CNN CORRESPONDENT

The female primate is believed to have drowned in a crater lake[12] and was discovered in a shale[13] mine outside of Frankfurt, Germany in 1983. It all makes for a very good TV show, doesn't it?

ANTHONY GEFFEN, ATLANTIC PRODUCTIONS

The story of a little girl who connects possibly to every person on this planet.

RICHARD ROTH, CNN CORRESPONDENT

Unknown to the primate named "Ida," numerous[14] TV and book deals were signed. The History Channel's special is called *The Link*, but is it really the missing link of evolution?

JOHN HURUM, UNIVERSITY OF OSLO

It's really, really hard to pinpoint[15] exactly who gave rise to humans at that point, but this is as good as it gets, really.

RICHARD ROTH, CNN CORRESPONDENT

The scientists call the primate one of the ancestors of all of us.

JENS FRANZEN, SENCKENBERG INSTITUTE

We are not dealing with our grand-grand-grand grandmother, but perhaps with our grand-grand grandaunt.

RICHARD ROTH, CNN CORRESPONDENT

Ida the primate will be on display at the Museum of Natural History. Mayor Michael Bloomberg got the first look.

物种：达尔文麦塞尔猴

Ida 艾达化石

存活年代：4 700 万年前古近纪第二期的始新世（Eocene）中期。

身长：约 58 厘米（含尾巴），推测成年约 68~73 厘米。

发掘：1983 年在德国麦塞尔化石坑（Messel pit）出土，该地为沥青页岩矿场，20 世纪以来即以发掘化石闻名。艾达最初因业余开采（excavation）断成两半分别出售，直到 2007 年才重新组合，科学家分析艾达是未成年雌性。

奥斯陆大学　英格·波斯塔

我记得我在学校的时候讨论过寻找空白期。

CNN 特派员　理查德·罗斯

这个雌性的灵长类据说是淹死在火山湖里，1983 年在德国法兰克福外的页岩矿脉中被发现。这就是个非常好的电视节目素材，不是吗？

亚特兰大制作公司　安东尼·吉芬

这个故事是，一个可能和这个星球上的每个人都有关系的小女孩。

CNN 特派员　理查德·罗斯

这个名叫"艾达"的灵长类动物不知道的是，许多的电视和书籍都订了合同。历史频道的特别节目叫做《那个环节》。但是这真的是进化中缺失的环节吗？

奥斯陆大学　约翰·赫伦

真的很难肯定地指出当时是什么让人类兴起。但是这已经算差强人意了，真的。

CNN 特派员　理查德·罗斯

科学家说这个灵长类是我们全体的祖先之一。

森克堡研究中心　杰恩斯·法兰兹

我们不是在处理我们的曾、曾、曾、曾祖母，但可能是我们的曾、曾、曾祖婶。

CNN 特派员　理查德·罗斯

艾达这个灵长类动物会在自然历史博物馆展出。迈克尔·布隆伯格市长先睹为快。

Language Notes

unknown to sb.　某人不知情的情况下

unknown 是形容词，可表示"未知的，陌生的，默默无闻的"，文中则是"不知道的"的意思。unknown to 后面加上人，表示"某人不知情"。

例 Unknown to Shelly, her ex-boyfriend was at the costume party.
雪莉不知道她的前男友在化装舞会。

as good as it gets　差强人意

as good as it gets 是口语中的惯用语，表示"所能得到的最好的结果或状况"，文中是"勉强可以接受，差强人意"的意思，有时则是"满意知足的"意思。

例 Jack feels that living on the beach is as good as it gets.
杰克觉得住在海边已经很满足了。

Vocabulary

12. crater lake ['kretə][lek] n. 火山湖
13. shale [ʃel] n. 页岩
14. numerous ['numərəs] adj. 许多的，为数众多的
The writer received numerous offers from publishers wanting to release his new novel.
15. pinpoint ['pɪn,pɔɪnt] v. 明确确定
The military used satellites to pinpoint the enemy.

炫酷时尚　寰宇星空　生命发现　绿色革命　生活嬗变

MICHAEL BLOOMBERG, NEW YORK CITY MAYOR

This is what Darwin was looking for, and it just reconfirms[16] the basic concept of Darwin.

RICHARD ROTH, CNN CORRESPONDENT

They may not have the missing link, but the investigators hope the hoopla[17] over the primate in a mine will lead to a gold mine[18] of interest in science.

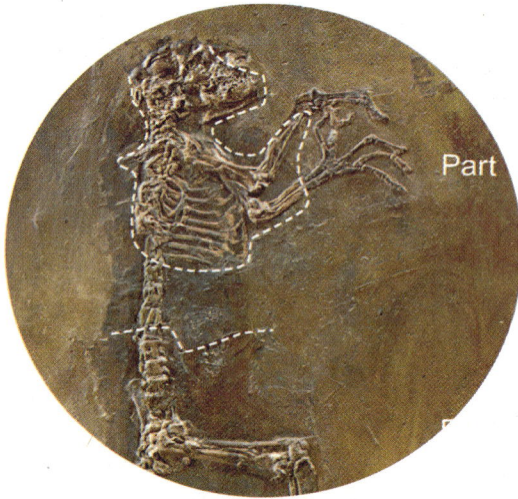

纽约市长　迈克尔·布隆伯格

这就是达尔文在寻找的，而它正好再次肯定了达尔文的基本理念。

CNN 特派员　理查德·罗斯

他们可能没有找到空白期的证据，但是研究人员希望，这个矿藏中的灵长类引起的旋风，会打开科学兴趣的金矿。CNN

Give It a Try 请选出正确答案

1. Donald _____ the source of the strange noise in his car's engine.
   a. pinpointed　　　b. beheld
   c. livened　　　　d. reconfirmed

2. Bonny didn't want any _____ over her upcoming birthday.
   a. evolution　　　b. primate
   c. fossil　　　　d. hoopla

3. This movie was five years in the _____ and not very successful.
   a. shale　　　　b. gateway
   c. making　　　d. goldmine

Answers: 1.a 2.d 3.c

Vocabulary

16. **reconfirm** [ˌriːkənˈfɜːm] v. 再确认
    The election officials reconfirmed the politician's victory.
17. **hoopla** [ˈhuːpˌlɑː] n. 喧闹
18. **gold mine** [gold][maɪn] n. 金矿，【喻】丰富的来源

炫酷时尚　寰宇星空　生命发现　绿色革命　生活嬗变

达尔文麦塞尔猴
——人类的祖先？

2 但该化石没有狐猴的尖锐爪子和梳齿，却具备类似人类的特征如指甲、拇指与其他手指分开、四肢较短、两眼前视，显示应该是灵长类分支演化前的哺乳类（mammal）。

3 科学家将该生物学名取为 Darwinius masillae "达尔文麦塞尔猴"，推测是小型哺乳类进化到猿类之间的物种。

1 在麦塞尔化石坑发现化石，形体与狐猴相似。

小型哺乳类
small mammals

达尔文麦塞尔猴
Darwinius masillae

猿
Apes

早期原始人
Early hominids

现代人
Modern humans

定做 DNA,

人造生命科技大跃进

Making Life in a Lab

Geneticist[1] Creates First Synthetic[2] Organism[3]

图片提供: J. Craig Venter Institute

JONATHAN MANN, CNN ANCHOR

We begin with a potentially startling[4] breakthrough in the world of science. A geneticist says he and his team have created artificial[5] life. Phil Black explains how they did it, the potential benefits and why critics are so concerned.

PHIL BLACK, CNN CORRESPONDENT

Craig Venter is a biologist with an international reputation[6] for breaking new ground and making sure the world hears about it. He claims he's done it again.

CRAIG VENTER, GENETICIST

So it's the first living, self-replicating[7] cell that we have on the planet whose DNA was made chemically and designed in a computer, so it has no genetic ancestors[8]. Its parent's a computer.

Language Notes

break new ground　开创新局面

break ground 原指"（工程、工地）破土、动工"，延伸有"创办，开始执行，着手"的意思。break new ground 则表示"突破传统、开创新局面"。此动词词组可组成复合形容词 groundbreaking，形容"不同于以往的，创新的，突破性的"。

例 The band broke new ground in the realm of pop music.
那支乐团在流行乐领域中开创了新局面。

例 In the 1970s and '80s, Martin Scorsese was known for his groundbreaking films.
在20 世纪 70~80年代，马丁•斯科西斯以其创新性电影著名。

Vocabulary

1. geneticist [dʒə'nɛtəsɪst] *n.* 遗传学家
2. synthetic [sɪn'θɛtɪk] *adj.* 人造的，合成的
   Darlene never wears synthetic fabrics.
3. organism ['ɔrgə,nɪzəm] *n.* 有机体，生物
4. startling ['stɑrtlɪŋ] *adj.* 惊人的，令人吃惊的
   The research revealed some startling data.
5. artificial [,ɑrtə'fɪʃl] *adj.* 人工的，人造的
   The patient was a candidate for an artificial heart.
6. reputation [,rɛpjə'teʃən] *n.* 名誉，名声
7. replicate ['rɛplə,ket] *v.* 复制，再造，再生
   The scientist found it difficult to replicate the results of the test.
8. ancestor ['æn,sɛstə] *n.* （动物的）原种，祖先

CNN 主播

我们以一项科学界的惊人突破开始节目。一位遗传学家表示他和他的研究团队已成功创造出人造生命。菲尔•布莱克进一步说明他们是如何办到的，可能会带来什么好处以及为何舆论如此关注这个议题。

CNN 特派记者　菲尔•布莱克

克雷格•文特是位享誉国际的生物学家，不断开拓新领域并公之于世。文特表示他又再度成功了。

遗传学家　克雷格•文特

这是我们在地球上现有的第一个可自我复制的活体细胞，它的 DNA 是用化学方法制造，并在计算机上设计而成，所以它并没有任何生物基因上的祖先。它的父母亲是台计算机。

PHIL BLACK, CNN CORRESPONDENT

This new synthetically designed bacteria DNA was inserted[9] into the living cell of a different bacteria and it began multiplying[10]. Each new cell now carries the new DNA.

CRAIG VENTER, GENETICIST

These bacteria are software-driven biological machines. If [you] put in different software, they do something different and they look different.

PHIL BLACK, CNN CORRESPONDENT

It's being called the creation of new life. Some scientists dispute[11] that because only the DNA was created, but they all agree it's a big step.

RICHARD KITNEY, PROFESSOR, IMPERIAL COLLEGE LONDON

What that says in a more fundamental[12] way is that you can actually instruct[13] cells using synthetic genomes[14], which you create to perform tasks which, in the future—and we're talking about the relatively near future here—will perform tasks which they don't naturally do.

PHIL BLACK, CNN CORRESPONDENT

Venter and other biologists believe reprogramming[15] cells synthetically is the way to solve some of the world's problems. They say it could result in[1] new vaccines, foods or an algae[16] that eats up greenhouse gases while also producing fuel.

RICHARD KITNEY, PROFESSOR, IMPERIAL COLLEGE LONDON

In theory, what you should be able to do with these algae is to modify[17] them using these basic techniques so that they have two inputs[18], namely CO_2 and sunlight, and the output[19] from the algae will be oil and oxygen.

PHIL BLACK, CNN CORRESPONDENT

The creation of life is a dramatic headline, and it has triggered[20] some passionate[21] criticisms and warnings about the potential dangers. Experts admit there are risks. Some critics are so worried, they want a moratorium[22] on the research.

CNN 特派记者　菲尔·布莱克

这个以人工方式设计出来的细菌的 DNA 被植入另一种细菌的活体细胞内，接着它便开始复制。每个新细胞现在都带有这种新的 DNA。

遗传学家　克雷格·文特

这些细菌是由软件控制的生物机器。如果你放入不同的软件，它们会执行不同任务，而且它们看起来也会不太一样。

CNN 特派记者　菲尔·布莱克

这被称作是创造新生命。有些科学家对此提出质疑，因为被创造的只有 DNA，不过他们都同意这前进了一大步。

伦敦帝国学院教授　理查德·基特尼

从更基本的角度来看，那表示你真的可以使用合成基因组来控制细胞，你可以创造它们执行某些任务，未来——而且我们认为是在不久的将来——就能用它们做某些本身做不到的事。

CNN 特派记者　菲尔·布莱克

文特和其他遗传学家相信以合成的方式改造细胞能够解决世界上一些问题。他们表示这可以产生新的疫苗、食物，或产生一种可以一边吸收温室气体并一边制造燃料的藻类。

伦敦帝国学院教授　理查德·基特尼

理论上，你应该可以用这些基本的技术来改变这些藻类，让它们可以吸收两种东西，也就是二氧化碳和阳光，而这种藻类可产出石油和氧气。

CNN 特派记者　菲尔·布莱克

创造生命是个引人注目的标题，也引发了一些对于潜在危险的激烈批评和警告。专家承认仍有些风险。也有一些评论家非常担心，希望这项研究能够暂停。

Phrases

1. result in 造成，导致
The traffic jam resulted in Jonathan missing his doctor's appointment.

Vocabulary

9. insert [ɪn'sɜt] v. 插入，嵌入
Danny inserted the power plug into the socket.
10. multiply ['mʌltə‚plaɪ] v. 成倍增加，繁殖
Germs multiply in a warm, damp environment.
11. dispute [dɪ'spjut] v. 对……表示异议，争论
Sally disputes Jim's version of events at the party.
12. fundamental [‚fʌndə'mɛntl] adj. 基础的，基本的
The politician promised to bring about fundamental changes if he was elected.
13. instruct [ɪn'strʌkt] v. 指示，命令
The teacher instructed the class on how to write a paragraph.
14. genome ['dʒinom] n. 基因体，染色体组
15. reprogram [rɪ'pro‚græm] v. 修改程序，重新设定
Engineers reprogrammed the satellite to change its course.
16. algae ['ældʒi] n.（复数形式）水藻，海藻
17. modify ['mɑdə‚faɪ] v. 调整，稍作修改
Steven modified his computer to make it run faster.
18. input ['ɪn‚pʊt] n. 输入，输入的信息
19. output ['aʊt‚pʊt] n. 输出，输出量
20. trigger ['trɪgə] v. 引起，触发
The bad news triggered a run on the banks.
21. passionate ['pæʃənət] adj. 热忱的，狂热的
Vanessa is passionate about her art.
22. moratorium [‚mɔrə'tɔriəm] n. 暂停，中止

DAVID KING, HUMAN GENETICS ALERT

Well, the worst-case scenario[23] is that they create an organism which multiplies, you know, out of control and can't be stopped, and that it takes over[2].

PHIL BLACK, CNN CORRESPONDENT

Dr. Venter believes that's all unlikely. He also dismisses[24] fears the technology could easily result in a new generation of bioweapons, because only his team knows how to manipulate[25] DNA in this way. Venter says the research will continue to focus on small cells and basic life forms in the years ahead, and synthetically altering[26] or creating something much more complex[27], like a human, remains in the realm[28] of science fiction.

人类遗传学警报　大卫·金

　　最糟的情况是他们创造出一种有机体，不受控制地复制而且无法阻止，接着它便掌控全世界。

CNN 特派记者　菲尔·布莱克

　　文特博士认为那是绝对不可能的。他也反对此技术可能轻易导致生物武器新时代的疑虑，因为只有他的团队知道如何依此方法操作 DNA。文特表示未来几年的研究将会持续侧重于微小细胞和基本生物体，至于以合成的方式改变或创造更复杂的生命，例如人类，将仍然只存在于科幻小说中。CNN

Phrases

2. take over 接管，接手
   I can take over driving if you are too tired.

Vocabulary

23. scenario [sə'nɛri,o] *n.* 预测，方案
24. dismiss [dɪs'mɪs] *v.* 消除，摒弃（思想、感情等）
    Ben dismissed the story as pure rumor.
25. manipulate [mə,nɪpjə'let] *v.* 控制，操纵
    Alex manipulated the dials on the mixing board until he got the sound he wanted.
26. alter ['ɔltə] *v.* 改变，更改
    The suspect altered his story during the interrogation.
27. complex [kɑm'plɛks] *adj.* 复杂的
    The instructions were too complex to understand.

人造细菌的制造过程

克雷格·文特研究中心利用计算机及化学的方法，合成出一种变种丝状霉浆菌（Mycoplasma mycoides）的 108 万对染色体，将其置入酵母菌载体（yeast vector）中，然后将载体置入基因体（genome）中。经由转化、复制及分离的过程，生成新的人造基因体，再将完整的丝状霉浆菌合成基因体转殖到山羊霉浆菌（Mycoplasma capricolum）的受细胞中。在细胞复制过程中，山羊霉浆菌的基因体渐渐被丝状霉浆菌的基因体取代，两天后，培养皿中明显可见含有人造染色体的丝状霉浆菌。

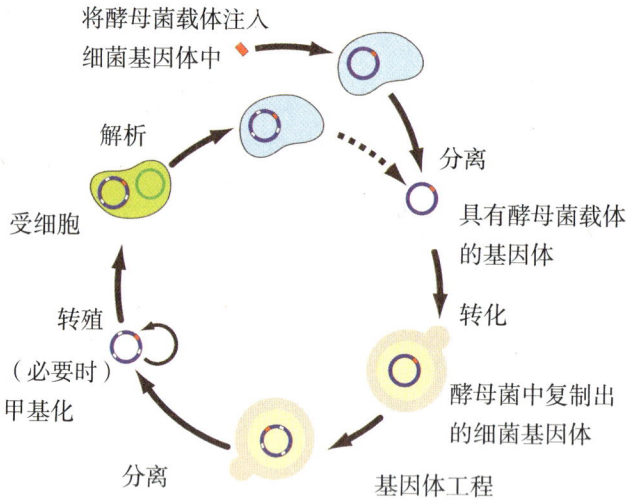

将酵母菌载体注入
细菌基因体中

解析

受细胞

分离

具有酵母菌载体
的基因体

转化

转殖
（必要时）
甲基化

酵母菌中复制出
的细菌基因体

分离

基因体工程

资料来源：J. Craig Venter Institute

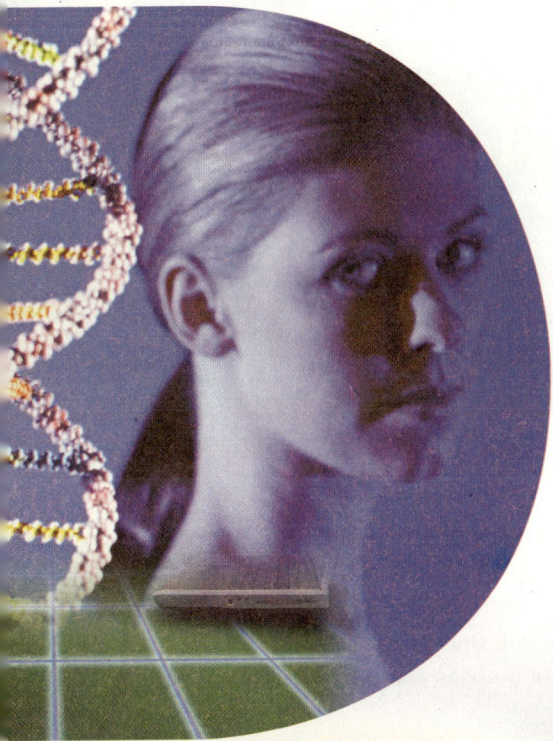

Human Genetics Alert　人类遗传学警报

　　人类遗传学警报是一个位于英国的非宗教独立团体，致力于监督基因工程的发展以及与社会大众一同探讨基因学方面的议题。他们并不是反对基因研究，而是反对基因歧视（genetic discrimination）、复制人（cloning）以及人类遗传基因工程。

炫酷时尚

寰宇星空

生命发现

绿色革命

生活嬗变

天文物理大师

史蒂芬·霍金

谈宇宙与人类的未来

The Final Frontier

Physicist[1] Stephen Hawking Journeys[2] into
the Future of Space Exploration

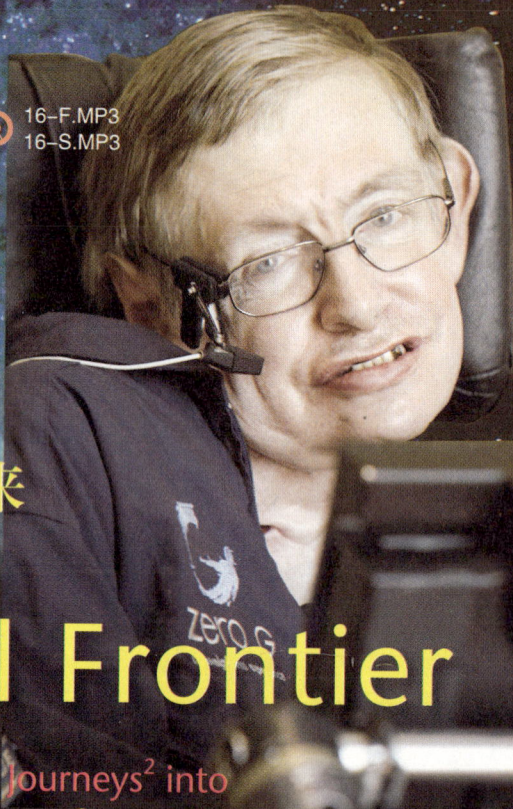

BECKY ANDERSON, CNN CORRESPONDENT

Professor Stephen Hawking is an unlikely celebrity. He achieved international fame with the publication of the scientific best seller[3] *A Brief History of Time*. He's disabled[4] by a condition that has left him almost completely paralyzed[5].

All right, well, I've just arrived here at Cambridge University at the Centre for Mathematical Sciences to interview Professor Stephen Hawking. The crew's already there, so let's see if we can find the door.

I started by asking whether his theories and beliefs had changed much in the last 20 years.

STEPHEN HAWKING, PHYSICIST

Over the last 20 years, observations have to a large extent confirmed the picture I painted in *A Brief History of Time*. The one major development that was not anticipated[6] was the discovery that the expansion of the universe is accelerating[7] now, rather than slowing down. However, it fits in[8] very well. I now understand why the universe is the way it is. We live in the most probable[9] of all possible worlds.

Language Notes

paint a picture　描绘，生动描述

字面意思是"画一张图画"，比喻"描绘，描述"某事物，通常是凭印象或想象，而且有"生动描述"的意思。

例 The article painted a picture of life in a Calcutta slum.
那篇文章描绘加尔各答贫民窟的生活。

Vocabulary

1. physicist ['fɪzəsɪst] *n.* 物理学家
2. journey ['dʒɜnɪ] *v.* 旅行
   Devon journeyed to India to learn yoga from a master.
3. best seller [bɛst]['sɛlə] 畅销作品（书、唱片）
4. disable [dɪs'ebl] *v.* 使失去能力，使伤残
   Someone disabled the virus protection on this computer.
5. paralyze ['pærə,laɪz] *v.* 瘫痪
   Fear paralyzed the audience as the lion attacked his trainer.
6. anticipate [æn'tɪsə,pet] *v.* 预期，预料
   Jeff anticipated that the economic collapse was coming before anyone else.
7. accelerate [æk'sɛlə,ret] *v.* 使加速，加快
   The car accelerated to pass the school bus.
8. fit in [fɪt][ɪn] 相符，符合
   The writer's philosophy fit in with Jim's world view.
9. probable ['prɑbəbl] *adj.* 很可能的，可能成真的
   Several statisticians tried to calculate the probable outcome of the election.

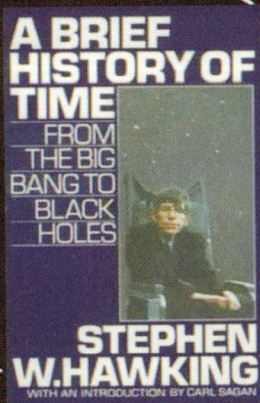

CNN 特派员　贝基·安德森

　　史蒂芬·霍金教授是一位意外成名的名人。他因为出版了科学畅销著作《时间简史》而名闻世界。他患有一种疾病，几乎全身瘫痪。

　　我刚抵达剑桥大学的数学科学中心，即将采访霍金教授。工作人员早就到了，看看我们能不能找到入口。

　　我首先问的问题是，他的理论和观念在过去二十年来有没有改变。

物理学家　史蒂芬·霍金

　　过去二十年来的观察，已经大大证实了我在《时间简史》里描绘的景象。当初没有预期到的一项重大发现，是宇宙的膨胀速度正在加快，而不是减缓。不过，这样的状况和我的理论也相当符合。现在，我已经了解宇宙为什么是这个模样了。我们生活的这个世界，是所有可能存在的世界当中最有可能出现的一个。

BECKY ANDERSON, CNN CORRESPONDENT

Why is your outlook[10] for humanity so pessimistic[11] and what are your solutions[12]?

STEPHEN HAWKING, PHYSICIST

I see great dangers for the human race. There have been a number of times in the past when its survival has been a question of touch and go. The Cuban Missile Crisis in 1963 was one of these. The frequency[13] of such occasions[14] is likely to increase in the future. We shall need great care and judgment[15] to negotiate[16] them all successfully, but I'm an optimist[17]. If we can avoid disaster for the next two centuries, our species should be safe as we spread into space.

BECKY ANDERSON, CNN CORRESPONDENT

I asked him whether the human race had a moral[18] obligation[19] to find out more about space.

STEPHEN HAWKING, PHYSICIST

I don't think the human race has a moral obligation to learn about space, but it would be foolish and shortsighted[20] not to do so. It may hold the key to our survival.

BECKY ANDERSON, CNN CORRESPONDENT

What expectations, Professor Hawking, do you have of the space flight that you hope to go on next year?

STEPHEN HAWKING, PHYSICIST

The Zero G flight I did last year was wonderful. After 40 years in a wheelchair, it was so good to be floating free, but that flight was just a warm-up for space. The real thing should be much better and last much longer. The sky will be black, and the stars will shine brightly. I'm a bit worried about the high g-forces on the way up and down, but I coped with[21] them OK on the Zero G flight.

BECKY ANDERSON, CNN CORRESPONDENT

And with that, we thank you very much indeed for your time.

STEPHEN HAWKING, PHYSICIST

Thank you.

CNN 特派员　贝基·安德森

你对人类的前景为什么这么悲观？你有什么解决的方法吗？

物理学家　史蒂芬·霍金

我看到人类面临着极大的危险。人类在过去也曾经数度遭遇生存危机，1963 年的古巴飞弹危机就是一个例子。这种危机的发生频率在未来可能会提高。我们必须要有较大的关注度和良好的判断力，才能安然度过所有的危机。但我很乐观。只要我们能够在未来 200 年间避开灾难，人类的生存空间即可拓展至太空，从此安全无忧。

CNN 特派员　贝基·安德森

我问他人类是不是有进一步了解太空的道德上的义务。

物理学家　史蒂芬·霍金

我不认为人类有了解太空的道德上的义务，可是如果不这么做，未免太过愚蠢也太过短视了。太空很可能是人类生存的关键。

CNN 特派员　贝基·安德森

霍金教授，你对自己明年的太空飞行有什么期待？

物理学家　史蒂芬·霍金

我去年参与的 Zero G 无重力飞行（注）非常棒。在轮椅上待了 40 年，能够自由漂浮实在感觉很好。不过，那趟飞行只是太空之旅的热身而已。实际上的太空旅行应该会更棒，持续得也更久。天空会是一片漆黑，星星会非常闪亮。我有点担心升空和降落期间高强的重力加速度，但我在无重力飞行中适应得还不错。

CNN 特派员　贝基·安德森

好的，非常谢谢你抽空接受访问。

物理学家　史蒂芬·霍金

谢谢。 CNN

> 注：Zero G 是全球唯一无重力飞行民营公司，1993 年成立，总部位于拉斯维加斯，除了与 NASA 合作训练航天员之外，也提供个人无重力飞行体验。

Language Notes

touch and go　紧张危急的情势

touch and go 当名词指不小心就会失控的"紧张而危急的情势"，也可以当形容词表示"非常紧张危急的"，类似中文的"一触即发"。

例 The patient's condition was touch and go after the operation.
那位患者手术后的情况非常危急。

Vocabulary

10. **outlook** ['aʊtˌlʊk] *n.* 前景，展望
11. **pessimistic** [ˌpɛsə'mɪstɪk] *adj.* 悲观的，悲观主义的
    Glen is pessimistic about his ability to afford college for his kids.
12. **solution** [sə'luʃən] *n.* 解决方法
13. **frequency** ['frikwənsɪ] *n.* 频率
14. **occasion** [ə'keʒən] *n.* 场合，时刻，起因
15. **judgment** ['dʒʌdʒmənt] *n.* 判断（力）
16. **negotiate** [nɪ'goʃɪˌet] *v.* 协商，谈判
    The star negotiated a new contract with the television studio.
17. **optimist** ['ɑptəmɪst] *n.* 乐观主义者
18. **moral** ['mɔrəl] *adj.* 道德的
    Dina took the moral high ground in her argument.
19. **obligation** [ˌɑblə'geʃən] *n.*（道德或法律的）义务
20. **shortsighted** ['ʃɔrtˌsaɪtɪd] *adj.* 短视的，目光短浅的
    Scientists blamed shortsighted environmental policies for global warming.
21. **cope with** [kop][wɪð] 应付，处理
    Darla coped with her anxiety by meditating.

A Brief History of Time:
from the Big Bang to Black Holes

《时间简史》

出版：1988 年美国 Bantam Dell 集团
类别：科普（popular science）
纪录：
· 翻译成 40 多种语言，全球销量超过 1 000 万册
· 伦敦《星期天泰晤士报》（Sunday Times）畅销榜停留长达 4 年
内容：
史蒂芬·霍金从研究黑洞（black holes）出发，探索宇宙的起源和归宿，向一般读者说明宇宙学（cosmology）的诸多主题，例如大爆炸（Big Bang）、黑洞、光锥（light cones）、超弦理论（superstring theory）等。2001 年出版《胡桃里的宇宙》（The Universe in a Nutshell），被认为是图画版的《时间简史》。

Stephen Hawking
史蒂芬·霍金

经历
1942 年出生于英国牛津，父母皆为研究学者。
1959 年 17 岁进入牛津大学攻读物理。
1962 年转往剑桥大学研究天文学和宇宙学。
1963 年被诊断患有肌萎缩性脊髓侧索硬化症（amyotrophic amyotrophic lateral sclerosis, ALS），全身逐渐瘫痪。
1985 年感染肺炎（pneumonia）开刀后失去发声能力，利用音质合成器（voice synthesizer）说话，通过抽动右脸颊肌肉，控制眼镜上的红外线感应器选择文字来输入数据。

重要天文学理论
1970 年奇异点（singularity）——与罗杰·彭罗斯提出宇宙大爆炸的起源。
1974 年霍金辐射（Hawking radiation）——黑洞会缓慢散发一种辐射能量，散尽后黑洞就会蒸发消失。
1983 年宇宙无边论（No Boundary Proposal）——与吉姆·何特勒提出，主张宇宙中没有 "空间" 存在。

Give It a Try 请选出正确答案

1. The scientist predicted the _____ outcome of the experiment.
   a. probable   b. pessimistic
   c. shortsighted   d. moral

2. he _____ of Jeff's headaches convinced him that he should see a doctor.
   a. outlook   b. frequency
   c. judgment   d. optimist

3. It was _____ of Helen to spend all her savings on gadgets and clothing.
   a. pessimistic   b. shortsighted
   c. probable   d. moral

Answers: 1.a 2.b 3.b

Notes

濒危物种新希望——DNA 冷冻方舟

The Bar Code[1] of Life

Creating a Genetic Ark[2] to Preserve[3] the Earth's
Endangered[4] Species

ANNA COREN , CNNN A NCHOR

   Well, this week and next, we are taking you on a journey to *Earth's Frontiers*[5]. Today, it's Madagascar where scientists have set themselves quite a challenge. Their objective[6] is to document[7] marine life and their sample size is the entire ocean. Becky Anderson has the story.

BECKY ANDERSON, CNN CORRESPONDENT

   Our oceans contain some of the oldest life on our planet and some of the most endangered. With species disappearing every day, a group of scientists from opposite corners of the globe have set themselves the task of cataloging[8] the DNA of every form of life in the ocean before it's too late.

   From Southern Madagascar, a cold region of fierce[9] promontories[10], open bays and extensive algal[11] belts, to England's North Sea, their common goal is to better understand the abundance[12] of life in our oceans—past, present and future—and use its DNA to create a bar code of life.

CNN 主播　安娜·科伦

　　本周和下周，我们将带你一起观看《地球先锋》。现在，科学家在马达加斯加迎接一个严峻的挑战。他们的目标是要记录海洋生物，样本范围则是整个海洋。贝基·安德森带来以下报道。

CNN 特派员　贝基·安德森

　　我们的海洋蕴藏了地球上一些最古老以及濒临绝种的生物。鉴于地球上每天都有物种消失，一群来自地球两端的科学家给自己定下任务，要把每一种海洋生物的 DNA 加以登记，以免为时太晚。

　　从马达加斯加南部气候寒冷恶劣的海岬地区、开阔的海湾、广阔的海藻带，到英国的北海，他们的共同的目标是更加了解海洋中丰富多样的生物，不论是已消失的、现存的还是未知的，并利用 DNA 建立生物条形码。

Vocabulary

1. **bar code** [bɑr][kod] *n.* 条形码
2. **ark** [ɑrk] *n.* 方舟，避难所
3. **preserve** [prɪˈzɜv] *v.* 保护，保育，保存
   Many people preserve meat by smoking or drying it.
4. **endangered** [ɪnˈdendʒəd] *adj.* 濒临绝种的
   The national park was established to protect endangered species.
5. **frontier** [ˌfrʌnˈtɪr] *n.* （学科活动的）尖端，边缘
6. **objective** [əbˈdʒɛktɪv] *n.* 目标，目的
7. **document** [ˈdɑkjəmənt] *v.* 记录，详细记载
   The film crew documented the politician's presidential campaign.
8. **catalog** [ˈkætəlɔg] *v.* 将……编目，登记
   The collector cataloged thousands of stamps.
9. **fierce** [fɪrs] *adj.* （天气）狂暴的，恶劣的，严苛的
   The competition between the cross-town rivals was fierce.
10. **promontory** [ˈprɑmənˌtɔrɪ] *n.* 海岬，岬角
11. **algal** [ˈælgəl] *adj.* 海藻的，藻类的
    Special paint prevents algal growth on the boat's hull.
12. **abundance** [əˈbʌndəns] *n.* 大量，充裕，丰盛

Professor Philippe Bouchet leads a team of scientists from around the world who have gathered here in Madagascar. He's dedicated his life to[1] discovering unknown species. On this day, he thinks he's made an important discovery.

PHILIPPE BOUCHET, MARINE BIOLOGIST

The catch of the day, not immediately identifiable[13] with one of the known species. Hmmm. I don't know. Maybe it's still something different.

BECKY ANDERSON, CNN CORRESPONDENT

Philippe and his team have already cataloged more than three and a half thousand specimens. Around one and a half thousand new marine species entered into literature[14] every year. At this rate, the process of discovering, verifying[15] and naming all remaining unknown marine species would take more than five centuries.

On the other side of the globe, Professor David Rawson is involved in a similar project, to collect material from endangered fish species in Britain using a pioneering[16] technique called cryopreservation to create a so called Frozen Ark.

DAVID RAWSON, UNIVERSITY OF BEDFORDSHIRE

This is to culture[17] cells from the fin, and we can take it back to the lab and we can get cells to grow up from the fin clippings we're about to take.

BECKY ANDERSON, CNN CORRESPONDENT

His research will enable future scientists to compare what once lived in the oceans with what lives there now and what will live there in the future.

DAVID RAWSON, UNIVERSITY OF BEDFORDSHIRE

The big concern is that certain groups are particularly vulnerable[18] to extinction[19] and fish probably most of all, of all the vertebrate[20] groups. Something like 30 percent of them are considered entirely vulnerable.

Frozen Ark is a way of preserving material in a more useful way than we did in the past. So it's a form of banking[21] in—banking cells in a state where they can be held for hundreds or thousands of years at very, very low temperatures, particularly because [of] liquid nitrogen[22], which is minus 196 degrees Centigrade, so extremely cold temperatures where, in effect[2], all life activity does . . . is in suspended animation.

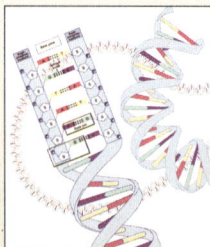

图片提供：National Human Genome Research Institute

菲利普·布薛特教授带领一支科学家团队，成员从世界各地聚集到马达加斯加。他将自己的生命奉献给发现未知的物种上。这天，他认为他有了重大的发现。

海洋生物学家　菲利普·布薛特

这是今天抓到的，无法立即辨别是某种已知的物种。我不知道。这可能是不同的物种。

CNN 特派员　贝基·安德森

菲利普和他的团队已经将超过 3 500 种样本编目。每年将近会有 1 500 种新的海洋物种编进文献中。照这样的速度，从发现、证实和命名其余所有未知的海洋物种，整个过程可能要花上五个多世纪。

在地球的另外一边，大卫·罗森教授参与了一项类似的计划，他们从英国濒临绝种的鱼类身上搜集物质，利用创新的超低温冷冻技术创造所谓的冷冻方舟。

贝德福德大学　大卫·罗森

这要用来培养鱼鳍上的细胞。我们把它带回实验室，然后就可以对待会儿剪下的鱼鳍中取得的细胞进行培养。

CNN 特派员　贝基·安德森

他的研究让未来的科学家能够比较海洋中曾经存在的、现存的和未来将会出现的物种。

贝德福德大学　大卫·罗森

目前最大的担忧是某些物种非常容易消失，而鱼类在所有的脊椎动物中又最有可能面临这项考验。大约30%的鱼类被认为十分脆弱。

冷冻方舟用一种比过去更有效的方式保存生物数据。这是存放细胞的一种方式，把细胞放在非常、非常低的温度状态下保存数百年，甚至达数千年之久。尤其因为液态氮只有零下196 摄氏度，在这样极度低温的状态下，事实上所有的生命活动都会……处于假死状态。

Phrases

1. dedicate . . . to　把（人生、事业等）奉献于
The politician dedicated his career to improving the lives of others.
2. in effect　实际上，事实上
In effect, Douglas became the guardian for his orphaned nephew.

Vocabulary

13. identifiable [aɪˌdɛntəˈfaɪəbl] adj. 可辨认的
Inspectors found 20 identifiable contaminants in the food.
14. literature [ˈlɪtərəˌtʃə] n. 文献，资料
15. verify [ˈvɛrəˌfaɪ] v. 核实，查对
The security guard verified everyone's identity before admitting them to the building.
16. pioneering [ˌpaɪəˈnɪrɪŋ] adj. 先驱的，开创性的
Ben's father is a pioneering scientist in cancer research.
17. culture [ˈkʌltʃə] v. 培养（细胞、细菌等）
Biologists cultured the mold spores in the lab.
18. vulnerable [ˈvʌlnərəbl] adj. 脆弱的，易受伤害的
Many ecosystems are vulnerable to climate change.
19. extinction [ɪkˈstɪŋkʃən] n. 绝种，灭亡
20. vertebrate [ˈvɜtəbˌret] n. 脊椎动物
21. bank [bæŋk] v. 存入，存到银行
Health workers banked the blood samples in a storage facility.
22. nitrogen [ˈnaɪtrədʒən] n. 氮，氮气

炫酷时尚　寰宇星空　生命发现　绿色革命　生活嬗变

Step by Step 听懂 CNN 先锋科技

BECKY ANDERSON, CNN CORRESPONDENT

It is estimated[25] that most species that become extinct have never been documented by scientists. Philippe and David know that they are in a race against time.

DAVID RAWSON, UNIVERSITY OF BEDFORDSHIRE

I think many nations now recognize that their fauna[26] and flora[27] are as valuable to them as their mineral reserves and their land. It's an enormous task to capture everything. But a start has been made. And I think it's making us recognize the value of our biology that's around us.

PHILIPPE BOUCHET, MARINE BIOLOGIST

And when I was a student, my dream was to discover one new species. And, well, that dream has been fulfilled, I mean, thousands of times. In fact, nearly everywhere in the world, you . . . especially in the tropics, there are [is] still plenty to discover. And my experience with the tropical islands in the Pacific—and I have seen places early in my career—20 years later, these habitats[28] were gone. So, yes, there is a race against time.

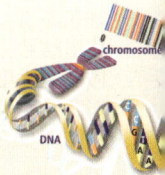

CNN 特派员　贝基·安德森

据推测，大部分绝种的物种都未曾被科学家记录。菲利普和大卫都知道他们在和时间赛跑。

贝德福德大学　大卫·罗森

我想许多国家现在意识到他们的动物群和植物群都很珍贵，就像他们的矿藏和土地一样。虽然要采集每个物种是一项浩大的工程，但是我们已经跨出了第一步。我认为这让我们正视周遭生物的价值。

海洋生物学家　菲利普·布薛特

当我还是学生时，我的梦想便是发现一个新的物种。而那个梦想早已实现，有数千次了。事实上，几乎世界上的每个地方，你……特别是在热带地区，仍有许多物种尚待发现。以我在太平洋热带岛屿的经历，在我工作初期曾到过某些地方，过了 20 年，这些栖息地都已经消失了。所以，是的，这是场与时间的赛跑。CNN

Language Notes

a race against time　与时间赛跑

比喻某件事情很紧急，需要尽快完成，仿佛在和时间比赛一样。against time 本身可表示"时间快来不及，赶快"，也可写成 against the clock。

例 The rescuers were in a race against time to reach the stranded hikers.
搜救人员与时间赛跑，想快点找到受困的登山者。

例 Doctors raced against the clock to save the patient's life.
医生和时间赛跑，抢救病人的生命。

Vocabulary

25. **estimate** ['ɛstə,met] *v.* 估计，估算
   Floyd estimated that the drive would take five hours.
26. **fauna** ['fɔnə] *n.* （某地区或时期）动物群
27. **flora** ['flɔrə] *n.* （某地区或时期）植物群
28. **habitat** ['hæbə,tæt] *n.* （动植物的）栖息地

炫酷时尚

寰宇星空

生命发现

绿色革命

生活嬗变

什么是 **DNA 条形码** ？

2003 年加拿大圭尔夫大学（University of Guelph）保罗·贺博特（Paul Hebert）的研究团队提出利用 DNA 序列（sequence）截取一小段基因组（genome）的数值编为条形码，便于鉴定比对物种。

用来辨识动物的部分是线粒体细胞色素氧化酶 1（CO1, cytochrome c oxidase subunit 1），只有 648 组碱基对（base pair）。编码以 C、A、T、G 四个字母组成，分别表示核酸（nucleic acid）中的胞嘧啶（cytosine）、腺嘌呤（adenine）、胸腺嘧啶（thymine）和鸟嘌呤（guanine），并用蓝、绿、红、黑色区别。例如极北柳莺的 CATG 编码如下：

CC TA TA CC TAA TC TT GG AG C ATG AG C GGG C A TGG TA GG C …

转成条形码为：

将数据存入 DNA 条形码数据库，用来进行全球物种保存、查询、比对及研究。陆地植物则以叶绿体（chloroplast）的 matK 及 rbcL 部分来编码。

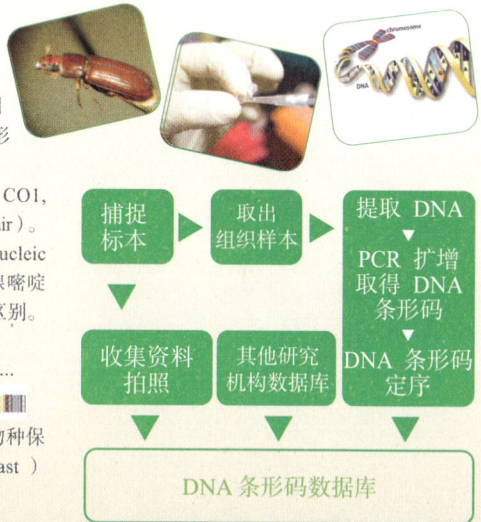

捕捉标本 → 取出组织样本 → 提取 DNA

PCR 扩增取得 DNA 条形码

收集资料拍照　　其他研究机构数据库　　DNA 条形码定序

DNA 条形码数据库

资料来源：International Barcode of Life

日本真的是为了研究捕鲸？
生物学家告诉你真相

A Whale of
a Discovery

Researchers Offer a Humane[1] Alternative[3] to Japan's Lethal[2] Science

KRISTIE LU STOUT, CNN ANCHOR

Every year, hundreds of whales are killed in the name of science, but there's a new method out there that suggests the same information can be found without actually harming the whales. Anna Coren looks at this new technique and what it could mean for the contentious[4] issue of whaling around the world.

ANNA COREN, CNN CORRESPONDENT

They're one of the most majestic[5] creatures of the deep. Growing up to 15 meters long and weighing in excess of[1] 40 tons, the humpback, known for its playful, curious nature, certainly knows how to put on a show. Among the adoring crowd, a group of Australian researchers working to come up with[2] evidence to try and save the whales from this. Japan will resume[6] its annual scientific hunt in the Southern Ocean at the end of the year. Under the International Whaling Commission, it's allowed to cull[7] 1,000 minkes[8], 50 fin whales, and in recent years, 50 humpbacks have been added to the list. While Japan claims it's in the name of science, critics say it's a crude[9] disguise[10] to sell and eat whale meat.

Language Notes

标题扫描：

> **a whale of** 巨大，大量

whale 原指"鲸"，延伸比喻"巨大、大量之物"，尤指体积硕大，a whale of 即"巨大、大量"的意思。

例 After the party, Tom woke up with a whale of a headache.
派对过后，汤姆醒来头痛得不得了。

Phrases

1. **in excess of** 超过
   Susan's debts are in excess of a year's salary.
2. **come up with** 想出，找到（答案）
   Brian came up with a solution to the problem.

Vocabulary

1. **humane** [hju'men] *adj.* 仁慈的，人道的
   The city is looking for a humane solution to its stray animal problem.
2. **alternative** [ɔ'tɜrnətɪv] *n.* 替代选择
3. **lethal** ['liθəl] *adj.* 致命的，危害极大的
   The man accidentally took a lethal dose of the drug.
4. **contentious** [kən'tɛnʃəs] *adj.* 有争议的
   Drug legalization is a contentious issue in many countries.
5. **majestic** [mə'dʒɛstɪk] *adj.* 雄伟的，壮观的
   Brian saw several majestic eagles soaring over the valley.
6. **resume** [rɪ'zum] *v.* 重新开始，（中断后）继续
   The game resumed after a short break.
7. **cull** [kʌl] *v.* 部分捕杀，宰杀
   National park officials culled dozens of feral sheep.
8. **minke** ['mɪŋkə] *n.* 小须鲸
9. **crude** [krud] *adj.* 粗陋的，粗糙的
   The child made a crude remark when his teacher left the room.
10. **disguise** [dɪs'gaɪs] *n.* 伪装，掩饰

炫酷时尚　寰宇星空　生命发现　绿色革命　生活嬗变

CNN 主播　克里斯蒂·卢·斯托特

　　每年，数以百计的鲸因科学的名义遭到杀害，但是有个新方法证明其实不用伤害鲸也可得到相同的资料。安娜·科伦带领我们看看这项新技术，以及这对全球备受争议的捕鲸议题会带来什么样的影响。

CNN 特派员　安娜·科伦

　　他们是海洋中最健壮的生物之一。座头鲸身长可达 15 米，体重超过 40 吨，也是出了名的生性好玩、好奇心重，座头鲸肯定知道如何进行一场表演。在喜爱鲸的人们之中，有一群澳大利亚的科学家正致力于找出证据，努力解救鲸免于捕杀。日本将于今年年底在南太平洋再度展开年度科学捕鲸。在国际捕鲸委员会的许可下，已核准捕杀 1 000 头小须鲸、50 头鳍鲸，这几年还有 50 头座头鲸已被加入清单。虽然日本声称这是为了科学研究，但批评声指出这只是贩卖和食用鲸肉的粗劣伪装。

PETER HARRISON, SOUTHERN CROSS UNIVERSITY

There is no science associated with the scientific whaling. There is no need to kill whales in order to get the so-called scientific information the Japanese claim they need to get.

ANNA COREN, CNN CORRESPONDENT

Dr. Peter Harrison from Southern Cross University is behind the groundbreaking[11] study. As the whales make their annual migration[12] along the east coast of Australia, he and his team of scientists collect very small but valuable whale DNA.

PETER HARRISON, SOUTHERN CROSS UNIVERSITY

In the whale footprint, the clear water that occurs after a big breach[13] has occurred, we then go in slowly and with a "highly technical" kitchen sieve[14] on the end of a long pole, we basically scooped[15] a little bit of sample out and then pop it into alcohol and then take it back to the laboratory to do the genetic analysis.

ANNA COREN, CNN CORRESPONDENT

These bits of skin can determine a whale's sex, genetic type, and potentially the secret to their age. Scientists believe they've found a connection between the length of the end of the chromosomes[16] and the age of whales. It's this key piece of information Japan claims can only be obtained through tissue located in the outer ear canal[17], and that requires killing them. In a statement released to CNN, Japan said, "Non-lethal research does not give enough information to find out the dynamics[18] and sustainability[19] of whales as resources in the longer term future."

南十字星大学　彼得·哈里森

科学捕鲸和科学并无关联。其实并不需要杀害鲸才能取得日本人声称他们需要的所谓的"科学数据"。

CNN 特派员　安娜·科伦

南十字星大学的彼得·哈里森博士是这项开创性研究的幕后推手。鲸沿着澳大利亚东海岸进行年度迁徙时，他和他的科学团队会搜集少量但却相当有价值的鲸的DNA。

南十字星大学　彼得·哈里森

在鲸的足迹中，也就是鲸大跳跃跃出水面过后的无波纹海水，我们会慢慢地接近，用一根尾端装有"高科技"厨房专用筛的杆子。基本上我们只取一点点样本，然后迅速放至酒精中，再带回实验室进行基因分析。

CNN 特派员　安娜·科伦

这些鲸皮碎片可以判定一头鲸的性别、基因类型，甚至有可能一探鲸的年龄秘密。科学家相信，他们已经发现染色体尾端的长度和鲸的年龄有关。这就是日本声称只能从外耳道里的组织得知的关键信息，而那样做需要杀害鲸。在一份发给 CNN 的声明稿中，日方表示，"非致命性的研究无法提供足够信息以查明鲸的生态和生机，这在长远的未来会是重要的资源。"

Vocabulary

11. **groundbreaking** ['graʊnd,brekɪŋ] *adj.* 开创性的
    The doctor made several groundbreaking discoveries.
12. **migration** [maɪ'greʃən] *n.* 迁徙，移居
13. **breach** [britʃ] *n.* 跃出水面（尤指鲸）
14. **sieve** [sɪv] *n.* 筛子
15. **scoop** [skʊp] *v.* （用勺子）舀起，（用铲子）铲起
    Billy scooped the ice cream into a cone.
16. **chromosome** ['kroməˌzom] *n.* 染色体
17. **canal** [kə'næl] *n.* 气管，食道
18. **dynamic** [daɪ'næmɪk] *n.* 相互作用的方式，动态
19. **sustainability** [səˌstenə'bɪləti] *n.* 持续性

Japan and several other pro-whaling nations tried to overturn[20] the commercial whaling ban[21] at this year's international whaling conference in Morocco and failed, but some believe it may only be a matter of time. Before commercial whaling began last century, there were an estimated 40,000 eastern Australian humpbacks. By the time the whaling station closed here in Byron Bay in 1962, as few as 100 remained. Researchers say, since becoming a protected species, those numbers have bounced[22] back to 12,000, but argue that does not justify[23] a return to the days of hunting the humpback. Dr. Harrison is confident he will soon have enough scientific data to potentially save his beloved whale.

PETER HARRISON, SOUTHERN CROSS UNIVERSITY
It will remove the last excuse that the Japanese are using to try and underpin[24] their scientific whaling.

日本和其他数个支持捕鲸的国家，试图推翻今年摩洛哥国际捕鲸会议中通过的商业捕鲸禁令，但是他们失败了。不过有些人认为这只是时间早晚的问题。在上个世纪商业捕鲸活动开始之前，估计澳大利亚东部海岸有 4 万头座头鲸。到 1962 年拜伦湾的捕鲸站关闭时，仅剩下 100 头座头鲸。研究人员表示，由于座头鲸已列为保护动物，数量已回升至 1.2 万，但他们也指出那并不能将重新猎杀鲸合理化。哈里森博士有信心很快就能有足够的科学数据，可能可以解救他心爱的鲸。

南十字星大学　彼得·哈里森

　　这就能打消日本人用来设法加强科学捕鲸活动的最后一个借口。CNN

全球捕鲸现况 ●●●●●●●●●●●●●●●

　　捕鲸活动可追溯到至少公元前 3 000 年，但自 19 世纪中以来，因科技发展使得捕鲸工具进步，加上鲸油（whale oil / train oil）及鲸肉的需求大增，演变成滥捕并造成鲸的数量锐减。

　　1946 年有 15 国在华盛顿签署国际捕鲸管制公约（International Convention for the Regulation of Whaling），并成立国际捕鲸委员会（IWC, International Whaling Commission），主要负责监督、评估各国的捕鲸数量及种类，目前共有 59 个成员国。目前主要的捕鲸地区包括环绕北极的加拿大北部、美国阿拉斯加、俄罗斯远东地区、挪威、冰岛、丹麦格陵兰岛（Greenland）、法罗群岛（Faroe Islands）、日本，此外还有两个印度尼西亚的部落仍维持捕鲸活动。

　　其中丹麦法罗群岛及日本捕鲸牵扯到文化议题，前者视捕鲸为传统庆典，有动物保护主义者曾潜入庆典活动秘密拍照，上网公布后引起关注。日本则是长久以来有食用鲸肉及生鱼片的传统，《国家地理杂志》前摄影师的纪录片《血色海湾》(*The Cove*)，就是拍摄日本渔村猎捕鲸豚的真相。

捕鲸的规范与种类 ●●●●●●●●●●●●

　　国际捕鲸委员会允许的捕鲸范畴主要有三类：维持原住民生活需求的原住民限制（aboriginal limits）、可买卖的商业限制（commercial limits）以及科学研究许可（scientific permits）。

　　限制捕猎的鲸鱼种类依海域及数量、用途等有不同数量的规定，主要包括抹香鲸（sperm whale）、长须鲸（fin whale）、小须鲸（minke whale）、座头鲸（humpback whale）、塞鲸（Sei whale）、北极鲸（bowhead）和布氏鲸（Brydes whale）。

Vocabulary

20. overturn [ˌovəˈtɜn] v. 推翻，撤销
The judge overturned the lower court's ruling.
21. ban [bæn] n. 禁令
22. bounce [baʊns] v. 弹跳，弹起
The economy eventually bounced back after the downturn.
23. justify [ˈdʒʌstəˌfaɪ] v. 证明……为正当、有理
Jenny justified the expense of the meal because she felt she deserved it.
24. underpin [ˌʌndəˈpɪn] v. 加强，巩固
The data underpinned the scientist's theory.

绿色革命

⑲ 实用又环保的超薄电子报纸

⑳ 替代能源新里程——生物燃料客机首航

㉑ 回顾环保科技 10 年轨迹

实用又环保的超薄电子报纸

Hot off the (Paperless) Presses

Eco-Friendly E-Reader Delivers the News While Saving Trees

CNN ANCHOR

Reading the front page over a cup of coffee might be headed[1] in a digital direction. On this week's *Eco Solutions*, Fred Pleitgen shows us how engineers are putting a new twist[2] on the morning paper, and how this new gadget[3] might help save trees around the world.

FREDERIK PLEITGEN, CNN CORRESPONDENT

Four billion—that's an estimate[4] of how many trees are cut down every year to make paper products. Gentlemen, put down your chain saws[5] because the Plastic Logic E-Reader is almost here.

RICHARD ARCHULETA, CEO, PLASTIC LOGIC

The device[6] is kind of very thin, very light. It is about the size and weight of a pad[7] of paper.

CNN 主播

一边看报纸头版，一边喝咖啡，这样的生活大概也要进入数字时代了。在本周的《生态解决方案》节目里，弗雷德里克·普里根要告诉我们工程师如何使早报呈现新变化，而且这种新产品可能有助于保护世界各地的树木。

CNN 特派员　弗雷德里克·普里根

40 亿——根据估计，每年为了生产纸张就必须砍掉这么多棵树。各位先生，请放下电锯吧，因为塑料材质电子阅读器就快要推出了。

塑料材质公司　CEO　理查德·阿丘列塔

这种产品很薄，很轻，大小和重量都和一本便笺本差不多。

Language Notes

标题扫描：

> **hot off the presses**

press 在这里是 printing machine "印刷机" 的意思。hot off the presses 原意是指 "刚刚印刷出来的"，通常是指报纸或杂志。此词组后衍生为 "最新消息或信息"。

例 The latest issue of Jim's newsletter is hot off the presses.
吉姆最新一期的通讯期刊刚刚出版了。

例 Word about her company's upcoming layoffs was hot off the presses when Jan decided to take the job offer from a competitor.
珍在她公司即将裁员的消息传出时，决定接受竞争公司所提供的工作。

Vocabulary

1. **head** [hɛd] v. （向特定方向）前进
   After the first act, the play headed in an unexpected direction.
2. **twist** [twɪst] n. 变化，花样
3. **gadget** ['gædʒɪt] n. 精巧的机械或器具
4. **estimate** ['ɛstəˌmet] n. 估计，估算
5. **chain saw** [tʃen] [sɔ] 链锯
6. **device** [dɪ'vaɪs] n. 设备，仪器，装置
7. **pad** [pæd] n. 垫子，便签本

FREDERIK PLEITGEN, CNN CORRESPONDENT

Due out next week, the e-reader says so long to all those piles of paper.

RICHARD ARCHULETA, CEO, PLASTIC LOGIC

It works by taking anything that you would normally print out or read on paper, like a newspaper or a magazine, and transfers them from either computer or wirelessly, you know, to the device so that you can read them.

FREDERIK PLEITGEN, CNN CORRESPONDENT

At this one-of-a-kind production facility[8] in Dresden, Germany, nanotech is saving Mother Nature, where an environmentally friendly process creates the e-paper's unique flexible[9] plastic design. And with the swipe[10] of a thumb, Plastic Logic hopes to usher in a green reading revolution.

CNN 特派员　弗雷德里克·普里根

预计下周上市，电子阅读器要向成堆的纸张说再见了。

塑料材质公司　CEO　理查德·阿丘列塔

电子阅读器可以通过计算机或无线设备下载通常印在纸上让人阅读的东西，例如报纸或杂志，然后把内容显示出来供你阅读。

CNN 特派员　弗雷德里克·普里根

这座独一无二的制造厂位于德国德勒斯登，纳米科技正在这里拯救大自然，通过无害环境的生产程序制造出独特的弹性塑料材质电子设备。只要拇指一按，塑料材质公司希望这样就能够促成阅读活动的绿色革命。

Language Notes

due out　预计上市

due 当形容词是"预定，预计"的意思，后面接副词 out/back/in 等来修饰 due。

例 An update to the security software is due out in about a week.
更新版的杀毒软件将在一周左右上市。

usher in　开辟，创始

usher ['ʌʃə] in 是"开创新局面"的意思。若写成 usher sb. in 则指"引领，迎接"。

例 Google ushered in the era of cloud computing.
谷歌开创了计算机云端计算的新纪元。

例 The butler ushered the guests into the sitting room.
那位男管家引领客人到起居室。

Vocabulary

8. facility [fə'sɪlətɪ] n. （供特定用途的）场所
9. flexible ['flɛksəbl] adj. 有弹性的，可弯曲的
The flexible hinge allowed the device to be folded up.
10. swipe [swaɪp] n. 猛打，擦过

炫酷时尚　寰宇星空　生命发现　绿色革命　生活嬗变

RICHARD ARCHULETA, CEO, PLASTIC LOGIC

No more cutting down trees, mass[11] production of paper, no big printing presses, and of course, no big trucks distributing[12] the paper.

FREDERIK PLEITGEN, CNN CORRESPONDENT

An estimated 1.7 billion people read one of these every day. If Plastic Logic has its way, selling a few e-readers might just save a few of these.

塑料材质公司　CEO　理查德·阿丘列塔

不必再砍树、不必再大量生产纸张，不必再大规模印刷，更不需要再有大卡车运送纸张。

CNN　特派员　弗雷德里克·普里根

据估计，每天有 17 亿人阅读这种东西。塑料材质公司如果心愿得偿，卖出几个电子阅读器，也许就能够省下不少纸张。**CNN**

Language Notes

have one's way　如某人所愿

way 在这里是"意愿，愿望"的意思。have one's way 则等同于中文的"得偿所愿"。

例 If Ted had his way, his birthday would be a holiday.

要是真能如泰德所愿，他的生日就是固定节日了。

Plastic Logic E-Reader　塑料材质电子阅读器
该阅读器创新的地方在于面板（display）比其他电子阅读器大（8.5×11 英寸）、画质好、耗电少（low power consumption），并强调轻和薄。此款阅读器可支持许多文本软件，如 Word、Excel、Powerpoint 和 Adobe PDF。市场上其他的电子阅读器还有 Sony Reader、Philips Readius、Amazon Kindle。

Vocabulary

11. **mass** [mæs] *adj.* 大量的
After safety testing, the new product went into mass production.
12. **distribute** [dɪ'strɪbjut] *v.* 运送，分发
The large film company distributes many small independently made movies.

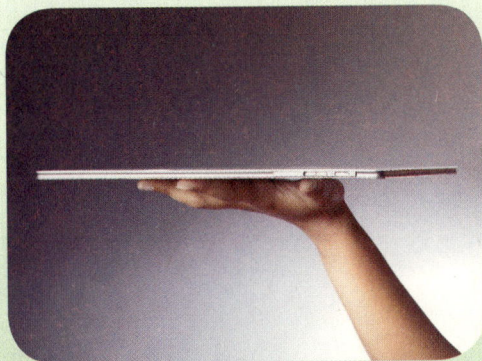

炫酷时尚　寰宇星空　生命发现　绿色革命　生活嬗变

149

替代能源新里程——
生物燃料客机首航

Virgin Atlantic Launches[1]
First Biofuel[2]-Powered Airliner

Green
Flight

图片提供：AFP

CNN ANCHOR

Well, Virgin Atlantic has become the first commercial airline to fly a plane partially[3] powered with biofuel. On Sunday, the Boeing 747 flew from London's Heathrow to Amsterdam. Virgin expects analysis of the test flight to show that a biofuel blend[4] produces much less CO_2 than regular jet fuel, but some environmental campaigners[5] say it is just a distraction[6] from more pressing[7] climate change issues. Owen Thomas has more.

图片提供：The Boeing Company

CNN 主播

维京航空成为第一家用生物燃料作为飞机部分动力的商用航空公司。该架波音 747 客机在周日从伦敦的希斯洛机场飞往阿姆斯特丹。维京航空预期这次试飞的分析结果将显示生物燃料混合油所产生的二氧化碳比一般航空煤油要少得多。但一些环保人士却表示，此举只会让更为迫在眉睫的气候变迁问题偏离正题。欧文·托马斯带来进一步报道。

Vocabulary

1. **launch** [lɔntʃ] *v.* 发射，起飞
   The military launched a missile test in the mid-Pacific.
2. **biofuel** ['baɪoˌfjuəl] *n.* 生物燃料（= biorganic fuel）
3. **partially** ['pɑrʃəlɪ] *adv.* 部分地
4. **blend** [blɛnd] *n.* 混合物，混合
5. **campaigner** [kæm'penə] *n.* 社会运动人士
6. **distraction** [dɪ'strækʃən] *n.* 分散注意的事物，分心
7. **pressing** ['prɛsɪŋ] *adj.* 紧迫的，迫切的
   I can't stay at the meeting long as I have a pressing engagement across town.

OWEN THOMAS, CNN CORRESPONDENT

Is the biofuel partly powering this Boeing 747 the future of aviation or an environmentally damaging publicity[8] stunt[9]? The jet had one of its engines connected to a biofuel tank providing 20 percent of its power. Remember this day, says Virgin's boss.

RICHARD BRANSON, PRESIDENT VIRGIN ATLANTIC

So today marks a biofuel breakthrough[10] for the whole airline industry.

OWEN THOMAS, CNN CORRESPONDENT

Don't be so sure, say Friends of the Earth.

KENNETH RICHTER, FRIENDS OF THE EARTH

We think it is a bit of a gimmick[11] and more than that, is a distraction from the real solutions to climate change.

OWEN THOMAS, CNN CORRESPONDENT

This is a babassu nut, which, with the coconut oil, makes up the biofuel on the flight. Branson, though, is keen to stress this is just the start. In three or four years' time, biofuel from algae[12] could be the most efficient fuel of the future. He told CNN, only a couple years ago no one believed it would be possible to power a jet on biofuel.

RICHARD BRANSON, PRESIDENT, VIRGIN ATLANTIC

With global warming, I'm afraid, happening so quickly, we've all got to use all our technical prowess[13] and all of our best minds to try to come up with technological breakthroughs like we've seen today. And today actually is an historic day, I think, where people will look back on it in 10, 20 years time and remember today as being the big breakthrough, the big start of this new revolution[14].

OWEN THOMAS, CNN CORRESPONDENT

Virgin says this is the first jet in the world to fly on renewable[15] fuel. No passengers on board, but technical advisers are there to analyze the jet's performance[16]. Environmental campaigners, however, believe carbon[17] saving some [from] biofuels are at best negligible[18] ,and biofuel crops compete with food production.

CNN 特派员　欧文·托马斯

提供这架波音 747 客机部分动力的生物燃料会是航空业的未来？还是对环境有害的宣传花招？这架喷气机有一个引擎和生物燃料油箱连接，供应 20% 的动力。维京航空的老板说，好好记住这一天。

维京航空总裁　理查德·布兰森

今天是整个航空业在使用生物燃料上有重大突破的日子。

CNN 特派员　欧文·托马斯

但是地球之友说，别那么笃定。

地球之友　肯尼斯·里克特

我们认为那只是个噱头，不只如此，这会把对气候变化问题真正解决之道的注意力分散了。

CNN 特派员　欧文·托马斯

这是巴巴苏棕榈树的果实，和椰子油混合成这架飞机使用的生物燃料。不过布兰森极力强调，这只是个开始而已。未来三四年内，由海藻制成的生物燃料将成为未来最具效能的燃料。他告诉本台，不过几年前，根本没人相信能用生物燃料作为喷气机的动力。

维京航空总裁　理查德·布兰森

由于全球变暖的速度如此之快，我们恐怕得穷尽一切科技力量，以最顶尖的人才，设法寻求像我们今天所见的科技突破。我认为今天真的是个历史性的一天，10 为年、20 年之后，人们会回过头来看这件事，会记得今天是个有重要突破的日子，是这个新革命的重要开端。

CNN 特派员　欧文·托马斯

维京航空表示，这是全球第一架使用再生燃料的喷气机。虽然机上没有乘客，但有技术顾问负责分析该架喷气机的飞行表现。然而环保人士认为，生物燃料能够节省下来的碳微乎其微，而且生物燃料作物会和粮食生产相互竞争。

Language Notes

be keen to v.　非常想……

keen 原本是形容 "锐利的，敏锐的" 或 "强烈的"，引申为 "热切的，渴望的"，后面加上 to V.，表示 "非常想做某事"。

例 Barbara is keen to start her new job at the music publishing company.
芭芭拉非常想在那家唱片公司上班。

look back on　回顾

look back 的字面意思是 "回头看"，引申为 "回顾，回想，追忆"，后面用介词 on 加上回想的事物。

例 Steve looked back on his tenure with the company as an unrivaled success.
史蒂夫回顾他为这个公司效力的时候，认为取得了卓越的成就。

Vocabulary

8. **publicity** [,pʌˈbəlɪsəti] n. 宣传，宣扬
9. **stunt** [stʌnt] n. 花招
10. **breakthrough** [ˈbrekˌθru] n. 突破性的进展
11. **gimmick** [ˈgɪmɪk] n. 花招
12. **algae** [ˈælˌdʒi] n. 水藻，海藻（单数形式为 alga [ˈælgə]）
13. **prowess** [ˈprauəs] n. 高超的本领、能力
14. **revolution** [ˈrɛvəˌluʃən] n. 革命性的剧变，变革
15. **renewable** [rɪˈnjuəbl] adj. 可更新的，可继续的
    Corn is a valuable renewable resource.
16. **prowess** [ˈprauəs] n. 高超的本领、能力
17. **performance** [pəˈfɔrməns] n. 表现，性能
18. **negligible** [ˈnɛglɪdʒəbl] adj. 微不足道的，极轻微的
    The profits from the sale were negligible when taking into account higher manufacturing costs.

炫酷时尚　寰宇星空　生命发现　绿色革命　生活嬗变

KENNETH RICHTER, FRIENDS OF THE EARTH

A lot more research needs to be done into how much emissions[19] these biofuels actually save. And, at the moment, the majority of biofuels actually have [a] very bad impact and they do little to combat[20] climate change.

OWEN THOMAS, CNN CORRESPONDENT

The jet successfully completed its journey and proved that biofuels can help power an aircraft. It'll take many more years of research before this new fuel will be commercially available and accepted as the way forward.

图片提供：The Boeing Company

地球之友　肯尼斯·里克特

　　这类生物燃料究竟能降低多少废气排放量，这点还必须进行更多研究。目前，绝大部分的生物燃料其实都会带来很不好的影响，在应对气候变化问题方面也没什么帮助。

CNN 特派员　欧文·托马斯

　　该架喷气机成功完成了旅程，证明了生物燃料可以用作为飞机的动力。还要经过多年研究之后，这种新燃料才能用于商业用途，并受到认可成为未来发展的出路。CNN

Language Notes

the way forward　未来的发展

字面上的意思是"向前的路"，比喻"未来的发展、方法，之后的方向"，后面可用介词 for 加上发展的事物或领域。

例 The newly elected president showed the way forward for reviving the economy.
新当选的总统指出今后经济复苏的方向。

Vocabulary

19. emission [i'mɪʃən] n. 发散（物），排放（物）
20. combat ['kɒmbæt] v. 对付，战斗
The organization combats poverty in developing countries.

炫酷时尚

寰宇星空

生命发现

绿色革命

生活嬗变

biofuel crop　生物燃料作物

定义：指作为生物燃料原料（feedstock）的能源作物（energy crop），一般是高密度（densely planted）、低投入（low-input）、高收成（highyield）的物种。

常见种类：玉米、黄豆、甘蔗、蓖麻籽、椰子等。最新技术是用水藻，但仍有成本过高（high-cost）的问题。

产品：生物柴油（biodiesel）、生物沼气（biogas）、生物乙醇（bioethanol）、生物甲醇（biomethanol）等。

生物燃料的争议

优点：可生物分解（biodegradable），对环境的破坏比较小。

缺点：燃烧后依然会产生二氧化碳等废气，需要大量农作物，造成滥砍滥伐（deforestation）、土壤破坏（soil erosion）、粮食短缺（food shortage）、食品价格上涨等问题。

可提炼生物柴油的作物及油量百分比

（依相同重量可出产的比例排行）

椰子干	copra	62
蓖麻籽	castor seed	50
芝麻	sesame	50
花生仁	groundnut	42
麻风树	jatropha	40
油菜籽	rapeseed	37
棕榈核	palm kernel	36
芥菜籽	mustard seed	35
葵花籽	sunflower	32
棕榈果仁	palm fruit	20
黄豆	soybean	14
棉花籽	cotton seed	13

jet fuel　航空煤油

　　现行最常用的商业航空燃料，是以无铅（unleaded）煤油（paraffin, kerosene）为基底的 JET A-1，颜色清澈呈麦褐色，挥发起火的燃点（flash point）约为 38℃，凝固点（freezing point）约为 −47℃。美国自20世纪50年代起则使用 Jet A 作为标准航空燃油，凝固点约为−40℃。

　　另一种民用机涡轮引擎（turbine engine）的燃料是 JETB，以石脑油（naphtha）与煤油混合制成，可提升天冷时的性能。研究发现，在美国交通工具排放的温室气体（greenhouse gas）中，航空废气就占了11%。欧盟研究则发现，每个飞机乘客平均每公里就会制造 191 克温室气体，而且直接排放到高层大气中，对臭氧层（ozone layer）的破坏非常严重。

图片提供: soknet

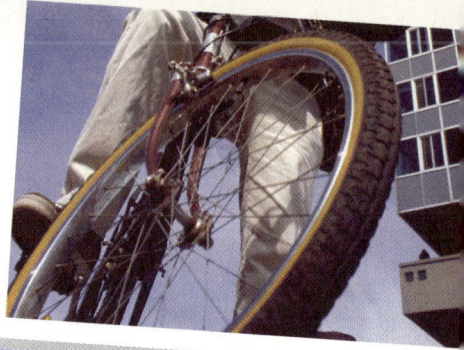

回顾环保科技 10 年轨迹

The
Tracking Environmental Advancements[1] of the Past 10 Years

Eco-Decade

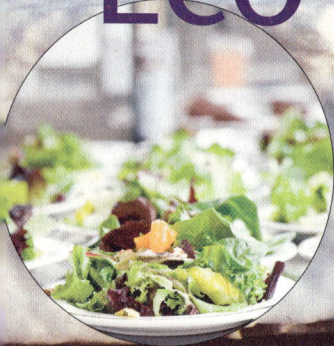

图片提供: J. Craig Venter Institute

ROSEMARY CHURCH, CNN ANCHOR

Let's raise our glass in honor of[1] the past decade with a look at environmental advancements over the last 10 years. Here's Kristie Lu Stout.

KRISTIE LU STOUT, CNN ANCHOR AND CORRESPONDENT

The Toyota Prius is a common sight on today's street, but that was not the case 10 years ago, and what a difference a decade makes. There're now over one million Prius' on the road. It was the first mass-produced hybrid vehicle and led the way[2] for other car manufacturers to go green. Industry insiders called the Prius a game changer, attracting buyers despite its higher than average cost and unique look. Developments in green technology have meant that recent models have included optional[2] solar panels on the roof and plug-in[3] technology to be released[4] in 2012.

图片提供：Toyota

片提供：World Resources Institute

CNN 主播　罗斯玛丽·邱尔吉

让我们举杯向过去这十年致敬，看看这十年来在环保方面取得的进展。克里斯蒂·卢·斯托特的报道。

CNN 特派员　克里斯蒂·卢·斯托特

如今丰田的 Prius 在街道上随处可见，但十年前却并非如此。十年来的变化相当大。现在路上行驶的 Prius 已逾百万辆。Prius 是首辆量产的油电混合车，它带领其他汽车制造商走向环保。汽车工业人士称 Prius 是一辆"改变游戏规则的车"，尽管它的要价高于平均价格且外形独特，却仍能吸引买家。而绿色科技的发展也意味着将于 2012 年问世的 Prius 最新车款会提供车顶太阳能板的选择配置以及插座式充电技术等功能。

Language Notes

game changer　改变游戏规则者

本指运动比赛中至关紧要，具有扭转比赛局面能力者，引申指"能扭转现有情况、想法、做法的人或事物"，类似我们常听到的"改变游戏规则者"。另外有形容词用法 game-changing，表示"具有改变游戏规则、颠覆现有局面能力的"。

例 The iPhone was a game changer in the mobile communication market.
iPhone 在手机通信市场是个改变游戏规则的产品。

Phrases

1. **in honor of** 向……致敬，纪念……
   Jack received an award in honor of his years of service to the school.
2. **lead the way** 带路，位居龙头地位，最受欢迎
   The country led the way in biomedical research.

Vocabulary

1. **advancement** [əd'vænsmənt] *n.* 发展
2. **optional** ['ɑpʃənl] *adj.* 可选择的
   The car comes with an optional DVD player.
3. **plug-in** ['plʌg,ɪn] *adj.* 可插入插头的，可插入（以扩充功能）的
   The camera has a plug-in adapter for connecting to your television.
4. **release** [rɪ'lis] *v.* 发表，发行
   The studio released the film during the summer blockbuster season.

炫酷时尚　寰宇星空　生命发现　绿色革命　生活嬗变

Step by Step 听懂 CNN 先锋科技

AL GORE, FORMER U.S. VICE PRESIDENT
The scientific consensus[5] is that we are causing global warming.

KRISTIE LU STOUT, CNN ANCHOR AND CORRESPONDENT
One of the most talked-about PowerPoint presentations[6], Al Gore's 2006 documentary[7] *An Inconvenient*[8] *Truth* was instrumental[9] in spreading the message and sparking[10] debate on climate change. As one of the highest grossing[11] documentaries of all time, it helped the green movement go mainstream[12]. Al Gore went on to get an unexpected[13] accolade[14] in 2007 for his climate change work—The Nobel Peace Prize.

For many of us, this is one of the ways of going green in the home. CFLs, short for compact fluorescent light bulbs, won over[3] consumers as a cost-saver. It uses 75 percent less energy and lasts 10 times longer then an incandescent[15] bulb. In 2007, sales of CFLs reached record heights worldwide. Countries like Australia have already implemented[16] a ban on traditional light bulbs, with Canada and the EU following suit.

图：Paul Keller

图：Clean Wal-Mart

美国前任副总统　阿尔·戈尔

人类正使地球变暖已是科学上的共识。

CNN 特派员　克里斯蒂·卢·斯托特

戈尔于 2006 年参与制作的纪录片《不愿面对的真相》是最常被人们探讨的幻灯片演讲稿，它在传播变暖警报和引发对气候变迁的讨论上扮演着重要角色。身为史上票房最佳的纪录片之一，这部影片帮助将环保运动推向主流。戈尔在气候变化上做出的贡献，也让他之后在 2007 年获得诺贝尔和平奖这项意外的荣耀。

对我们许多人来说，这是在家做环保的方法之一。简称为 CFLs 的调光节能荧光灯因为能省钱颇受消费者青睐。它消耗的能源比白炽灯泡少 75%，且寿命长 10 倍。2007 年，CFLs 灯泡在全球销售创新高。澳大利亚等国家已立法禁用传统灯泡，加拿大和欧盟也要跟进。

Language Notes

follow suit　效仿某人

suit 在纸牌游戏中是指"同花色的牌"，所以 follow suit 是指"跟着前一位发牌者打出同花色的牌"。后来便以此引申指"仿效别人，跟着别人做"。

例 When Jeff donated money to the charity, several of his coworkers followed suit.
杰夫一给这家慈善机构捐钱，他的几个同事就跟着做了。

Phrases

3. win over 赢得……的支持、同意
The speaker won over the crowd with a few jokes.
4. head off 避开，逃避不好的事
William headed off a disaster by backing up his computer.

Vocabulary

5. consensus [kən'sɛnsəs] *n.* 共识
6. presentation [ˌprizɛn'teʃən] *n.* 演说，发布会
7. documentary [ˌdɑkjə'mɛntərɪ] *n.* 纪录片
8. inconvenient [ˌɪnkən'vinjənt] *adj.* 引起麻烦的，造成困难的
9. instrumental [ˌɪnstrə'mɛntl] *adj.* 起重要作用的
Several celebrities were instrumental in raising awareness about famine relief.
10. spark [spɑrk] *v.* 点燃，激励
11. gross [gros] *v.* 总共收入
The film grossed significantly more after its international release.
12. mainstream ['menˌstrim] *n.* 主流思想、群体
13. unexpected [ˌʌnɪk'spɛktɪd] *adj.* 出乎意料的，始料未及的
Several flights were hit with unexpected delays.
14. accolade ['ækəˌled] *n.* 表扬，赞赏
15. incandescent [ˌɪnkən'dɛsṇt] *adj.* 白炽的
Joanna prefers incandescent light to fluorescent.
16. implement ['ɪmpləˌmɛnt] *v.* 实施，执行
The company implemented a new dress code.

It was a seven-trillion-dollar wake-up call—the price of climate change if the world does not act, according to former chief economist at the World Bank Sir Nicholas Stern.

SIR NICHOLAS STERN, THE STERN REVIEW

So, crude[17] economics of what does it cost you to head off[4] the risks, what is the damage associated with the risks, points very strongly that the investments in mitigation[18] have a very high payoff[19].

注：compact fluorescent light bulb 调光节能荧光灯；小型荧光灯泡在相同亮度下，与传统白炽灯或卤素灯相比，调光节能荧光灯用电量较少。不过由于省电技术日益精进，LED 这类用电效率更高的照明设备已陆续推出，人们的选择也更加多元化。

这是一次价值 7 兆美元的警钟。根据世界银行前首席经济学家尼古拉斯·斯特恩的说法，如果不采取行动，气候变化将让整个世界付出如此高的代价。

《斯特思报告》 尼古拉斯·斯特恩

所以，大概要付出多少成本才能避开风险？风险所带来的损害有多大？就这两者看来，很明显地，用在缓和气候变化方面的投资将有极高的回报。

Language Notes

wake-up call　警告，警报

wake-up call 本来是指旅馆、饭店人员叫房客起床的电话，后来引申指"警告，警报"，使某人警觉到某个问题、危险、处境或需求，进而采取行动，想办法避免恶果。

例 The mortgage crisis should have been a wake-up call to the whole financial industry.
房贷危机对整个金融业来说是个警报。

Vocabulary

17. **crude** [krud] *adj.* 大略的
18. **mitigation** ['mɪtəgeʃən] *n.* 缓和，减轻
19. **payoff** ['pe,ɔf] *n.* 收益，好处

炫酷时尚　寰宇星空　生命发现　绿色革命　生活嬗变

KRISTIE LU STOUT, CNN ANCHOR AND CORRESPONDENT

In 2006, the Stern Review gave the first idea of the financial fallout[20] of a warming planet. According to the 700-page report, the worst-case scenario means that climate change will cause 20 percent of global GDP each year. So while the past 10 years have shown that going green has come a long way, there's still a long road ahead for the next 10.

图片提供：jurvetson

CNN 特派员　克里斯蒂·卢·斯托特

　　2006 年，《斯特恩报告》首先提出地球变暖可能造成的经济损失。这份 700 页的报告指出，最糟的情况是，气候变化将会导致全球国内生产总值每年减少 20%。因此，虽然过去这 10 年显示环保工作已有长足进展，但未来 10 年仍有很长的一段路要走。CNN

Language Notes

worst-case scenario　最坏的情况

scenario 指"事态，局面，预测某事件、行为的可能发展情况"。worst-case 则是指"最坏的（可能）情况下的"。所以 worst-case scenario 是指"最坏的情况，最恶劣的事态发展"。

例 The worst-case scenario is the company declares bankruptcy.
最糟的情况是公司宣布破产。

have come a long way　大有进步

字面上是"走了相当长一段路"，比喻"某人、某事物已有相当进展或大有进步"，用法为 sb./sth. has come a long way。也可写成将来时 sb. will go a long way，表示"某人将大有成就"。

例 The city has come along way since its early days as a small fishing village.
例 从一个小渔村开始，这座城市至今已大有进步。

Vocabulary

20. fallout ['fɔl,aut] *n.* 后果，余波

生活嬗变

㉒ 爱它就为它装上义肢——动物义肢新科技

㉓ 从 Walkman 到 iPod，随身听走过 30 年

㉔ "以牙还眼" 创新手术让盲人重见光明

㉕ 新型手机揭示通信科技新风貌

㉖ 信息时代的噩梦——无线网络

㉗ 顺应高龄化时代的护理机器人登场

㉘ 3D 科技带你游历古罗马

㉙ 瘫痪病人的新希望——鳗鱼

爱它就为它装上义肢——

动物义肢新科技

Pet Prosthetics

Technology Gives Furry[2]
Friends a Leg Up

CNN ANCHOR

In the months leading to the Beijing Olympics, there was much attention on South Africa's double-amputee[3] sprinter[4], Oscar Pistorius, whose nickname became "the Blade Runner." More specifically[5], the focus was on the prosthetic legs that enabled[6] him to compete with athletes with normal legs. Now a surgical[7] procedure could enable pets with limb[8] disabilities[9] to function[10] normally. Jacqui Jeras has the details.

JACQUI JERAS, CNN CORRESPONDENT

It's a delicate[11] procedure, but researchers at North Carolina State University are helping a few pets get a new leg on life.

ERIKA EDWARDS, DOG OWNER

He's a good, very good candidate for the surgery, so we're hoping everything turns out well for him.

Language Notes

标题扫描：

give someone a leg up 帮助某人成功

give someone a leg up 原指"助某人一臂之力"，leg 在这里有双关的含意，也就是标题所说的"义肢"。

例 Jeff gave his friend a leg up by arranging a job interview at his company.

杰夫帮了他朋友一把，在他的公司安排了一个工作面试的机会。

Vocabulary

1. prosthetics [prɑs'θɛtɪks] n. 修复学，装补学
2. furry ['fɜɪ] adj. 毛茸茸的
   The furry rabbit curled up in the little boy's arms.
3. amputee [,æmpjə'ti] n. 截肢者
4. sprinter ['sprɪntə] n. 短跑选手
5. specifically [sprɪ'sɪfɪklɪ] adv. 明确地，具体地
6. enable [ɪ'nebl] v. 使能够
   The GPS enabled Ann to avoid getting lost.
7. surgical ['sɜdʒɪkl] adj. 外科的
   The company specializes in surgical tools.
8. limb [lɪm] n. 肢，臂，脚，翼
9. disability [,dɪsə'bɪlɪti] n. 残疾，残障
10. function ['fʌŋkʃən] v. 工作，运行
    Without a battery, the clock can't function.
11. delicate ['dɛlɪkət] adj. 精细的，脆弱的
    The sculpture was carved from a delicate egg shell.

CNN 主播

在北京奥运会前几个月，南非的双腿截肢短跑健将奥斯卡·佩斯托瑞斯备受瞩目，被人昵称为"快刀跑者"。说得精确一点，大家瞩目的是让他得以和正常运动员场上竞技的义腿。现在，有一种手术方法可能会让肢体残障的宠物正常行动。雅基·洁拉斯带来以下报道。

CNN 特派员 雅基·洁拉斯

这是非常精细的手术，但北卡罗莱娜州立大学的研究人员正帮助几只宠物展开新的生命旅程。

狗主人 艾瑞卡·爱德华兹

他是这种手术的极佳对象，所以我们希望会有好的结果。

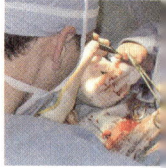

JACQUI JERAS, CNN CORRESPONDENT

Erika's dog, Nubby, is missing part of one leg, but may soon be able to walk like a normal dog again, thanks in part to an artificial[12] titanium[13] limb that is surgically attached to the leg bone. It's a procedure that takes practice.

DR. DENNIS MARCELLIN-LITTLE, NCSU

Well, the surgery is really done on a plastic model beforehand[14], so we get to know the patient very well before we bring him to the operating room.

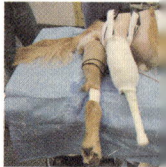

JACQUI JERAS, CNN CORRESPONDENT

Practice models are custom-made from three-dimensional scans of the animal's bone structure.

OLA HARRYSSON, PROFESSOR, NCSU

You're building your models one layer at a time, and we can custom design[15] anything, and we can build it in a one step.

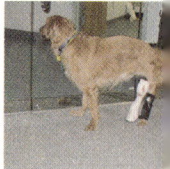

JACQUI JERAS, CNN CORRESPONDENT

In 2007, a cat named Mr. France underwent[16] surgery for the experimental artificial limb. The cat's muscle and skin tissue eventually grew onto the implant, making the prosthetic part of the bone. Mr. France walked around with a temporary foot for several months before being fitted with a custom-made one.

His owner says he's a different cat, and now runs around and socializes[17] with others in her household[18].

And that's good news for Erika, who is looking forward to Nubby's operation.

ERIKA EDWARDS, DOG OWNER

He's going to benefit[19] from it quite a bit. Um, we're excited about doing it.

CNN 特派员　雅基·洁拉斯

艾瑞卡的狗儿努比有一条腿缺了一部分。不过，多亏通过手术接在腿骨上的钛金属义肢，努比可能很快就能够再像正常狗儿一样走路了。这项手术必须要有熟练的技术。

北卡罗莱娜州立大学　马西林利特尔博士

手术其实会先用塑料模型模拟一遍。所以，我们把患者推进手术室之前，就已经对他非常熟悉了。

CNN 特派员　雅基·洁拉斯

模拟用的模型是通过立体扫描狗儿的骨头结构量身特制的。

北卡罗莱娜州立大学教授　欧拉·哈里森

模型是一层层构建起来的，所有东西都可以量身设计，而且能够用一个步骤制作完成。

CNN 特派员　雅基·洁拉斯

2007年，一只名叫法国先生的猫接受了这种实验性义肢手术。猫的肌肉和皮肤组织慢慢长在植入物上，义肢于是成为骨头的一部分。法国先生先前几个月先以临时脚走路，然后才装上量身特制的脚掌。

他的主人说，他现在已经变了个模样，在屋里跑来跑去和大家玩耍。

对艾瑞卡来说，这是个好消息，因为他正期待着努比的手术。

狗主人　艾瑞卡·爱德华兹

这项手术一定会对他大有好处。我们觉得很兴奋。CNN

Language Notes

in part 在某种程度上，部分地

词组 in part 相当于副词 partly/partially，也就是"在某种程度上，部分地"。

例 Brenda's novel was a success, in part because of her famous mother.

布兰达的小说之所以成功，在某种程度上是因为她那位有名的母亲。

Give It a Try　请选出正确答案

1. Tina raises a variety of _____ creatures on her ranch.
   a. surgical　　b. furry
   c. specific　　d. artificial
2. Rex likes to go to trade conferences and ___ with his peers.
   a. enable　　b. undergo
   c. socialize　　d. benefit

Answers: 1.b 2.c

Vocabulary

12. artificial [ˌɑrtə'fɪʃəl] adj. 人工的，人造的
   The drink contains artificial sweeteners.
13. titanium [taɪ'teniəm] n. 【化】钛
14. beforehand [bɪ'fɔr,hænd] adv. 预先，事先
15. custom design ['kʌstəm][dɪ'zaɪn] 量身定做
   A jeweler custom designed Angela's wedding ring.
16. undergo [ˌʌndə'go] v. 接受（治疗，检查等）
   Phil's Aunt underwent a hip operation.
17. socialize ['soʃə,laɪz] v. 交际，参与社交
   Jan socialized with guests at the party.
18. household ['haus,hold] n. 一家人，家眷，家庭，户
19. benefit ['bɛnəfɪt] v. 得益，受惠
   Danny benefited from his father's political connections.

23–F.MP3
23–S.MP3

从 Walkman
到 iPod,
随身听走过 30 年

Hasta la vista, baby!

Walking Away from Walkman

Sony Pulls the Plug on the Original Personal Music Player

PAULINE CHIOU, CNN ANCHOR

Well, it is the end of an era[1] .Three decades after it transformed[2] the music industry, Sony is retiring[3] the classic Walkman, but as Zain Verjee tells us, a lot of people say they won't even notice it's gone.

ZAIN VERJEE, CNN CORRESPONDENT

Thirty years ago, it was cutting-edge[4] technology. Now it's nearly forgotten.

UNIDENTIFIED CORRESPONDENT

Do you know what a Walkman is? Did you ever use one?

UNIDENTIFIED MALE

Yeah, I know what a Walkman is. With a CD? Like to play CDs? Yeah.

Language Notes

标题扫描：

> **pull the plug** 结束，终止

字面上是"拔掉插头"的意思，引申比喻"结束，终止"计划、活动等，后面可加 on 再接结束的事物。

例 The network pulled the plug on the popular television series.
那家电视网停播了这部热门电视剧。

CNN 主播　邱波林

这是一个时代的结束。在它改变音乐市场 30 年之后，索尼公司将停止生产经典的 Walkman 随身听。但是洁茵·维尔吉告诉我们，许多人表示他们甚至没有注意它已经消失了。

CNN 特派员　洁茵·维尔吉

30 年前，这可是尖端科技，但是现在几乎已被遗忘。

不知名特派员

你知道随身听是什么吗？你曾经使用过随身听吗？

不知名男性

嗯，我知道随身听。听 CD 的吗？播放 CD 用的吗？嗯。

Vocabulary

1. era [ˈɛrə] n. 时代，年代
2. transform [ˌtrænsˈfɔrm] v. 使改变形态，使改观
   The Internet transformed the retail industry.
3. retire [rɪˈtaɪr] v. 撤离，撤退
   The team retired the player's number when he entered the hall of fame.
4. cutting-edge [ˈkʌtɪŋˌedʒ] adj. 尖端的，最先进的
   The video game system boasts cutting-edge graphics.

UNIDENTIFIED CORRESPONDENT
Or tapes.

UNIDENTIFIED MALE
Tapes?

ZAIN VERJEE, CNN CORRESPONDENT
That's right. Tapes.

SONY WALKMAN AD
The world's smallest cassette player.

ZAIN VERJEE, CNN CORRESPONDENT
In the past 30 years, Sony has sold more than 200 million Walkmen [Walkmans].

UNIDENTIFIED FEMALE
Twenty years ago, yes, yes, and I did use a Walkman and it was good.

ZAIN VERJEE, CNN CORRESPONDENT
But now, it's pulling the plug.

UNIDENTIFIED MALE
It's . . . there's no use for them anymore, except in maybe in museums.

UNIDENTIFIED FEMALE
I used to have one when they were in fashion[1], but I don't have one anymore. This one, my MP3s . . . and downloading and iPods.

ZAIN VERJEE, CNN CORRESPONDENT
Sony stopped producing the Walkman in Japan. The last batch[5] was made in April. The times they are a changin'. Sony revolutionized[6] the electronics industry with the Walkman in 1979. It was the first ever portable[7] music device. As cassette tapes gave way to CDs, Sony followed up with the Discman.

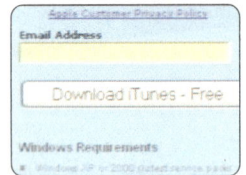

不知名特派员

或是录音带。

不知名男性

录音带？

CNN 特派员　洁茵·维尔吉

没错。录音带。

索尼随身听广告

世界上最小的卡式播放器。

CNN 特派员　洁茵·维尔吉

在过去 30 年，索尼公司卖出了超过 2 亿个随身听。

不知名女性

20 年前，对，我确实用过随身听，那很好用。

CNN 特派员　洁茵·维尔吉

但是现在，那正在吹熄灯号呢。

不知名男性

这……它们已无用武之地了，除非可能在博物馆里。

不知名女性

当它们还很流行的时候，我曾经有过一个。但我已经没有了。这个是我的 MP3……下载的方式和 iPod。

CNN 特派员　洁茵·维尔吉

索尼公司停止在日本生产随身听。最后一批货已在 4 月生产完毕。时不我待啊。索尼公司在 1979 年以随身听彻底改造电子产业。它是第一台可携式音乐装置。当 CD 取代录音带时，索尼公司也以 Discman 跟进。

Language Notes

give way to ...　让步，被取代

原是"退让，屈服，让位"的意思，在这里比喻磁带退出市场，被 CD"取代"。

例 After a few hours of driving, the city's tall buildings gave way to suburban homes.
开了几个小时的车后，城市高楼的景色被市郊房屋取代了。

例 After 10 minutes of arguing, Peter eventually gave way to his wife's wishes.
经过 10 分钟的争吵，彼得终于让步顺从了太太的意思。

Phrases

1. **in fashion**　正流行
Flannel shirts were **in fashion** in the early '90s.

The times they are a changin'

知名创作歌手鲍伯·迪伦（Bob Dylan）于 1964 年推出的同名专辑中的歌曲曲名，这首歌对 20 世纪 60 年代的社会、政治动乱有详细刻画，因此曲名常被引用来感叹时代变迁。

Vocabulary

5. **batch** [bætʃ] *n.* 一批，一批生产的量
6. **revolutionize** [ˌrɛvəˈluʃəˌnaɪz] *v.* 彻底改变，改革
The Wii **revolutionized** the video game industry.
7. **portable** [ˈpɔrtəbl] *adj.* 可携式的，手提的
Danny brought a **portable** DVD player on the long flight.

But when Apple burst into[2] the market with its first iPod back in 2001, there was no turning back. In the nine years since, Apple has sold about 275 million iPods, making it the undisputed[8] leader in portable music.

Sony says there's still some demand for the classic Walkman in parts of Asia and the Middle East. To accommodate[9] those customers, it will produce a limited number of Walkmen [Walkmans] out of China, but many music lovers went digital a long time ago and say they won't even notice the Walkman is gone.

UNIDENTIFIED MALE
Walkmans with cassettes, right? No, I don't even have any cassettes anymore.

ZAIN VERJEE, CNN CORRESPONDENT
Like crimped[10] hair and Pacman, a classic of 1980s culture now banished[11] to the history books and the memories of nostalgic[12] fans.

图解词汇　音乐储存媒体

(compact) cassette / tape
磁带/录音带

long-playing record / LP
黑胶唱片

eight-track tape
8轨磁带

compact disc / CD
光盘

mini disc / MD
迷你光盘

但是当苹果公司在 2001 年以第一代 iPod 杀入市场走红后，就已经没有回头路了。在那之后的 9 年里，苹果公司卖出了 2.75 亿台iPod，这项纪录使它毋庸置疑稳居可携式音乐市场的龙头。

索尼公司表示，亚洲和中东的部分地区仍有一些随身听的需求。考虑到这些顾客，它将会在中国限量生产随身听，但是许多音乐爱好者很久以前便跟随数字化的脚步，并表示他们甚至不会注意到随身听已经在市场上消失了。

不知名男性

听录音带的随身听，对吗？没有，我甚至连录音带都没有。

CNN 特派员　洁茵·维尔吉

就像烫卷发和小精灵一样，一项 20 世纪 80 年代文化的经典产物现在消失了，只留存在历史书和怀旧迷的回忆中。CNN

Phrases

2. **burst into**　突然出现
The stage actor burst into films with a summer blockbuster.

Vocabulary

8. **undisputed** [ˌʌndɪˈspjutɪd] *adj.* 不容置疑的，毫无疑问的
The boxer became the undisputed heavyweight champion after winning the fight.
9. **accommodate** [əˈkɑməˌdet] *v.* 容纳，顾及
The restaurant accommodated our party even though they were quite busy.
10. **crimp** [krɪmp] *v.* 用电烫夹烫曲头发
Wendy used to crimp her hair in the '80s.
11. **banish** [ˈbænɪʃ] *v.* 放逐，赶走
Steven succeeds by banishing negative thoughts from his mind.
12. **nostalgic** [nɑˈstældʒɪk] *adj.* 怀旧的
That song makes me nostalgic for my college days.

Hasta la vista, baby!

图解词汇 音乐播放器实物

jukebox
自动点唱机组合

phonograph / gramophone
留声机

eight-track player
8轨磁带播放器

tape recorder /
compact cassette recorder
卡式录放音机

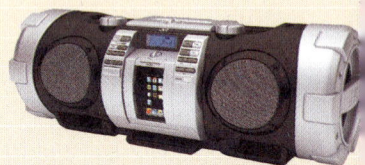

boom box / ghetto blaster /radio-
cassette player
手提音响

cassette deck
卡式录放音机台

㉓ 从 Walkman 到 iPod，随身听走过 30 年

Give It a Try 请选出正确答案

1. The electronics trade show highlights
   _____ technology.
   a. cutting-edge   b. edgy
   c. cut-up   d. cut-out

2. We _____ on the project when it began
   running over budget.
   a. plugged in   b. unplugged
   c. plugged up   d. pulled the plug

Answers: 1.a 2.d

MD Walkman
迷你光盘随身听

MP3 player
MP3 播放器

portable CD player
CD 随身听

stereo system
立体音响组合

Walkman /
portable cassette
磁带随身听

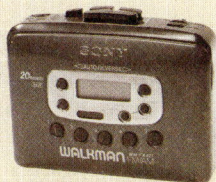

portable media player
多媒体随身播放器

右下角图片提供：Apple Inc.

179

"以牙还眼" 创新手术让盲人重见光明

A Tooth for an Eye

Florida Woman Gives Her Eyetooth[1] to Regain Sight

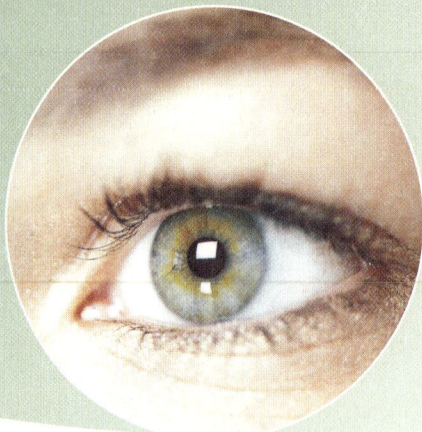

图片提供：Bascom Palmer Eye Institute

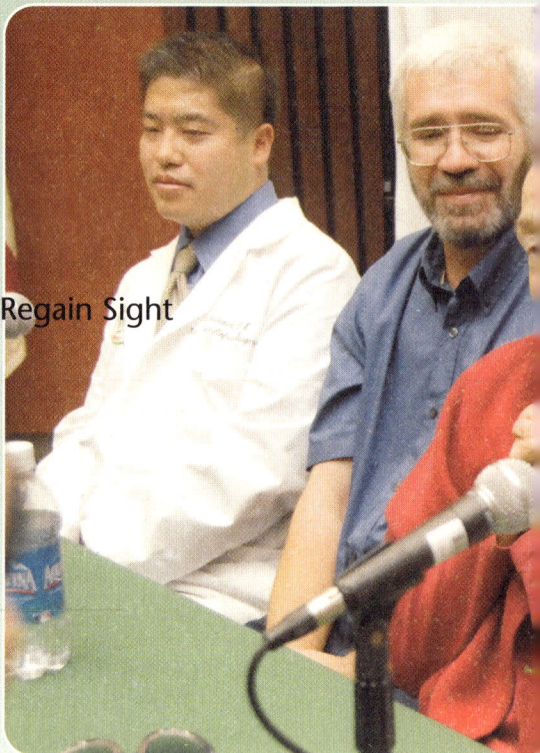

PAULINE CHIOU, CNN ANCHOR

Doctors in Miami have given a woman back her sight by using, of all things, her tooth. It's the first time this procedure[2] has been performed[3] in the United States. Our senior medical correspondent, Elizabeth Cohen, explains how this was done.

KAY THORNTON, VISION PATIENT

I thought about suicide . . . but then I thought, I can't.

ELIZABETH COHEN, CNN MEDICAL CORRESPONDENT

Kay Thornton lost her sight nine years ago when a bad reaction[4] to a drug scarred[5] her cornea[6], the clear covering of the eye. It was so bad, even a cornea transplant[7] wouldn't help. Doctors gave her no hope, but Kay believes in miracles.

Did you ever think a miracle would involve a tooth?

CNN EYE INSTITUTE
U UNIVERSITY OF MIAMI HEALTH SYSTEM

Language Notes

标题扫描：

a tooth for an eye

标题将英文谚语 an eye for an eye, a tooth for a tooth "以牙还牙，以眼还眼"前后句结合，点出文中患者是以牙齿植入眼睛换得视力。该谚语出自旧约《圣经》的"申命记"（Deuteronomy 19:21），全文为：

"And thine eye shall not pity; but life shall go for life, eye for eye, tooth for tooth, hand for hand, foot for foot."
"你眼不可顾惜，要以命偿命，以眼还眼，以牙还牙，以手还手，以脚还脚。"

标题扫描：

give one's eyeteeth　不计代价

eyeteeth "犬齿"因为有撕咬食物的功能，被认为很宝贵，所以用"交出犬齿"比喻"为了……不惜牺牲宝贵之物，不计代价"，后面接 for N. 或 to V. 表示想达到的目的，也常写成 give one's right arm。

例 Donna would give her eyeteeth to see her favorite band in concert.
唐娜愿意不计代价只求能去演唱会看她最喜欢的乐队。

Vocabulary

1. eyetooth ['aɪˌtuθ] *n.* 犬齿
2. procedure [prə'sidʒə] *n.* 手术，程序，步骤
3. perform [pə'fɔrm] *v.* 做，执行
   The medical examiner performed an autopsy on the murder victim.
4. reaction [rɪ'ækʃən] *n.* 副作用，反应
5. scar [skɑr] *v.* 损伤，留下伤痕
   A lifetime of cuts and burns scarred the chef's hands.
6. cornea ['kɔrniə] *n.* 眼角膜
7. transplant ['træns,plænt] *n.* 器官移植，移植

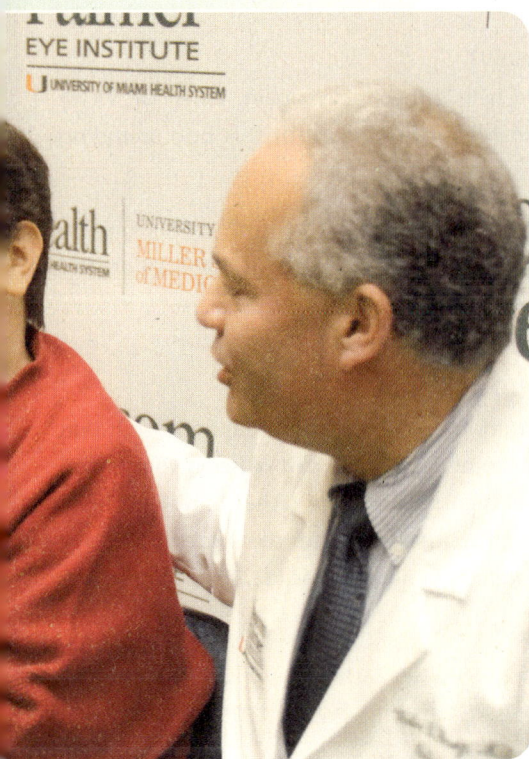

CNN 主播　邱波林

迈阿密的医生为一名妇女恢复了视力，使用的不是其他东西，而是她的牙齿。这种手术在美国是首例。本台的资深医学特派员伊丽莎白·科恩为我们说明这项手术是如何做的。

低视力患者　凯·桑顿

我想过要自杀……但后来又觉得我不能这么做。

CNN 医学特派员　伊丽莎白·科恩

凯·桑顿在 9 年前丧失视力，原因是她对一种药物产生不良反应，损伤了角膜这个包覆眼球的透明物。损伤的情形非常严重，连移植角膜都无法治疗。医生没有给她任何希望，但凯相信奇迹。

你有没有想过奇迹会和牙齿扯上关系吗？

KAY THORNTON, VISION PATIENT

Uh-uh. No.

ELIZABETH COHEN, CNN MEDICAL CORRESPONDENT

It's amazing that a tooth—a tooth!—could help someone see again. When Dr. Victor Perez at the Bascom Palmer Eye Institute in Miami first heard of this odd sounding procedure, he couldn't believe it either.

DR. VICTOR PEREZ, THE BASCOM PALMER EYE INSTITUTE

We thought, "Oh my God, how can that ... how can people do that?" And, you know, that seems to be a very, you know, far-fetched[8] idea.

ELIZABETH COHEN, CNN MEDICAL CORRESPONDENT

First, Dr. Perez removed the scar tissue[9] from Thornton's left cornea, because it was blocking her vision. Then, get this, he took her canine tooth[10] and part of her jawbone[11] and whittled it down. This is the actual surgery. He then used a piece of her tooth and bone to hold in place[12] a new lens that acts as her cornea. Just hours after the surgery, Dr. Perez removed Thornton's bandages[13], and for the first time in nearly a decade, she could see her best friend, Rick Brister.

KAY THORNTON, VISION PATIENT

He was the prettiest thing I believe I've ever seen.

ELIZABETH COHEN, CNN MEDICAL CORRESPONDENT

This procedure won't work for most blind people, and Thornton can't see perfectly.

KAY THORNTON, VISION PATIENT

I can't tell exactly what color you have on, either a blue or black.

低视力患者　凯·桑顿

哦，没有。

CNN 医学特派员　伊丽莎白·科恩

真是神奇，牙齿竟然能够让人重见光明！迈阿密巴斯康帕默眼科医院的维克特·佩雷兹医生初次听到这种奇特的手术也不敢置信。

巴斯康帕默眼科医院　维克特·佩雷兹医生

我们心想，"老天，怎么……这怎么做得到？"听起来实在是个异想天开的想法。

CNN 医学特派员　伊丽莎白·科恩

首先，佩雷兹医生移除桑顿左眼角膜受伤的组织，因为这片组织阻挡了她的视线。接着，听好了，他取出她的犬齿还有部分的颌骨，然后削薄。这实际上处于手术过程中。他利用牙齿和骨头固定一片新的镜片，用来作为她的角膜。手术后几个小时，佩雷兹医生就拆下了桑顿的绷带。过了将近 10 年，她终于第一次看到了她最好的朋友，瑞克·布里斯特。

低视力患者　凯·桑顿

我认为他是我看过的最美丽的事物。

CNN 医学特派员　伊丽莎白·科恩

这种手术对大多数的盲人无效，而且桑顿的视力还是有缺陷。

低视力患者　凯·桑顿

我不太确定你衣服的颜色，不是蓝色就是黑色。

Language Notes

whittle down　削薄，削减

whittle 是将某物"逐渐削薄，削弱"的意思，也可指"削减，削弱"。若接人，则表示"折磨，使精神不佳、苦恼"。

例 The human resources department whittled down the number of candidates for the job to six applicants.
人力资源部把该职位空缺的征选名额减为四名。

例 Julia whittled Max down with her scathing criticism of his work.
朱莉亚对麦克斯的作品提出严苛批评，让他大受打击。

Vocabulary

8. **far-fetched** ['fɑr,fɛtʃt] *adj.* 难以置信的，牵强的
Conspiracy theorists often come up with **far-fetched** explanations for mysterious phenomenon.
9. **tissue** ['tɪʃu] *n.* （生物）组织，薄织物
10. **canine tooth** ['kɑnaɪn][tuθ] 犬齿
11. **jawbone** ['dʒɔ,bon] *n.* 颌骨
12. **in place** [ɪn][ples] 在正确位置，适当地
Plans are **in place** to merge our company with its main competitor.
13. **bandage** ['bændɪdʒ] *n.* 绷带

ELIZABETH COHEN, CNN MEDICAL CORRESPONDENT
Yeah, black. I'm wearing black.

KAY THORNTON, VISION PATIENT
C-A-V.

DR. VICTOR PEREZ, THE BASCOM PALMER EYE INSTITUTE
Uh-huh, that's really good.

ELIZABETH COHEN, CNN MEDICAL CORRESPONDENT
Her vision will get better, and meanwhile[14], she's thrilled[15] by what she can see right now.

KAY THORNTON, VISION PATIENT
That is amazing! Rick, just look at those clouds!

CNN 医学特派员　伊丽莎白·科恩

　　没错，是黑色。我穿的是黑色。

低视力患者　凯·桑顿

　　C-A-V。

巴斯康帕默眼科医院　维克特·佩雷兹医生

　　没错，很好。

CNN 医学特派员　伊丽莎白·科恩

　　她的视力会越来越好。现在，她对自己能够看见的事物兴奋不已。

低视力患者　凯·桑顿

　　真是太神奇了！瑞克，你看那些云！ CNN

炫酷时尚　寰宇星空　生命发现　绿色革命　生活嬗变

Vocabulary

14. meanwhile ['min,hwaɪl] *adv.* 同时
15. thrill [θrɪl] *v.* （使）非常兴奋或激动，战栗
The animal trainer thrilled his audience by putting his head in a lion's mouth.

骨齿人工角膜手术 MOOKP—— Modified Osteo-Odonto-Keratoprosthesis

① 患者角膜受损严重，丧失视力

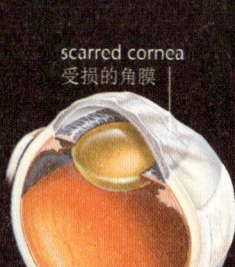

② 取一块口腔黏膜移植于眼球上，等待两个月让血管增生。

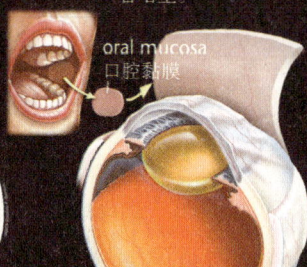

③ A 取整颗犬齿和部分齿槽骨，切除齿冠。
B 纵向削成薄片、凿洞，嵌入光学圆柱透镜。
C 齿骨人工角膜完成。

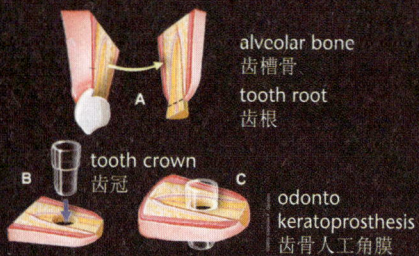

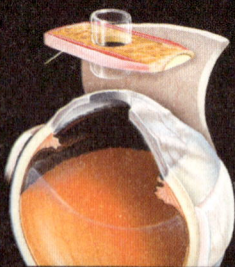

scarred cornea
受损的角膜

oral mucosa
口腔黏膜

alveolar bone
齿槽骨

tooth root
齿根

tooth crown
齿冠

odonto keratoprosthesis
齿骨人工角膜

artificial eye shell
义眼外壳

④ 将眼球上的口腔黏膜掀开，角膜切一个开口，切除玻璃体，植入齿骨人工角膜。

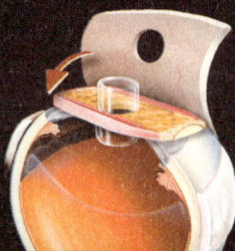

⑤ 将口腔黏膜切一个开口透光，覆盖在齿骨人工角膜上。

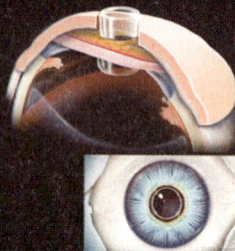

⑥ 移植的口腔黏膜能避免齿骨坏死，外层可戴上义眼外壳来修饰。

图片提供：Bascom Palmer Eye Institute © 2009 Stephen F. Gordon

Notes

新型手机揭示

通信科技新风貌

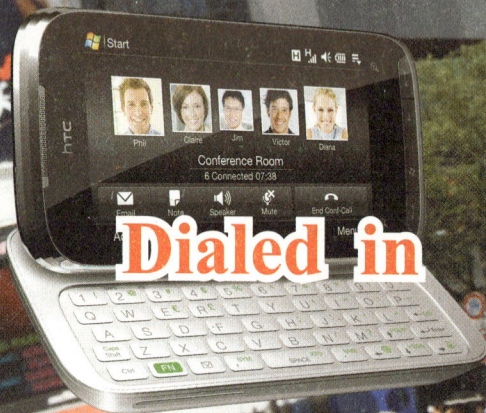

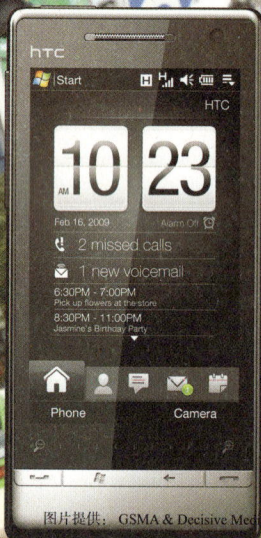

Dialed in

图片提供：GSMA & Decisive Media、HTC

Connecting to the Future of Mobile Communication in Barcelona

CNN ANCHOR

Now, the cell phone (was a long time ago) was once just a luxury[1] for a few, but now it's a must-have for the masses, and in Barcelona a phone fair[2] is showing off all the latest handsets[3] and gadgets. Adrian Finighan has more.

ADRIAN FINIGHAN, CNN CORRESPONDENT

Barcelona, home to the biggest mobile phone fair on the planet, a technological melting pot brimming[4] with the latest handsets, high-tech wizardry[5] and gadgets galore[6]. From the latest innovation to the quirky[7] designs to the downright[8] bizarre[9], The Mobile World Conference [Congress] has something for all tech tastes.

25 新型手机揭示通信科技新风貌

Mobile World Congress
巴塞罗那全球移动通信展

全名：GSM Mobile World Congress / 3GSM
　　　Mobile World Congress

首次举办：1987 年法国戛纳（Cannes）

搬迁：2006 年搬迁至西班牙巴塞罗那

下届日期：2010 年 2 月 15 日至 18 日

　　由全球移动通信联盟协会（GSM Association，简称 GSMA）主办，为全球规模最大的移动通信展，把会议（congress）和展览（exhibition）结合起来，让全球电信行业从业者齐聚，通过会议发布（unveil）最新技术与规格（specifications），在会议结束后就能直接到展位上现场展示及操作（demonstrate），是每年通信业从业者互动交流的国际盛事。

Vocabulary

1. **luxury** [ˈlʌɡdʒəri] *n.* 奢侈
2. **fair** [fɛr] *n.* 展览会，博览会
3. **handset** [ˈhænd͵sɛt] *n.* 电话听筒，手机
4. **brim** [brɪm] *v.* 充满，充溢
   Many of the young graduates are brimming with ideas.
5. **wizardry** [ˈwɪzədrɪ] *n.* 巫术，魔法，奇才
6. **galore** [ɡəˈlɔr] *adj.* 大量的（用在名词后）
   The traditional market was filled with bargains galore.
7. **quirky** [͵kwɜkɪ] *adj.* 古怪的
   Jenny likes to wear T-shirts with quirky slogans on them.
8. **downright** [ˈdaʊn͵raɪt] *adv.* 完全地，彻底地
9. **bizarre** [bəˈzɑr] *adj.* 古怪的，新奇的，不寻常的
   The lab is well-known for its bizarre inventions.

CNN 主播

　　以前手机只是少数人的奢侈品，现在却成了大众的必需品。在巴塞罗那，一场手机展览展示了最新的手机和器材。艾德里安·费尼根带来进一步报道。

CNN 特派员　艾德里安·费尼根

　　巴塞罗那是全球最大手机展的举办地，堪称是个科技大熔炉，充斥着最新型手机、高科技成果和许多科技产品。从最新的创新发明到奇特的设计，再到新奇古怪的产品，移动通信世界大会能够满足各种不同科技爱好者的品位。

What once was the must-have accessory for the business elite is now a personal portal[10] for all with access to movies, pictures, information, locations and social networking in an instant. And if you believe all the chatter[11] among the titans[12] of tech here in Barcelona, the mobile phone industry is set to continue growing at a rampant[13] pace with mobile applications, location-based services set to be the next big growth area.

MICHAEL O'HARA, CHIEF MARKETING OFFICE, GSMA

I think we're seeing an emerging[14] trend also that people are moving away from excitement on the device to actually moving to excitement around the services that you can consume on the device. So, having established that broadband[15] network infrastructure[16], people are able to do cool things like watch YouTube, like connect to Facebook, like Tweet using Twitter.

ADRIAN FINIGHAN, CNN CORRESPONDENT

As more and more people try to cash in on the social networking craze[17], relative newcomer INQ is weighing in with a specifically tailored[18] handset. This is called the INQ1. It claims to be the world's first social networking mobile, and it's affordable[19] too. It doesn't feel cheap and nasty[20], although this costs less than the average PDA, and you can do a whole load of things on it.

You can go onto Facebook, you can go to Windows Live Messenger, Skype, Last.fm, for instance, and it stays rather like a BlackBerry, permanently[21] connected to the social networking Web sites.

手机在过去曾是商业精英必备的物件，现在则是大众的个人通信方式，瞬间即可获得电影、图片、信息、地点及社交网络。如果你相信科技巨擘在巴塞罗那所说的话，那么手机产业仍将继续迅速成长，以移动应用软件及定位服务为下一波的主要成长领域。

全球移动通信联盟协会市场营销总监
迈克尔·欧哈拉

我认为目前还有一股新兴的趋势，就是大众对硬件的兴奋感已经转移到通过硬件能运用的服务。所以，宽带网络的基础建设既然已经存在，大众就能够在手机上使用各种炫酷的功能，例如观看 YouTube、连接到 Facebook 网站，或是上 Twitter 网站留言使用 Tweet。

CNN 特派员　艾德里安·费尼根

随着越来越多人想要利用社交网络热潮获利，新的厂商 INQ 也推出了一款特制的手机加入战局。这款手机名为 INQ1，号称是全世界第一款社交网络服务手机，而且价格不贵。这款手机的价钱虽然比一般的个人掌上电脑便宜，却不会让人觉得廉价低劣，而且可以使用很多功能。

例如上 YouTube 网站、使用微软实时通、打 Skype 电话、听 Last.fm 频道等等。此外，这款手机也像黑莓手机一样，可随时联机到社交网络网站。

Language Notes

cash in on　利用……赚钱

cash 作动词时解释为"将支票、汇票等兑成现金"，词组 cash in on sth. 则是"利用、靠……来赚钱"的意思。

例 Marty cashed in on his singing talent.
马蒂靠他的歌唱才华赚钱。

weigh in　提出（论点），加入……

weigh in 是指"在对话或讨论中提出意见"，后面用 with 加上论点、建议，文中表示在社区网络狂潮中，以具体的行动加入战局与竞争。

例 Climate experts weighed in with their theories on the causes of global warming.
气候专家们针对地球变暖的原因提出他们的理论。

a whole load of　很多，大量

load 是"某物的量"，a whole load of sth. 则是特别强调有"一大堆的……"。

例 Andrew bought a whole load of junk at a yard sale.
安德鲁在院子旧货拍卖中买了一大堆废物回来。

Vocabulary

10. portal ['pɔrtl] *n.* 入口
11. chatter ['tʃætə] *n.* 喋喋不休
12. titan ['taɪtn] *n.* 巨擘，重要人物
13. rampant ['ræmpənt] *adj.* 蔓延的，猖獗的
14. emerging [ɪ'mɜdʒɪŋ] *adj.* 新兴的
    Dan likes to invest in emerging markets.
15. broadband ['brɔd,bænd] *adj.* 宽带的
    The hotel has broadband Internet access.
16. infrastructure ['ɪnfrə,strʌktʃə] *n.* 基础建设
17. craze [krez] *n.* 狂热，风尚
18. tailored ['teləd] *adj.* 定做的，合身的
    Donny always wears tailored shirts.
19. affordable [ə'fɔrdəbl] *adj.* 负担得起的
    The couple is looking for an affordable home in Southern California.
20. nasty ['næstɪ] *adj.* 不好的，令人作呕的
21. permanently ['pɜmənəntlɪ] *adv.* 永久地

Meanwhile, Microsoft is sharpening its knives, hoping to mimic[22] the success its Windows brand has had in the PC market. It's just unveiled a massive change to its mobile business, trying to improve information sharing between a computer, handset and the Internet. It's also rolling out a new touch-screen interface[23], which ships late 2009, and an online application store with thousands of downloads and space to store and synchronize[24] personal information.

But all is not well in tech town as operators brace for a drawn-out[25] downturn. While demand for entry-level[26] phones in the emerging world is still strong, mature markets are straining[27]. The figures show customers are hanging onto handsets longer or switching to pre-pay deals. Research in Motion, the company behind BlackBerry, is feeling the sting[28]. The company's latest models, like the touch-screen Storm and the Bold, are still selling, but cash-strapped[29] corporate customers are trying to slash costs, and that means cutting back on upgrades.

JIM BALSILLIE, CO-CEO, RESEARCH IN MOTION
And the prudent[30] person pays attention to that, and you try to be factor that into your thinking, and we did our guidance thinking. Let's be prudent for our subscribers in late December, and then last week we had to announce our subscribers[31] are 20 percent higher than we expected. You know, our sales will grow 15 percent quarter over quarter.

ADRIAN FINIGHAN, CNN CORRESPONDENT
As the global recession sets in and purse string[s] tightens[32], it's mobile phone users like you and me who hold the power to get the right handset and the right applications at the right price.

另一方面，微软也摩拳擦掌，希望能效仿 Windows 系列品牌在个人计算机市场上的成功案例。该公司刚宣布了一项移动业务的重大变革，希望改善计算机、手机与因特网之间的信息分享。微软也推出新的触控屏幕接口，将于 2009 年底上市，还有一家在线应用软件商，提供数千种软件下载，以及可同步更新个人数据的储存空间。

不过，科技业界目前状况并不理想，从业者纷纷准备应对长期衰退的局面。新兴世界对入门级的手机虽然仍有大量需求，成熟的市场却已达饱和。统计数据显示，消费者保留手机的时间增长，或转用预付制消费。黑莓手机制造商移动研究公司已经感受到痛楚。该公司最新款式的产品，例如有触控屏幕的 Storm 和 Bold，虽然还是相当热卖，但是现金吃紧的企业客户却试图削减成本，也就是减少升级的花费。

移动研究公司联合 CEO　吉姆·贝尔斯利

谨慎的人会注意到这种现象，也会试着把这种情形加以考虑。我们做了指导性思考，把 12 月底的用户数预估得较保守，结果上周我们宣布用户数比预估高出 20%。我们的销售额将按季增长 15%。

CNN 特派员　艾德里安·费尼根

全球经济陷入衰退，大家看紧了钱包，像你我这样的手机使用者就握有主动权，可以用适当的价格得到适当的手机与应用软件。CNN

Language Notes

sharpen one's knives　摩拳擦掌

sharpen one's knives 字面上的意思是"将某人的刀子磨利"，比喻要"准备面对激烈的情况"，例如竞争、战斗等。

roll out　推出

roll out 原指"以滚动的方式展示物品"，通常是有轮胎的东西，如汽车。常见文中的用法，解释为"推出新产品"。

hang onto　保留，保住

hang onto 指"紧抓，紧守"或"保留，保住某物"的意思，也就是 keep "（长期）持有，保有"，也可写成 hang on to。

factor sth. into　将……计入，将……考虑在内

factor 当名词是"因素"，在这里当动词，factor sth. into 是指"将……计入，将……考虑在内"的意思。

Vocabulary

22. mimic ['mɪmɪk] v. 模仿
    The bird mimics nearly every sound it hears.
23. interface ['ɪntəˌfes] n. 界面
24. synchronize ['sɪŋkrənaɪz] v. 使同步，使协调
25. drawn-out ['drɔnˌaut] adj. 冗长的
    Both parties settled the lawsuit to avoid a drawn-out court case.
26. entry-level ['ɛntrɪ'lɛvl] adj. 入门的，初级的
    Tom got an entry-level job at a film studio.
27. strain [stren] v. 拉紧
    The movers strained to carry piano out of the house.
28. sting [stɪŋ] n. 痛楚，刺痛
29. cash-strapped ['kæʃˌstræpt] adj. 缺乏现金的
    Samuel was cash-strapped throughout most of college.
30. prudent ['prudnt] adj. 谨慎的，节俭的
    Stu is prudent in his financial planning.
31. subscriber [səb'skraɪbə] n. 订阅者，申请者，用户
32. tighten ['taɪtn] v. 使变紧
    The prison tightened security after two convicts escaped.

信息时代的噩梦——无线网络

Hijacked[1] Data

Airport Wi-Fi May Expose Your Laptop to Lurking[2] Hackers[3]

ANJALI RAO, CNN ANCHOR

It is a dangerous cyber[4] world out there, and one of the roughest[5] neighborhoods for the innocent computer user is the average airport. Business travelers surf[6] away on unprotected networks, leaving themselves open to hackers who may be sitting just a few feet away. Phil Black explains.

PHIL BLACK, CNN CORRESPONDENT

It's the most efficient way to use those hours lost in airports—sending e-mails, researching, buying, selling, closing deals. The air here is thick with[7] sensitive information transmitted across wireless Internet connections, and much of that sensitive information can be read by anyone who knows how.

This man looks innocent enough—a business traveler on his laptop. But Kiran Deshpande is an expert in wireless security, and he's watching everything I do online.

So, I'm connected to one of the open Wi-Fi networks here at Heathrow Airport, and I'm just having a browse around my favorite site.

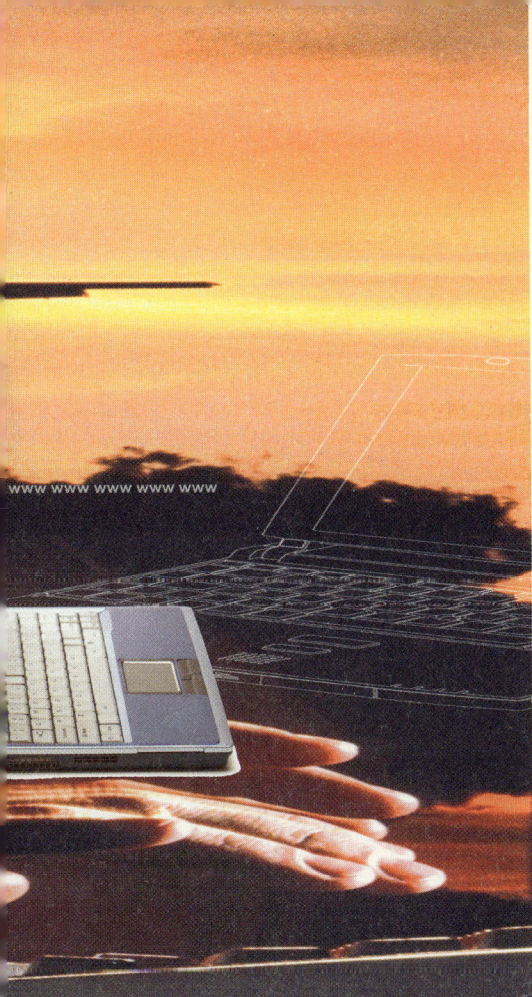

CNN 主播 安姿丽

网络世界危机四伏。对于无辜的计算机使用者来说，最危险环境之一就是一般机场。商务旅行人士会在无保护的网络上随意浏览，但这却会让他们对那些可能就坐在几英尺外的黑客毫无防备。菲尔·布莱克带来报道。

CNN 特派员 菲尔·布莱克

要利用在机场浪费的几小时，这是最有效率的方式：发送电子邮件、进行研究、买卖东西、完成交易。这里的空气充满了用无线网络传送的敏感信息，而知道个中诀窍者就能读取其中大部分信息。

这个人看来没什么，只是个正在使用笔记本电脑的商务旅客。但是基兰·德斯潘迪却是个无线网络安全方面的专家，他正在监察我上网做的每一件事。

我连上希思罗机场公共无线网络中的一个，浏览我最喜爱的网站。

Vocabulary

1. hijack ['haɪˌdʒæk] v. 劫持，抢劫
   The thieves hijacked a truckload of valuable electronics.
2. lurk [lɜːk] v. 潜伏
   Many dangerous animals lurked in the forest.
3. hacker ['hækə] n. 黑客
4. cyber ['saɪbə] n.【计算机】与计算机或网络相关事物
5. rough [rʌf] adj. 犯罪盛行的，危险的，粗野的
   Julie avoids walking in some of the rougher parts of town.
6. surf [sɜːf] v. 浏览（网络）
   Megan surfs the Internet on her new PC.
7. be thick with 充满
   The city dump was thick with rats and other vermin.

炫酷时尚　寰宇星空　生命发现　绿色革命　生活嬗变

As I casually surf, Kiran sees all.

KIRAN DESHPANDE, PRESIDENT, AIRTIGHT INTERNATIONAL
You actually went to the *Business Traveller* page. That's what you've been doing.

PHIL BLACK, CNN CORRESPONDENT
It's all there on his screen. This was pretty harmless spying[8], but it could have been much more serious.

But if I was sending an e-mail or doing some banking[9], would you be able to see that as well?

KIRAN DESHPANDE, PRESIDENT, AIRTIGHT INTERNATIONAL
If you send some passwords and some other stuff[10], anything that you're doing in HTTP is pretty much visible to me here.

PHIL BLACK, CNN CORRESPONDENT
Using open, public Wi-Fi is one security risk at airports. There's another, and it's more sinister[11]. Sean Remnant is a white hat hacker. He's a good guy in the hacking world. First, he shows me how easy it is to scan the terminal's[12] available networks.

SEAN REMNANT, INTERNET SECURITY EXPERT
And then instantly, I've got . . . I'm seeing probably 20 wireless networks with four or five of those having relatively weak security.

PHIL BLACK, CNN CORRESPONDENT
Among this list of Wi-Fi networks, there's a fake, a trap.

SEAN REMNANT, INTERNET SECURITY EXPERT
I have a colleague that sets up a . . . what we call a rogue access point to lure[13] someone in. And he's basically called it "Public WiFi," that we can see here. Now, that's my colleague's rogue access point. He's got a little access point that's no bigger than a matchbox that he's just got sitting on his lap. And that's now, basically, a public wireless service that somebody could use.

PHIL BLACK, CNN CORRESPONDENT
That's how easy it is?

就在我随意浏览的时候，基兰看得一清二楚。

Airtight 国际总经理　基兰·德斯潘迪

你刚上了《商务旅游人士》的网页，这是你刚才在做的事。

CNN 特派员　菲尔·布莱克

一切都在他的屏幕上。这只是无伤大雅的窥探行为，但这可能会造成相当严重的后果。

但是如果我正在发电子邮件或进行银行账务活动，你也能看得到吗？

Airtight 国际总经理　基兰·德斯潘迪

如果你发送了密码和其他一些东西，你在网页上的一举一动，我这里都看得一清二楚。

CNN 特派员　菲尔·布莱克

在机场里使用开放的公共无线网络是有安全风险的。还有另一种危险，这个更邪恶。西恩·雷南特是个白帽黑客，他是黑客世界中的好人。他先向我展示要在航站楼中扫描可用的网络有多容易。

网络安全专家　西恩·雷南特

我马上就看到了大约二十个无线网络，其中有四五个的安全性相对比较差。

CNN 特派员　菲尔·布莱克

在这张无线网络清单中，就有个假货，一个陷阱。

网络安全专家　西恩·雷南特

我有个同事建了一个我们称之为恶意存取点的东西来诱骗别人。基本上他把它称为"公共无线网络"，就是我们看到的这个东西。那就是我同事的恶意存取点。他有个小小存取点，体积没有火柴盒大，刚插上他的笔记本电脑。现在这个存取点就成了有人会使用的公共无线上网设备。

CNN 特派员　菲尔·布莱克

就这么简单吗？

Vocabulary

8. **spy** [spaɪ] *v.* 暗中监视，搜集情报，进行间谍工作
   The corporation often **spies** upon its competition.
9. **bank** [bæŋk] *v.* 存款
   William **banks** at several local financial institutions.
10. **stuff** [stʌf] *n.* （无特定的）东西
11. **sinister** [ˈsɪnəstə] *adj.* 邪恶的
    The detective believed that there may be **sinister** circumstances behind the recent string of mysterious deaths in the city.
12. **terminal** [ˈtɜmən] *n.* 航站楼
13. **lure** [lʊr] *v.* 引诱，诱骗
    The con artists **lured** unwitting victims to invest in a fictitious company.

SEAN REMNANT, INTERNET SECURITY EXPERT
That's how easy it is.

PHIL BLACK, CNN CORRESPONDENT
How hard is it to tell the difference between a genuine wireless hotspot and a rogue hotspot?

SEAN REMNANT, INTERNET SECURITY EXPERT
If somebody really wants to capture your traffic, they will pretend to be the public hotspot service service provider. So they will pretend to be your BT Openzone, your T-Mobile, your Cloud Network. From an everyday traveler's point of view, you're going to find it very difficult to differentiate between good and bad.

PHIL BLACK, CNN CORRESPONDENT
So are Wi-Fi zones best avoided? The expert advice is to surf securely using VPNs. However, when in a rush, we tend to sacrifice security for speed. Remember to stay alert. A cyber thief may be waiting to mug[14] you in the most clean and bloodless way.

网络安全专家　西恩·雷南特
　　就这么简单。

CNN 特派员　菲尔·布莱克
　　要分辨真正的无线热点和恶意热点有多难?

网络安全专家　西恩·雷南特
　　如果有人真的想要收集你的网络传输数据，他们会假装是公共热点的服务提供者。他们会假扮成你的 BT Openzone（注1）、你的 T-Mobile（注2）或你的云端网络（注3）。从一个经常进行商务旅行的人的角度来看，你要分辨热点服务提供者的真假并不容易。

CNN 特派员　菲尔·布莱克
　　所以最好还是别碰无线网络？专家建议使用 VPNs 安全上网。然而当你赶时间时，我们常会为了速度而牺牲安全。记住要保持警觉，某个网络小偷可能正等着要用干净而不见血的方式洗劫你。 ⓒ

注1：即英国电信（British Telecom）旗下的商业无线网络热点总称，多见于咖啡馆、旅馆、车站、机场等公共区域。
注2：T-Mobile 是一家跨国电信公司，是世界最大电信公司之一，旗下也有网络业务，其无线网络热点遍布欧洲、美国两地。
注3：Cloud Network "云端网络"即共同进行云端运算的众多计算机系统所形成的网络。而云端运算其实就是由众多计算机系统连接成一个大型数据库，使用者可通过网络将数据储存于此数据库中，或是让数据库分析、处理数据。所以使用者不需高级配备，只需上网便可完成极复杂的工作。

Vocabulary

14. mug [mʌg] *v.* （公开）行凶，抢劫
Carl was mugged on his last trip to New York and vowed to never go back.

炫酷时尚

寰宇星空

生命发现

绿色革命

生活嬗变

Internet Terms 网络词汇

hotspot
hotspot
热点，热区

无线网络使用者可连上网络的连接点或区域。而文中所提到的 rouge hotspot 则是黑客伪造的热点，目的在于骗取上网者的数据。

http
http (= hypertext transmission protocol)
超文本链接协议

使用最广泛的网络协议，也是所有www 文件所需遵守的传输标准。利用这个统一标准，我们不仅可让数据传输速度更快，还可以提高正确率。

rogue access point
rogue access point
恶意存取点，非法无线存取点

· 未经网管人员同意，私下设立的无线网络存取点。
· 由黑客伪造的网络存取点，用来诱骗上网者使用并骗取其个人信息。

white hat hacker
white hat hacker
白帽黑客

相对于入侵他人系统以犯罪牟利的黑帽黑客（black hat hacker），白帽黑客通常是公司组织聘用者，他们会测试、找出系统漏洞，好让该公司得以改善、修正其系统。

VPN
VPN (= virtual private network)
虚拟个人网络，虚拟专用网络

通过公共网络架构进入公司网络等内部网络的方式。这种通信方式会通过加密方式提高通信保密性、安全性。

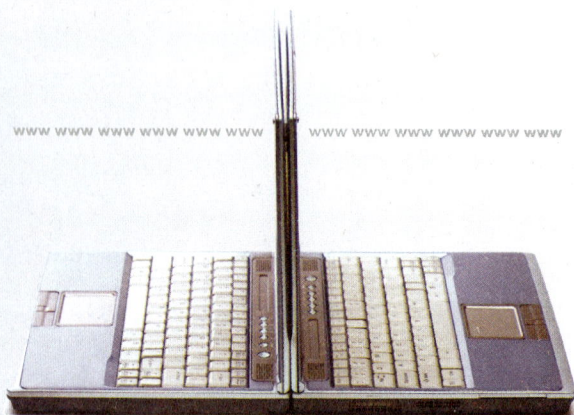

Notes

顺应高龄化时代的
护理机器人登场

Mechanical[1] Helper Lends a Hand[1] to the Elderly

Robo-
Nurse

图片提供：Reuters 杂志

MONITA RAJPAL, CNN ANCHOR

Well, most of us would like a little extra help around the house, right? Especially seniors. Now there's someone who can pitch in[2] in the most high-tech way possible. Kyung Lah went to meet TWENDY-ONE in Tokyo.

KYUNG LAH, CNN CORRESPONDENT

The helping hands here are metal and silicone[2] designed to assist a person to a wheelchair. Her name is TWENDY-ONE, robot for the elderly. She may look like E.T., but inventor Shegeki Sugano says she's more than just a cute friend: "[She can] cook an egg and have [has] the dexterity[3] to delicately[4] pick up food and serve[5] it."

图片提供：Reuters

CNN 主播　莫妮塔·拉吉波

　　大多数人都希望家里能多点帮手，不是吗？尤其是老年人。现在有人能以最尖端科技来提供帮助。拉赫去东京见了 TWENDY-ONE。

CNN 特派员　拉赫

　　这个帮手是由金属和硅制作而成，专门设计来帮人坐上轮椅。她的名字叫做 TWENDY-ONE，是为老年人设计的机器人。她或许外观看似像 E.T.，但发明人菅野茂木却说，她不只是个可爱的朋友而已，"她会煮蛋，还能灵巧优雅地拿起食物端上桌。"

Phrases

1. **lend a hand** 提供帮助
   The boy scout lent a hand to the elderly woman.
2. **pitch in** 参与，支援
   Jeff pitched in to help his dad rake the leaves.

Vocabulary

1. **mechanical** [mə'kænɪk!] *adj.* 机械的，运用机械的
   A mechanical arm placed items on the assembly line.
2. **silicone** ['sɪlɪˌkon] *n.* 硅
3. **dexterity** [dɛk'stɛrətɪ] *n.* 灵巧，技能
4. **delicately** ['dɛləkətlɪ] *adv.* 动作轻巧地，优雅地
5. **serve** [sɜv] *v.* 端上（食物）
   The waiter served the first course of the meal.

So, the goal of TWENDY-ONE isn't necessarily to replace[6] a human caretaker[7] but to simply assist someone, in this case to help me toast this piece of bread.

The aging[8] baby boomers[9] in the U.S. and Japan are who Sugano says will need this robot. By 2050, 40 percent of Japan's population will be over the age of 65 and [there will be] fewer young people to care for[3] them because Japan has one of the lowest birth rates in the world.

So what man can't, machine can, says graduate student Atomu Maeshiro. "I believe this robot will be a big help in the near future," he says.

It is definitely a work in progress[4].

Right now, the robot needs a team of researchers and a screen full of computer prompts[10] to work. The inventor believes a commercial version will be ready to go by 2020, giving the elderly a hand up for independent living.

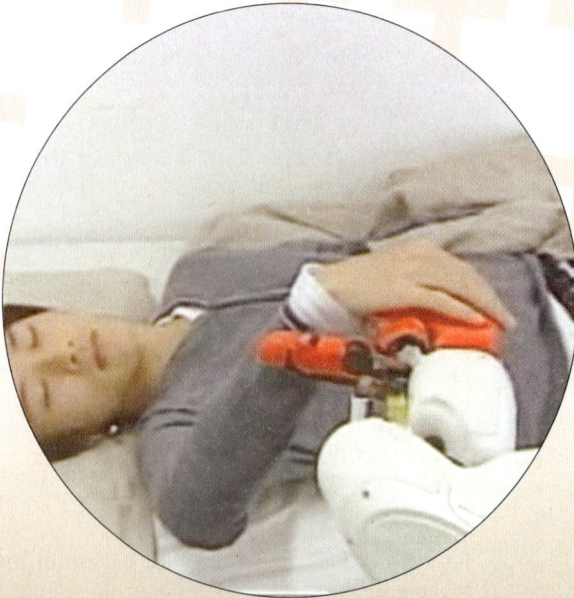

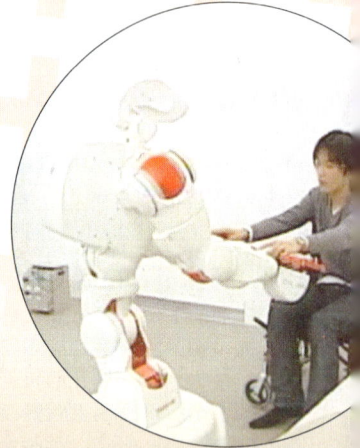

所以，TWENDY-ONE 的目标并非要取代真人看护，而是要去帮助人，就像现在她要来帮我烤这片面包。

菅野表示，美国和日本年纪渐长的婴儿潮时代的出生者将会是这款机器人的需求者。到了 2050 年，日本将有 40% 的人口超过 65 岁，能照顾他们的年轻人将越来越少，因为日本是全球生育率最低的国家之一。

因此研究生前城说，人类不能做到的，机器却能。他说，"我相信这个机器人在不久的将来肯定会帮上大忙。"

当然，这个机器人还是正在研发中的产品。

现在，这个机器人需要一组研究人员和一个写满计算机指令的屏幕才能工作。发明者相信 2020 年之前便能推出商业款，帮助老年人过上独立的居家生活。CNN

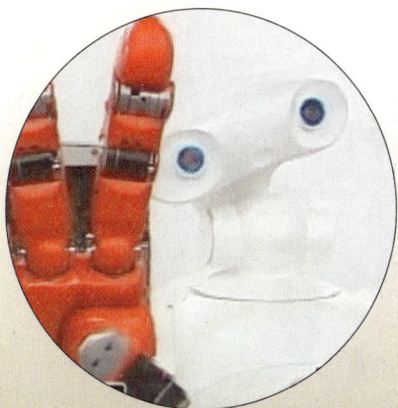

Phrases

3. care for 照料
The nurse cared for several older patients.
4. in progress 正在进行中
No one can enter the theater while the play is in progress.

Vocabulary

6. replace [rɪˈples] v. 取代，替换
Max replaced the old light bulb.
7. caretaker [ˈkɛrˌtekə] n. 看护者
8. age [edʒ] v. 变老，成熟
The cheese aged in a cool cellar.
9. baby boomer [ˈbebɪ][ˈbumə] 婴儿潮时代（第二次世界大战后的出生者）
10. prompt [prɑmpt] n. 提示

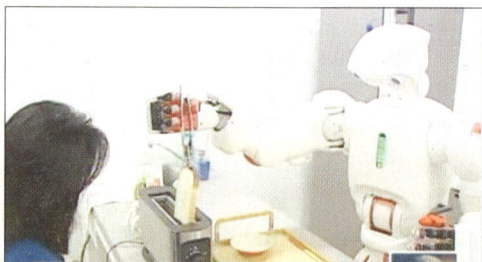

Give It a Try 请选出正确答案

1. The aircraft was grounded because of
   _____ problems.
   a. mechanical   b. methodical
   c. metaphysical   d. metaphorical

2. A _____ delivers food to Donna's
   grandmother every afternoon.
   a. dexterity   b. silicone
   c. caretaker   d. prompt

3. The crowd was delighted by the sheer
   _____ of the acrobats.
   a. prosperity   b. dexterity
   c. silicone   d. caretaker

Answers: 1.a 2.c 3.b

✚ TWENDY-ONE's Specs

宽：73.4 厘米　高：146.7 厘米
重量：111 千克
特色：共有 47 处可全方位（omni-directional）转动的关节（joint），使 TWENDY-ONE 能灵活稳定地拿取东西、弯腰清扫地板。TWENDY-ONE 的头部及躯干有超音波侦测器（ultrasonic sensor）、力度侦测器（force sensor）等，能观测人类碰触的力量，而提供适当的回应力度，并且能侦测四周环境，避免碰伤人类。另外，由于装有强力传动装置（actuator），TWENDY-ONE 不但能抬起重物，还能搀扶人类。

Notes

Virtual[1] 3D 科技带你游历古罗马

3D Technology Takes Visitors on a Walk Through the Ancient City

Rome

图片提供：3D Rewind Rome™. Virtuality Group srl.

CNN ANCHOR

Well, have you ever imagined what life was like in ancient Rome? Now you have a chance to experience it, thanks to 3D technology. Rome bureau[2] chief Alessio Vinci takes us on a tour.

ALESSIO VINCI, CNN CORRESPONDENT

What the glorious[3] Roman Empire looked like in the old days has been pretty much left to your imagination, until now.

SAPIENTINUS, VIRTUAL GUIDE, 3D REWIND ROME

Ladies and gentlemen, I give you the Colosseum[4]!

ALESSIO VINCI, CNN CORRESPONDENT

Just a stone's throw away from the real Colosseum …

SAPIENTINUS, VIRTUAL GUIDE, 3D REWIND ROME

Step this way, folks, for your chance to peek into the Temple of Vesta[5].

ALESSIO VINCI, CNN CORRESPONDENT

… entertainment and history merged[6] into a 30-minute interactive journey.

㉘ 3D 科技带你游历古罗马

Language Notes

a stone's throw   不远，近在咫尺

字面上的意思是"投石可及的距离"，表示距离不远，类似中文里的"一墙之隔"，后面通常接 away from 加上相距的地方。

例 The subway station is just a stone's throw from my house.
地铁站离我家仅有一墙之隔。

Vocabulary

1. virtual ['vɜtʃʊəl] *adj.* 虚拟的
   The architect used a computer to create a **virtual** model of the building.
2. bureau ['bjʊro] *n.* 联络处，分社，局，处
3. glorious ['glorius] *adj.* 荣耀的，辉煌的
   Workers restored the cathedral to its **glorious** original splendor.
4. Colosseum [ˌkɑlə'siəm] *n.* 罗马圆形大剧场，（c-）大型体育场
5. Vesta ['vɛstə] *n.* 罗马女灶神，（v-）短火柴
6. merge [mɜdʒ] *v.* 融合，结合
   The design **merges** efficiency with simple beauty.

CNN 主播

你有没有想象过生活在古罗马会是什么样？有了立体绘图科技，现在你有机会体验一番了。罗马分部的组长亚勒席欧·芬奇要带我们去走一趟。

CNN 特派员　亚勒席欧·芬奇

辉煌的罗马帝国以前究竟是什么样子，原本只能任人想象，直到现在。

3D 重回罗马虚拟导游　萨皮恩提诺斯

各位女士先生，为您介绍罗马竞技场！

CNN 特派员　亚勒席欧·芬奇

这里距离真的罗马竞技场并不远……

3D 重回罗马虚拟导游　萨皮恩提诺斯

各位，请往这边走，将有机会一窥维斯塔神庙内部。

CNN 特派员　亚勒席欧·芬奇

……娱乐与历史融合成一场 30 分钟的互动旅程。

炫酷时尚　寰宇星空　生命发现　绿色革命　**生活嬗变**

SAPIENTINUS, VIRTUAL GUIDE, 3D REWIND ROME
This loose stone should give us an undisturbed[7] view.

ALESSIO VINCI, CNN CORRESPONDENT
Starting with a replica[8] of today's excavations[9], visitors can take a virtual tour of ancient Rome with some surprises.

OLIVIA MENAGUALE, 3D REWIND ROME
You are back in time. You are smelling the history.

ALESSIO VINCI, CNN CORRESPONDENT
You actually reproduce the smells, as well?

OLIVIA MENAGUALE, 3D REWIND ROME
We do. You can smell the mold[10]. You can see a little powders coming from the top. You can hear water going around your sides, and you can even hear the squeaky[11] noise of animals scurrying[12] around.

ALESSIO VINCI, CNN CORRESPONDENT
Rats? Animals—rats?

OLIVIA MENAGUALE, 3D REWIND ROME
You know, we'll leave the surprise for the people that are coming.

ALESSIO VINCI, CNN CORRESPONDENT
You actually use real rats?

OLIVIA MENAGUALE, 3D REWIND ROME
I can't tell you, you know.

ALESSIO VINCI, CNN CORRESPONDENT
3D technology allows visitors to walk through the hustle and bustle of Roman life.

SAPIENTINUS, VIRTUAL GUIDE, 3D REWIND ROME
It's the poorest part of Rome, where us ordinary mortals[13] live.

MAXENTIUS, VIRTUAL ROMAN EMPEROR, 3D REWIND ROMAN
Brave gladiators[14], give us a day to remember.

ALESSIO VINCI, CNN CORRESPONDENT
The sensation[15] is like walking through a virtual time machine. Olivia Menaguale is one of the partners in the project, but also an art historian.

3D 重回罗马虚拟导游 萨皮恩提诺斯
这块松脱的石块应该能让我们好好看个清楚。

CNN 特派员 亚勒席欧·芬奇
一开始是刚刚出土古迹的模拟画面，接着游客即可踏上一场惊奇的古罗马虚拟实境之旅。

3D 重回罗马 奥莉维亚·孟纳古瓦勒
你回到了过去，嗅闻着历史的气息。

CNN 特派员 亚勒席欧·芬奇
你们真的连气味都仿造出来了？

3D 重回罗马 奥莉维亚·孟纳古瓦勒
没错。你可以闻到霉味，可以看到粉状物从上面飘下来，可以听到水在你四周流动，甚至还可以听到动物跑来跑去的声音。

CNN 特派员 亚勒席欧·芬奇
老鼠吗？你说的动物是老鼠吗？

3D 重回罗马 奥莉维亚·孟纳古瓦勒
这个惊喜就留给来访的游客去发掘吧。

CNN 特派员 亚勒席欧·芬奇
你们用真的老鼠吗？

3D 重回罗马 奥莉维亚·孟纳古瓦勒
这我无可奉告。

CNN 特派员 亚勒席欧·芬奇
立体绘图科技让游客能穿梭在罗马喧嚣生活的大街小巷。

3D 重回罗马虚拟导游 萨皮恩提诺斯
这里是罗马最贫穷的地区，就是我们这些平凡百姓住的地方。

3D 重回罗马虚拟罗马皇帝 马克森提
英勇的角斗士，带给我们精彩难忘的一天吧。

CNN 特派员 亚勒席欧·芬奇
这种感觉就像走进虚拟的时光机器一样。奥莉维亚·孟纳古瓦勒是这项计划的其中一名合伙人，她同时也是艺术史学家。

Language Notes

hustle and bustle 熙熙攘攘

hustle ['hʌsl] 指"奔忙，赶忙，忙碌"，bustle ['bʌsl] 指"喧嚣，忙乱"，将意义相似且押韵的名词连在一起制造强调的效果，表示非常忙碌的状态，即中文"忙忙乱乱"、"熙熙攘攘"的意思。

例 Nancy moved to the countryside to escape the hustle and bustle of the big city.
南西搬到了乡间，以避开大城市的喧嚣。

Vocabulary

7. **undisturbed** [ʌndɪs'tɜbd] *adj.* 不受干扰的
The ruins of the ancient city laid undisturbed for hundreds of years.
8. **replica** ['rɛplɪkə] *n.* 复制品
9. **excavation** [ˌɛkskə'veʃən] *n.* 古迹，出土文物
10. **mold** [mold] *n.* 霉，霉菌
11. **squeaky** ['skwikɪ] *adj.* 吱吱响的，发出短促尖声的
Jack put oil on the squeaky door hinge.
12. **scurry** ['skɜrɪ] *v.* 匆匆地跑，急匆匆地走
Something scurried by Andy's foot while he walked through the dark alley.
13. **mortal** ['mɔrtl] *n.* 人，凡人
14. **gladiator** ['glediˌetə] *n.*（古罗马）角斗士
15. **sensation** [sɛn'seʃən] *n.* 感觉，知觉

OLIVIA MENAGUALE, 3D REWIND ROME

So, we are just an enhancement[16] to the classic tour that you should do, because here ... that's why we are just 80 meters away from the Colosseum. We don't want to be detached[17] from the real thing; we want to be part of it.

ALESSIO VINCI, CNN CORRESPONDENT

And through this wireless[18] device[19], actually, the audio is in eight different languages, right? Chinese, Russian, German, French, Spanish, English ... right?

OLIVIA MENAGUALE, 3D REWIND ROME

Italian at the moment.

ALESSIO VINCI, CNN CORRESPONDENT

Arabic, maybe, in the future?

OLIVIA MENAGUALE, 3D REWIND ROME

Yeah. Yeah, of course, will be the next one, possibly.

ALESSIO VINCI, CNN CORRESPONDENT

Most of it, though, doesn't really need a translation.

3D 重回罗马　奥莉维亚·孟纳古瓦勒

我们等于是古典罗马传统游的加强版，但你应该去实际走一走，因为这里……这就是为什么我们距离大剧场只有 80 米。我们不希望和真实的古罗马脱节，而是要成为它的一部分。

CNN 特派员　亚勒席欧·芬奇

这个无线装置可以播出 8 种不同语言的解说，对不对？中文、俄语、德语、法语、西班牙语、英语……是吗？

3D 重回罗马　奥莉维亚·孟纳古瓦勒

现在播放的是意大利语。

CNN 特派员　亚勒席欧·芬奇

未来也可能增加阿拉伯语吧？

3D 重回罗马　奥莉维亚·孟纳古瓦勒

是啊，是啊，当然。我们下一个增加的很可能就是阿拉伯语。

CNN 特派员　亚勒席欧·芬奇

不过，大部分的解说其实并不需要翻译。

CNN

Language Notes

at the moment　现在，在此刻

at the moment 就是 now "现在，在此刻"的意思，但是 at the moment 通常用在目前状况可能随即会改变的时候。

例 At the moment, Bill doesn't have any plans for New Year's Eve.
比尔现在还没为除夕夜做任何计划。

Vocabulary

16. enhancement [ɪnˈhænsmənt] n. 提高，加强
17. detach [dɪˈtætʃ] v. 分开，分离
Silvia detached the headphones from her MP3 player before putting it in her coat.
18. wireless [ˈwaɪrləs] adj. 无线的
Tom uses a wireless headset for his mobile phone when driving his car.
19. device [dɪˈvaɪs] n. 仪器，装置，设备

炫酷时尚　寰宇星空　生命发现　绿色革命　生活嬗变

瘫痪病人的新希望
——鳗鱼！

Eels[1] that Heal

Lampreys Offer New Hope to Spinal Injury Patients

图片提供：Dept. of Electrical and Computer Engineering, Johns Hopkins University

FEMALE NARRATOR

Three months after his trip to Peru, Dr. Drew Seibert's life changed.

DR. DREW SEIBERT, FORMER PARALYTIC

Somehow I fell forward, hit the my forehead on the edge of a shower. My body kept going, threw my neck back and broke some vertebrae[2] in my neck. I woke up from my coma[3] three days later and was on a ventilator[4], and I was paralyzed[5] from the neck on down completely, just lying there, couldn't move anything.

FEMALE NARRATOR

Seibert has been rehabilitating[6] here at the Shepherd Center in Atlanta, Georgia for three years. He has made great progress, but continues to hope for scientific breakthrough.

DR. DREW SEIBERT, FORMER PARALYTIC

I'm constantly reading about new things on the Internet to see if there's any … anything that, first of all, might get me back to normal, but also, secondly, that I might be able to be involved in[1] to help other people, even if it's not necessarily gonna help me. There's gotta be an answer to this, and eventually they're gonna figure it out[2].

Phrases

1. **be involved in** 参与，涉入
   Several vehicles **were involved in** the crash.
2. **figure out** 搞清楚，弄懂
   It took hours, but Bill **figured out** the puzzle.

Vocabulary

1. **eel** [il] *n.* 鳗鱼，鳗、鳝等蛇状鱼类
2. **vertebrae** ['vətəbrə] *n.* 脊椎，脊骨
3. **coma** ['komə] *n.* 昏迷
4. **ventilator** ['vɛntə,letə] *n.* 呼吸器
5. **paralyze** ['pɛrə,laɪz] *v.* 使瘫痪，使麻痹
   The accident **paralyzed** the car's driver from the waist down.
6. **rehabilitate** [rɪə'bɪlə,tet] *v.* 使康复
   The center **rehabilitates** injured animals.

女声旁白

　　秘鲁之旅 3 个月后，德鲁·希伯特博士的人生改变了。

曾瘫痪病人　德鲁·希伯特博士

　　我不知道为什么往前跌倒，前额撞到淋浴间的边缘。我的身体继续前倾，以致脖子后仰，折断了几节颈椎骨。3 天后我才从昏迷中醒来，身上接上了呼吸器，而且脖子以下完全瘫痪，只能躺在床上，一动都不能动。

女声旁白

　　希伯特在佐治亚州亚特兰大的谢波德中心进行康复训练已经有 3 年的时间。他已经大有进步，但仍然盼望科学能有突破性的进展。

曾瘫痪病人　德鲁·希伯特博士

　　我持续上网查阅新消息，看看有没有什么……能够使我恢复正常，这是最重要的，其次是能够让我帮助别人，就算对我没有帮助也没关系。这个问题一定有解决办法，而且最终一定会有人找出答案。

FEMALE NARRATOR

Dr. Avis Cohen and Dr. Ralph Etienne-Cummings may just have Seibert's answer.

DR. AVIS COHEN, UNIVERSITY OF MARYLAND

What happens in a spinal cord[7] injury is that the brain is no longer able to come down to the spinal cord and turn it on.

FEMALE NARRATOR

Cohen is a biologist who has been studying the spinal cords of lamprey eels.

DR. AVIS COHEN, UNIVERSITY OF MARYLAND

In the lamprey, we can test devices to control the spinal cord below a lesion[8] site and design those devices which can then be transported to mammalian[9] animals and then to humans as a means[10] of controlling the spinal cord of a human that has had a spinal cord injury.

The reason that the lamprey's is a model system is because, even though it's very primitive[11], being at the bottom of the vertebrate tree, it is a complete vertebrate. It has all of the features[12] that your spinal cord has and your nervous system has, only it's much simpler.

We thought about controlling the legs of these robotic limbs using the same principals that the spinal cord of the lamprey used. And that was how it was born, because Ralph had designed a chip that would generate the same pattern[13] of activity.

DR. RALPH ETIENNE-CUMMINGS, JOHNS HOPKINS UNIVERSITY

So what we have here is inside of this box we have a silicon model of the spinal cord you guys saw a little bit earlier on[3]. And what that means is that we have a piece of silicon which is fabricated[14] in the same foundry[15] that you fabricate your Pentium chips, but instead of making logic circuits[16] here, we are making mimics[17] of biological circuits.

FEMALE NARRATOR

Cohen and Etienne-Cummings' chip could help Seibert walk more naturally.

女声旁白

艾薇丝·科恩博士与雷夫·埃田康明斯博士可能正握有希伯特想要的答案。

马里兰大学　艾薇丝·科恩博士

脊髓损伤造成的结果，就是大脑再也无法传达到脊髓去激活它。

女声旁白

科恩是一位生物学家，研究七鳃鳗的脊髓已有一段时间。

马里兰大学　艾薇丝·科恩博士

我们可以在七鳃鳗身上测试仪器，设法控制损害处以下的脊髓，然后再经过设计，让这种仪器能够移植使用在哺乳类动物身上，最后再用于人类身上，让遭受过脊髓损伤的人借此控制脊髓。

七鳃鳗的身体构造之所以被视为模范系统，原因是这种生物虽然非常原始，属于脊椎动物最底层的生物，却是完整的脊椎动物。它具备了所有你的脊髓和神经系统拥有的一切特征，只是简单了许多。

我们想到套用七鳃鳗脊髓工作的控制原理，来控制这些机械肢体的腿部。这套机器就是这么诞生的，雷夫设计了一个能够产生相同活动模式的芯片。

约翰霍普金斯大学　雷夫·埃田康明斯博士

这个盒子里有个硅晶制作的脊髓模型，根据你们刚刚看过的脊髓设计而成。意思就是，这片硅晶就是在制造奔腾芯片的铸造厂中制造的，但这里不是用来制作逻辑电路，我们是要制作生物线路的仿造品。

女声旁白

科恩与埃田康明斯的芯片也许能够协助希伯特走路时更加自然。

Phrases

3. **early on** 早先，初期
   Early on, there were signs of trouble in Matt and Bonnie's relationship.

Vocabulary

7. **spinal cord** ['spaɪn]['kɔrd] 脊髓
8. **lesion** ['liːʒə] n. （身体或器官）损伤
9. **mammalian** [mə'melɪən] adj. 哺乳动物的
   The zoo has numerous **mammalian** species on display.
10. **means** [miːnz] n. 方法，手段，工具
11. **primitive** ['prɪmətɪv] adj. 原始的
    Many **primitive** creatures live in the deepest parts of the ocean.
12. **feature** ['fiːtʃə] n. 特征，特色
13. **pattern** ['pætən] n. 范例，模式，样本
14. **fabricate** ['fæbrɪˌket] v. 制造，装配，组装
    Phil **fabricated** a roof for his hut out of palm leaves.
15. **foundry** ['faʊndrɪ] n. 制造厂
16. **circuit** ['sɜːkət] n. 电路，线路
17. **mimic** ['mɪmɪk] n. 模仿者，模仿物

DR. RALPH ETIENNE-CUMMINGS, JOHNS HOPKINS

It's not just an outgoing pathway. If that was the case, you know, then you would not need to have any sensors on your limb, right? You'd just kind of walk abnormally[18], right? So it's also getting this signal coming back telling you how well you're doing. Did I stub[19] my toe? Do I need to run faster? Did the ground change?

FEMALE NARRATOR

The chip still needs to be tested on larger mammals before it would be ready for human trial[20]. ~~That's outlooked for~~ [The outlook[21] is for it to be completed] 10 to 15 years down the road.

DR. AVIS COHEN, UNIVERSITY OF MARYLAND

I think that within my lifetime I could see that we could have this.

DR. DREW SEIBERT, FORMER PARALYTIC

If they could get me up walking, that would be fine with me. I don't care how pretty it looks. You know, if I can get from here to there on my own power and not have to have people assist me, that's fantastic.

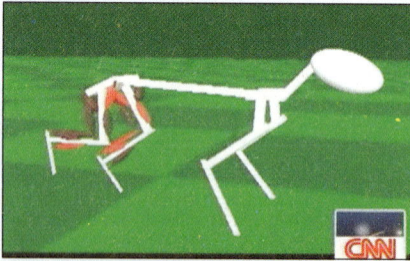

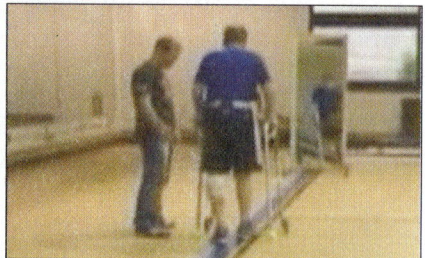

约翰霍普金斯大学　雷夫·埃田康明斯博士

这不只是一条发出信息的渠道。如果是这样的话，你的肢体就不需要有任何感应器，对不对？而且这样你走起路来也会不太正常，对不对？所以，这个系统也会接收回馈的信息，让你知道自己做得怎么样。我是不是踢到脚趾了？我需不需要跑快一点？地面是不是改变了？

女声旁白

这种芯片仍然必须在大型哺乳类动物身上测试，之后才能进行人体试验。目前看来还需要10到15年才能完成。

马里兰大学　艾薇丝·科恩博士

我想在我有生之年可以看得到成果。

曾瘫痪病人　德鲁·希伯特博士

如果有人能够让我起身走路，对我来说就够了。我不在乎外观好不好看。只要我能够凭自己的力量从这里移动到那里，而不需要别人扶持，那就太好了。CNN

Language Notes

down the road　未来，以后

原本指"沿路下去"，常用来比喻事情发展下去"将来有一天，未来，以后"。

例 We don't have any job openings at the moment, but we may have something down the road.
我们目前没有任何职位空缺，不过以后可能会有。

on one's own power　独力，靠一己之力

power 是"力量，能力，权力"的意思，on one's own power 指"靠某人自己的力量"完成某事，即 by oneself。

例 By bicycling, Jane gets around on her own power.
珍骑自行车就能自己到处跑了。

Vocabulary

18. **abnormally** [æb'nɔrməlɪ] *adv.* 反常地，不正常地
19. **stub** [stʌb] *v.* 脚趾踢到
    The boy stubbed his toe while running barefoot.
20. **trial** ['traɪəl] *n.* 试验，试用
21. **outlook** ['aut,luk] *n.* 前景，可能性

Spinal Cord Injury　脊髓损伤

定义：
指脊髓神经受到撞击、压迫或病变造成全部或部分伤害，导致下肢或四肢瘫痪、感觉异常或无知觉、自律神经失控、器官功能降低或丧失。

原因：
外伤性撞击，如车祸、高处跌落、运动伤害等。
非外伤性压迫，如肿瘤、神经病变等。

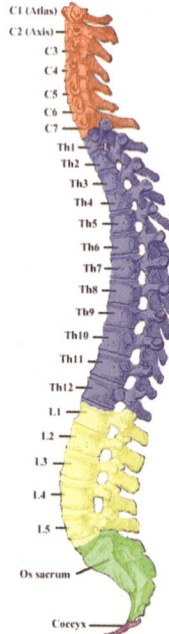

脊椎分为五大部分：

颈椎（cervical vertebrae，共 7 节）

胸椎（thoracic vertebrae，共 12 节）

腰椎（lumbar vertebrae，共 5 节）

骶骨（sacrum，5 节闭合的椎骨）

尾骨（coccyx，4 节未退化的椎骨）

Lamprey 七鳃鳗（八目鳗）

学名：Lampetra japonica

分类：脊椎动物亚门、圆口纲（Cyclostomata）、七鳃鳗目、七鳃鳗科、七鳃鳗属

特征：外形与辐鳍鱼纲（Actinopterygii）的鳗鱼或鳝鱼相似，无鳞、无颌、无胸鳍或腹鳍，两侧眼睛后有一排7个鳃孔，故俗称八目鳗。头部下方口部有漏斗状吸盘，中央和舌头有黄色角质齿。

生态：以口部吸附于其他鱼类身上，用角质齿刮破鱼体吸食其血和肉，并可借此长距离移动。寿命约为7年，幼时在河中生活4年，变态（metamorphose）后游入海中生活2年，溯源回游（migrate）产卵后不久死亡。

奇闻：

· 现存七鳃鳗的形态与3.6亿年前相差无几，为目前发现的活化石（living fossil）之一。

· 最早在古罗马时期就有食用七鳃鳗的记载，中世纪时成为欧洲上层阶级普遍的食材。

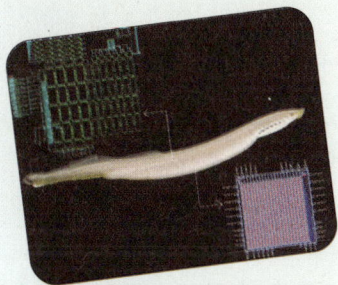

Give It a Try 请选出正确答案

1. The doctor prescribed a treatment for Ron's painful skin _____.
   - a. reasons
   - b. lessons
   - c. lesions
   - d. legions

2. When Phil broke his leg, he _____ a splint from two sticks.
   - a. fabricated
   - b. purchased
   - c. extricated
   - d. demonstrated

Answers: 1. c 2. a